The Deepest Roots

Contents

The Deepest Roots

strawberries—Marshall strawberries so luscious they were famously served to the Queen of England when she visited Victoria, British Columbia. After World War II and the incarceration of Japanese American farmers, Bainbridge shifted its production to organic vegetables and wine grapes. Today, farmers on Bainbridge turn to temporary help for harvesting. These include farmers, seasonal workers, interns, and volunteers who move systematically from farm to farm in "crop mobs," using their mass to bring the harvest in quickly.

As I learned more from greengrocers, farmers, and chefs about where our food now comes from, I found tendrils reaching out from Bainbridge to my parents' country of Mexico and back again, in a north–south relationship along trade routes that have probably existed for thousands of years. Because of improved transportation, the reach from Bainbridge now stretches as far as Ometepe, Nicaragua, in a unique arrangement based around coffee. North or south, the principles of food production remain the same: more sun equals a longer growing season, more labor equals a larger harvest. Politics and economics complicate, but do not negate, these fundamentals.

In the course of researching this book, I began to learn about concepts I had not heard of before, or at least had not listened to: community resiliency, value-added, factory organic, food security. I found myself squinting at those tiny stickers on the fresh vegetables in groceries stores, and visiting the websites listed there. Really, who are these people? Where were these turkeys and chickens free-ranging? Who are the farmers on whom I am dependent for oranges in winter and watermelons in summer? And why did my doctor think that eating dark chocolate and drinking green tea would lower my sky-high cholesterol?

Other questions arose as well: Should I admire or disdain the friend who picks up and eats roadkill? Am I asking these questions to ingratiate myself with my food-producing friends just in case? How do the relatively wealthy inhabitants of Bainbridge Island differ from the survivalists I knew in Western Colorado? Do the same dangers haunt them?

While I had done a lot of research for my novels, this was a different type of sleuthing, a search for the source of the Great American Dinner. In some ways, this exploration was as forbidding as Marlow's trip up the Congo in search of the heart of darkness. After all, eating meat, or "protein animals," involves the death of another creature on our behalf. Was I ready to confront this? In other ways, my search was both enlightening and reassuring. There are rituals around our relationship with food, both secular and religious, that enable us to fit the physical world together with our cultures and belief systems. Not surprisingly, religious beliefs often support best practices in the farming and preparation of food. After my hours and years of sleuthing, I am humbled by each and every one of the people who get up early and go outside to work in the fields every day, rain or shine, while I struggle to get out of bed in the dark.

I also took the time from my questioning to contemplate the pleasures, beauty, and pain of certain foods. We have memories, associations, and practices with everything that we eat, and I'll admit I got a little obsessed with tracking some of them down. People answered my questions with patience and good humor. I am not a farmer, a scientist, a gourmet chef, or even a very good cook. However, meeting these people forever changed the way I look at this overcast sky, this rocky soil, these trees, these plants and animals. Our food comes directly from all these sources, and learning that changed my understanding of our place in the world.

While reading *High Country News,* I came across a quote from James Lovelock's book *The Vanishing Face of Gaia: A Final Warning* that brought these elements into focus for me: "There will be great clamor from climate refugees seeking a safe haven in those few parts where the climate is tolerable and food is available. . . . We will need a new set of rules for (limiting the population in) climate oases."

I'm not ready to declare the end of the world, much less set the rules for it, but I now realize that I live in what Lovelock would call a climate oasis. At some level, I must have known this all along, and this is in part why my neighbors and I expend so much energy tracking development and land use on our island. It is an abundant but fragile environment, and on an island it is easy to see who is responsible for preserving it: we are. Bainbridge simply provides a microcosm of the choices we will all have to make as members of the human race.

Paul and Lorraine Svornitch, commercial fishers,
aboard the *M/V Ocean*.

What We Have
Always Known

THE GIRL IN THE CORN

WHEN I WAS VERY LITTLE, my family moved from
Santa Ana, California, out to Devore Heights. This was
an unincorporated community in the San Bernardino
Mountains, about seventy miles east of Los Angeles. After the private school where my father taught, the Spanish American Institute,
closed for lack of funds, he became the superintendent of the Optimist Boys Ranch, a residential facility for boys who needed more
guidance than their parents could provide at home.

In the 1950s, it was thought that fresh air and hard, physical labor
would straighten out any boy, so up to twenty of them between the
ages of twelve and eighteen might stay with us at any given time. The
boys slept in a dorm upstairs with a counselor, while our family of
five lived downstairs in a small apartment that had been carved out
of the back of the house. The boys were given farm chores, such as
growing a garden, taking care of chickens and horses, and weeding
the flowerbeds.

Let me describe this house: it was large and white, surrounded
by a lawn and beautiful plants, and had chickens, geese, and horses
on the grounds. A huge porch with white pillars graced the front, inspiring, I think, romantic notions in my older sisters. Yes, it was Tara
from *Gone with the Wind*. I don't know who built it, but it now served

as home to twenty juvenile delinquents, my father and mother and their three daughters.

The day we moved was my first birthday, and they say I blew spit all over the cake, so no one else wanted any. I don't remember that, but I do remember the dark apartment where we lived, the big dining room where we all ate together, and the chicken coop in the back that the boys were supposed to take care of. Mysteriously, the chickens often got loose, which meant several boys had to wander off into the adjacent woods looking for them. These boys were my playmates, and the ranch was the closest some of them ever got to a stable home. Years later, they would bring their families to our home in San Bernardino to visit.

After about three years, a small home came up for sale a quarter mile from the ranch, on "four square acres." I didn't know what an acre was, but my parents were very pleased with the idea and bought the property. My father hired someone to add an extra bedroom, a bath, and a dining room with a brick fireplace. I slept in my parents' walk-in closet, lying at an angle in my now too-small crib until I moved onto the floor in the living room.

Devore was known for the strong winds that blew through Cajon Pass. It was windy all the time, as cool air from the Pacific Ocean blew east to the desert, where it heated and rose. But it was most famous for the Santa Ana winds that blew when the pattern reversed and hot air blew west from the desert out to Los Angeles. These are the famous winds that Joan Didion wrote about in her essay, "Dreamers of the Golden Dream," so irritating that "every noise becomes a scream."

Four square acres was a bounty to my family. The house was set back from the road, up a long driveway. A neglected orchard stood on the front acreage. The property line on one side ran down the middle of an arroyo filled with rocks, boulders, cactus, and wild creatures, including beautiful yellow, brown, and white rattlesnakes. One of the first things my father did was plant a big square of corn behind the house.

As the corn ripened one year, a very persistent pheasant decided to help himself to it. I was told to go outside and scare him away. The pheasant seemed about as big as I was, and stood his ground whenever I rushed toward him flapping my arms and shouting. I guess he figured he could take me if it came to blows.

I finally stopped in frustration and peeled an ear of corn to taste for myself. It was so delicious, I could not understand why we bothered to cook it. My father came out to see why I had not returned, and began to sample the corn himself. Finally, my mother came out to find all three of us, my father, myself, and the pheasant, eating the raw corn. I've since learned that raw corn is perfectly edible, but contains so much sugar that it quickly turns to starch unless the process is stopped by cooking.

We lived there until I was six, when the Optimist Boys Ranch was closed, and my father became a substitute teacher in the San Bernardino schools. The twenty or so miles were considered a long distance in those days, so my family sold the house and four square acres to rent a home in town. By then, my sisters were in high school and junior high, so it was easier for them to get to school and participate in other activities.

Those few years in the mountains have stayed with me forever. I spent hours observing the plants and animals, from the glowworms in the yucca seeds to the lone condor that sometimes drifted inland to ride the thermals above us. At night, the stars spread like a sequined shawl across the sky, and we would sit outside and sing songs in Spanish while my mother played the guitar. When the Santa Anas were bad, the wind just howled, with winds up to sixty miles per hour. An elderly neighbor who used to visit died during that time, and we took in his orange cat. It was always leaning on someone's legs, and we said that it was a habit from resisting the wind.

Devore was rural enough that none of the nearby stores carried ready-made tortillas. My father expected my mother to make them, my sisters tell me, and she was very unhappy about it. She had never learned to make tortillas while growing up. Her family was so large that the children had specialized in certain tasks—my mother was the chauffeur and pianist. When her family acquired a Model A, she was the one who learned to drive it. I don't think they all fit in the car.

I once found a nest of just-hatched baby rattlers and brought one home in a jar because it was so beautiful, but the cat killed it. A neighbor and my father then went out and killed the rest, and I was sorry I had told anyone. There was no idea, then, of the balance of nature, chemical-free farming, or "letting nature take its course." Intervention was good, and people needed to impose order on nature's messy ways. It's always difficult when people live near wild creatures, harder on them than on us.

I was happy there, watching the first pale blue butterflies that heralded the spring, riding a bus to our two-room schoolhouse, and once even checking books out from a bookmobile that was sent to serve our small community. The *Sun Telegram* sent a photographer out to document the new service, and took a photo of me in baggy hand-me-downs and messy braids, clutching my Dr. Seuss books.

"I feel like I'm five but I'm six," said the caption. I had just celebrated a birthday, and in September or October, we would leave that house and move into the city of San Bernardino.

I could not know then that my aunt who, along with her husband, lived with us for a time, would die within two years of cancer, or that my parents liked to grow food at home because we had so little money. Nor could I know that two of my uncles had died of diabetes long before I was born. When we talk about food and people, there is so much to consider.

WHAT WE HAVE ALWAYS KNOWN

The title of this chapter makes me feel as though I should cue an orchestra to play Stravinsky's "Rite of Spring"—you know, the music Walt Disney used for the dinosaurs in *Fantasia*, with the frenzied drums and the dissonant horns as the old order unraveled.

But it's true, there are things we have known for a long time about food and community, our relationship to the earth, and our ability to wrest a living by tilling the soil, fishing the oceans and streams, and of course, applying the alchemy of cooking.

One way to tell this story, which is starting to feel like the Story of Everything, is to tell it through several stories, much the way it was told to me. It is a story of abundance, and it is a story of sorrow and scarce times. As everywhere, people who lived on Bainbridge Island for generations developed specialized knowledge that allowed them to take full advantage of what is possible based on the resources at hand.

As time passed, new people arrived with new skills, but perhaps not with the deep knowledge held by people who have lived through lean times, and who understand that the bounty is not limitless.

As I talked to people and learned to pay attention to the features of the land in a new way, the most obvious things came to light right away. That fish can sustain a nation, in fact several nations, along the West Coast. That berries can provide the vitamins I was used to getting by eating citrus fruit. That cedar trees can provide the raw materials for canoes, baskets, cooking utensils, hooks, and spears— all the tools needed to harvest, store, and prepare food.

But some things were less obvious: until I looked extensively for a source of carbohydrates in the local indigenous diet, I could not find one. People did not grow wheat or harvest rice. There was almost no grain in their diets. Talk about gluten-free! Instead, people cultivated camas roots, which not only provided a source of starch but also acted as a binder when dried, ground, and mixed with dried salmon to form patties that could be stored or taken along on travels by the "People of the Clear Salt Water," the Suquamish people's name for themselves. For up to ten thousand years, women have harvested the camas root by wading into the water and feeling for it with their toes. They dug up the roots and put them in baskets made especially for this task. The camas prairies, planted in shallow freshwater, were maintained by keeping the overgrowth down, usually through controlled burns. Another plant that filled the need for starches was the *wapato*, or arrowhead, a tuber with white flowers that could be grown in a wider range of conditions than camas.

Some foods were available for only a brief period of time and had to be gathered and eaten immediately. Others were also available fresh for only a short time, but could be prepared for storage during the long, dark winters. Today, food that was once valued for its high fat content, making it a crucial part of an indigenous diet, is viewed as unnecessary, unpalatable, or difficult to prepare.

Sadly, one of the things that came up over and over again in my conversations and research was the depletion of formerly abundant foods and food sources on the island. By ignoring the seasonal cycles of plants, fish, people, and ocean currents, we have destroyed much of the bounty that was once spread like a banquet at low tide.

Until recently, it was assumed that humans first formed and built permanent settlements in order to grow food. However, what might be the oldest place of permanent settlement in the world, Göbekli Tepe, in Turkey, was not built for agricultural purposes, as was once thought. Rather, as essayist Elif Batuman explains in a *New Yorker* article, it may have been built solely as a religious site by a hunter-gatherer civilization. There are no nearby fields of grain, or sources of food. There are no houses, only concentric circles of tall, almost modern-looking statues. These statues were all covered up at once, presumably by the departing worshippers, hence the settlement's name, which means "Large Hill." As Batuman notes, "the findings at Göbekli Tepe suggest that we have the story backwards—that it was actually the need to build a sacred site that first obliged hunter-gatherers to organize themselves as a workforce, to spend long periods of time in one place, to secure a stable food supply, and eventually to invent agriculture."

As a result of these findings, archaeologists are looking at other sites with a new eye. Stonehenge is now thought to be a really nice cemetery. In other words, we might have come to a fixed-in-place lifestyle later than we thought. On Bainbridge, most of us (except for the "snowbirds" who migrate to Mexico and Arizona every

Most of the Almazan acres are now owned by the Sears family ("trust funders," said Dan) and used as equestrian fields. Highway 305 took three acres, and the Morales farm, a public trust, occupies the rest, just to the east of the highway. Dan and Doreen's son still owns and lives on the original five acres.

After the Japanese families on Bainbridge were sent to internment camps in 1942, the Filipino farmers became caretakers for much of the farm property owned by the Japanese. The original immigrants, like Felix Almazan, were too old to be drafted to serve in World War II. Both Doreen and Dan's fathers worked instead as welders for the Hall Brothers shipyards during the war.

Felix and four other Filipinos—Felix Narte, Daniel Bucsit, Anacleto Corpus, and Toby Memberi—founded the Filipino American Hall in 1941. They all spoke Ilocano, the dominant language of the southern Philippines. The five purchased property on Strawberry Hill for the hall with their own money ("It was strawberry money!") as the Filipino Farmers of Bainbridge Island. It cost five dollars a year to become a member, and the other Filipino farmers on the island soon joined.

Shortly thereafter, the Army requisitioned most of the property, paying each of the original purchasers for it. The five founders took the money and invested it in Town & Country Market, the eventual successor to Eagle Harbor Market. In the late 1960s, when the federal government reclassified as surplus much of the land it had requisitioned for use during World War II, the Strawberry Hill property was sold to the Parks and Recreation District for one dollar, without offering it back to the Filipino community. In more recent years, the Parks District returned two and a half acres to the Filipino community, on which it built a new community hall next to the original shed used for shipping and receiving strawberries.

Felix Almazan and the other farmers supplemented what they grew by fishing off the piers at Point White and the ferry dock. They caught perch, red snapper, big cod of several varieties, octopus, and sea urchins.

"There used to be lots before," said Doreen. Sometimes her father would let the children go with him to the beach at Fay Bainbridge Park at night to catch Dungeness crab. There also used to be lots of shrimp in Eagle Harbor by the ferry terminal—but no one eats fish out of Eagle Harbor, now that it is a Superfund waste site due to heavy concentrations of creosote once used in the shipbuilding industry.

Today, the mouth of the harbor is taken up by the ferry slip and a repair yard maintained by the Washington State Ferry system. Visitors can gaze across the harbor and see what looks like construction in and close to the water on Bill Point. But the cheerful orange buoys and markers instead delineate the Superfund site, and the seemingly endless efforts to mitigate the seeping creosote as it bubbles up from the harbor bottom.

The Indipino families also foraged for wild food, although it wasn't called that at the time. When Doreen's mother went to work in the packing shed, her grandmother came from Canada to watch the children. She took them out to gather berries as they came into season. Doreen recalled that they ate huckleberries, salmonberries, dingleberries, thimbleberries, and salal berries, which she pronounced the old way, "slahal." Where logging had occurred, they found the small, dark, indigenous blackberries that her grandmother, or "Ta'a," preferred. They ate them raw and made pies or pudding cakes out of them—placing the berries on the bottom of the pan and covering them with batter. "The children would go outside and eat berries, or peel fern shoots and eat them as snacks," Doreen said. The young sprouts were called *saskis*, and they look like asparagus when small. "There used to be three kinds of salmonberries," said Doreen. "We'd stop for dessert."

Ta'a was a member of the Squamish tribe. Stanley Park in Vancouver, British Columbia, used to belong to them, and the Queen leased it from the tribe. Now, a ceremonial gun is discharged daily at the spot where Doreen's grandfather, Ta'a's husband, once maintained a salmon-drying shed. He was born in Capalano, a district of the larger population. Before, each family had about five acres. When the berry prices dropped and taxes increased, most Filipinos sold their farmland. The problem of this ratio of land to people is something that other farmers echoed as I continued my interviews.

AROUND THE ISLAND

One summer, I joined a group of Bainbridge Islanders circumnavigating the island in the *Virginia V*, an old ferry that has been restored and now serves as a tour boat. Our guide was Dennis Lewarch, the tribal historic preservation officer for the Suquamish Tribe, which recently opened a new museum.

Echoing Dan Rapada, Lewarch said that because the Suquamish have no major rivers in their territories—meaning, no major sources of salmon—their arrangement with other saltwater tribes was once that the Suquamish had a far greater range, allowing them to fish as far north as the Fraser River and to access more shorelines.

Fish spawns move north to south as they enter the cul-de-sac of Puget Sound, and the canoe people had about three months in which to gather most of their food for the year. Even the small streams on Bainbridge produced pinks and chum during September, October, and November. The Suquamish would fish all day, and smoke the fish at night, telling stories around the fires. Shellfish were gathered and smoked, then strung on cedar rope like necklaces, to be saved or traded for other goods in places like Muckleshoot and Nisqually.

Intimately acquainted with its rocky shoreline, the Suquamish designated over thirty-seven place names along the edges of Bainbridge Island. These are based on usage, appearance, or geological history. In English, Eagle Harbor and Eagledale are named after eagles, of course, but the latter already had the name "Elaledaltx" in Lushootseed, or Proto-Salish, as Lewarch called it. This is one case where the sound and the meaning almost line up in two very different languages. Lushootseed, the main coastal language, glides and leaps between consonants, with sounds that don't exist in English.

It is the language of water. I remember Vi Hilbert, a much-revered keeper of the language, trying to get me to spit out the consonant that slithers down the sides of your tongue, the true ending for "Seattle." It is somewhat like the soft "x" sound in Mayan.

The geology of Bainbridge reveals an equally slidey and slippery set of rocks. Within human memory, Laxelks, now called Wing Point, the long, trailing arm of rock that juts into Eagle Harbor, fell about three feet during an earthquake. Today it compels ferries to thread their way along a set course around it. Sometimes the rocky spine shows, and sometimes it doesn't. This can be disconcerting to first-time visitors, as the ferry seems ready to land on Rockaway Beach before it turns to enter the harbor.

On May 19, 1792, Captain George Vancouver dropped anchor on the British ship *Discovery* off Restoration Point at the south end of the island. Chief Seattle's father, Shweabe, and uncle brought deer from nearby Blake Island, and the Suquamish spent the day trading with the crew; the bounty must have seemed endless to the British sailors. Today, tribal leaders like Billy Frank Jr. of the Nisqually, arrested more than fifty times during his lifetime trying to protect family fishing rights, would find little to cheer about. The water is acidic, and salmon runs continue to decline. The day-to-day losses—of trees cut, land paved over, and shorelines hardened into fish-repellent slabs—have taken their toll. But a few people still look to the future, trying to maintain a sensible, sustainable way to harvest the sea. A tangled net of agencies work separately and together to clean up the sound, enforce regulations concerning chemical and septic discharges into the water, and restore the wetlands that once filtered the water and provided cover for small fry.

DEEPER ROOTS

I first met Gary Paul Nabhan in the basement of the Elliott Bay Book Company in downtown Seattle. I had stumbled across his work while researching the indigenous Opata people of the Sonoran desert for my second novel, *The Flower in the Skull*, based on family stories about my grandmother and great-grandmother. Nabhan, an ethnobotanist with an international following, is the author or editor of over twenty books exploring the history and science of New World plants. He lives in Arizona, which is part of Opata territory.

On the night of the reading I wasn't feeling well, coming down with a sinus infection, as it turns out, and almost skipped introducing myself, but my friend Lenore pushed me forward. After all, I was leaving shortly for Arizona to do further research on the Opata. I screwed up my courage and talked to him before the reading. This was the first time I had spoken with someone outside my family who had even heard of the Opata. Nabhan proved to be a kind and generous man. He confirmed many of the things I had guessed, and pointed me to other resources.

When researching my books, I am a voracious consumer of information. It turned out that these indigenous people of the Sonoran desert, among them my ancestors, were keepers of the landscape—cultivators, farmers, and *curanderas* who used the plants of the desert as their extended pantry and pharmacy. I could tell that the connection with the land was especially important for the Opata, but I needed the specifics, not vague "connections" and "spiritual legacies." Once I situated the people in my novel in their habitat, I felt that I could imagine their lives, predict what sorts of decisions they would make, the worldview they would have espoused at the turn of the twentieth century. My great-grandmother would have known both the beauty and the sorrow of it. And there was a lot of sorrow.

A few years after that first reading, Nabhan returned to the Northwest to discuss the importance of preserving wild food diversity. Nabhan is also a champion of the Slow Food movement, an international effort to get people to eat locally, and with intent. "Although we typically think of local or regional food communities as being focused on accessing place-based crops," he told the audience, "the Pacific Northwest is perhaps the ecosystem with the most wild food."

The auditorium at the University of Washington was packed. And not just with middle-aged activists in socks and sandals, their gray hair pulled back in ponytails, but with college students enthusiastically pursuing careers as scientists, agronomists, and social activists. Plants and people cannot be considered as separate entities, Nabhan told us; we are locked together in systems that depend on each other.

Nabhan's talk focused on whether or not the continued use of wild food should be encouraged as biologists try to restore wild ecosystems. Some eco-restorationists are wary of serving humans at the same time. But, as Nabhan pointed out, "Most indigenous cultures and many of the immediate cultures of this region wouldn't necessarily pit one against the other." He quoted food writer Georgia Pellegrini as saying that wild foraging and fishing have far lower carbon footprints than the way we now grow our food.

The almost entirely artificial agribusiness of California, said Nabhan—dependent on water pumped from the ground, pesticides, elaborate temperature control, packaging, and transportation—is among the most costly in dollars and energy in the world.

However, in certain areas, keystone species must be restored to a wild habitat before use can resume. "In regions such as the Gulf [of Mexico]," he explained, "the long-term recovery of fisheries and their fishermen can no longer be separated. Fishermen are doing much of the cleanup and ground work for species recovery."

In the fall of 2005, of a list of 180 foods unique to the Northwest, one-third were at risk of "falling off our tables" due to overharvesting or adverse environmental conditions. Rather than declaring everything off-limits, however, Ecotrust, an environmental advocacy group established in 1991, released a book by Nabhan called *Renewing Salmon Nation's Food Traditions,* pairing chefs with foragers. This partnership gave chefs insight into the foods they demand and prepare. Foragers know the habitats, where to look and what conditions are best for the plants and animals they seek. According to Nabhan, among all the "food nations" of North America—he gives them names like Clambake Nation and Chile Pepper Nation—Salmon Nation is the richest in mushrooms, berries, wild roots, fish, and shellfish. Native American traditions are at its core, but other culinary accents—from Spanish to Japanese—have added to the mix.

Today, one-third of the fish runs and shellfish beds in and around Puget Sound are depleted or contaminated. Eighty percent of the wetlands that once sustained developing fish and many of the indigenous food sources have been destroyed.

But there are people fighting back. Nick Bottner of the Home Orchard Society grows forgotten fruits in Oregon, Nabhan said. And Jerry Warren, professor emeritus at the University of Washington, who is also involved with the Slow Food movement, has worked with the Makah Tribe on cultivating potatoes.

All of these Northwest foods—blue potatoes, shellfish, native or adopted fruits—even those that were less preferred, should be accorded a high degree of cultural significance because of their adaptation and survival value. Some provided critical nutrients, such as vitamin C, as well as limited food energy. Some would have been potentially toxic if eaten in excess or without adequate preparation. The cultural aspects of the use of plant foods in times of scarcity are complex and multifaceted. Although modern living in North America seems to preclude the possibility of famine for most of us, the cultural knowledge surrounding food scarcity has great significance, and is rendered even more important because this knowledge is quickly disappearing.

SUSTAINABLE FISHING

Other people came to the Pacific Northwest over the years to escape war and famine in their own countries. My theory of migration is that people usually flee from the known, rather than toward the unknown. Things at home have to be pretty bad to drive people away from the land, climate, relatives, and customs they have known all their lives, often for many generations.

Among those who settled on Bainbridge Island were Croatians. Their history has been documented by Barbara Winther and Gary Loverich in their book, *Let It Go, Louie: Croatian Immigrants on Puget Sound.*

Croatia is a Baltic country made up in part of thousands of small islands, and many people there make a living by fishing. As do some of their descendants on Bainbridge.

The power was out when I went to meet Paul Svornich, a third-generation fisherman of Croatian descent on Bainbridge Island. By the light of a flashlight and a lantern, his wife, Lorraine, was carefully pasting labels on cans of tuna caught by Paul from his sailboat, fifty miles off the Oregon coast.

No one goes tuna fishing in a sailboat, except Paul Svornich.

"My family was involved in purse seining. They came from Croatia, but there are more fish here."

His grandfather's name was Anton Svornich, and his father was Matt. Paul's grandfather met Mary Kataich on Bainbridge, when she came to live with her uncle Dragich, while the rest of her family went to San Pedro, California, in 1928. All came out of a starvation environment in Croatia—too many people, and not enough fish.

"The Croatians devised this type of fishing here, pioneered and developed it. My dad, both uncles, and both grandfathers were fishermen. I grew up in that environment. It's pretty cool, but I wanted to try something different—something low-impact, with a small footprint. I developed a unique fishtrap design. It could be used by pulling rowboats just off-island.

"The traps came from my Grandpa's design. It was a cylinder of chicken wire about three feet across and six feet long. I found it after Grandpa was long dead, and I asked my dad how it worked. Grandpa would wreath the mouth in cedar boughs, he said. This was around 1977, 1978 that I asked. I did that and hung it off the porch of my houseboat. I caught way more fish than we could eat. I refined it into collapsible fishnets, using monofilament instead of chicken wire. I got a commercial fishing license and caught rockfish. At that time, I only sold rockfish and perch to Chinese restaurants. . . . Everyone knew I got fish."

Svornich initially used an outboard motor to fish, but he was looking for a sailboat. "All of them were way too plastic. I looked for a commercial boat, but couldn't find any that worked.

"In the Bahamas, I saw the sloops that they used with beach seines. That winter, I decided to look for a little sloop. In Puerto Rico, I saw a man carrying a sextant case, so I knew he was a sailor.

"'Go to Belize,' he said, where there are lots of working sloops. I found a thirty-two footer, very third world. It used rocks for ballast. It was crude, but robust.

"I fished around Bainbridge Island [in that boat] for a year. To comply with Department of Fisheries regulations, I sold to myself and to wholesalers. The Department saw the number of rockfish that I caught, the high number, and sent an observer. They closed the fishery a week later, and I agree with their decision. We were very low-impact, but if regular fishermen came in, they would have destroyed the rockfish population.

"When using a line, we caught no fish. But with the trap, we caught hundreds.

"Nevertheless, I still wanted to fish with a sailboat. The purse seiners were big operations. They used eight men per boat, then six as the use of machinery made them more efficient. On Dad's purse seiner, I didn't feel like a real fisherman, fishing one or two days a week, regardless of the weather.

"In Puget Sound, the boats are forty-five to sixty-five feet long. In Alaska, they are limited to fifty-eight feet, although they are wider as a consequence. They catch exclusively salmon. In the tropics, they catch tuna with two-hundred-foot boats.

"The Department could have done a lot of things to make catching rockfish in the Sound sustainable. It's a publicly owned resource, but we cannot access it without going through the commercial fisheries."

What little ambient light from outside was almost gone by now, and I was blindly taking notes. Paul's voice became that of a storyteller in dim firelight.

"After that, I knew I wanted to fish, but not in the Bering Sea. Most American fisheries have quotas. I'm not opposed to that at all. If a certain user group has a quota, and I don't catch it, someone else will. I'm just another seagull fighting over fish. So, I chose another area that was wide open. I chose albacore tuna, and deep-sea fishing."

"Albacore is still sustainable. Salmon are so vulnerable because their migration upstream takes them into the realm of man. No one even knows where tuna spawn or how. [There are] other tunas—yellowfin *(ahi)*, skipjack *(aku*, or tiny), big eye, bluefin. Bluefin are giant, and are going extinct. Then there are albacore, which I fish for. They are the species that lives in the coldest water. They are a warm-blooded fish. They like to live in a very specific temperature zone, around sixty-two degrees.

"They live mostly off the coast of Oregon. There is a belt of cold, green water that goes out forty or fifty miles, then warm, blue water. Tuna migrate like elk off the mountains: in the summer and fall, they are off the Oregon Coast, [traveling up] along the West Coast of North America, from California to Canada. When they arrive, they are lean and hungry. By fall, they are fat and lazy, and migrate across the Pacific to the Philippines and Japan. These are the Northern Pacific stock.

"I built a really small boat with a good refrigeration system—no one had done that. I wanted to own my product, not sell it to canneries. My father got a loan from a cannery to get a boat built. Canneries, big corporations, pay poorly.

"If they use ice, boats have to come in and sell at current market price. I fillet my own fish to sell to Japanese restaurants, and to individuals. It's really hard. It took me ten years to develop a market. Now, twenty-five years later, I sell 50 percent to Japanese restaurants, and the rest at our farmers market. I sell two products: 90 percent is frozen tuna loins, the rest is canned. I sell it to restaurants on the island. I sell it for sushi at Central Market, Ichi-Zen, and Hakata Sushi in Mukilteo.

"Purse seiners are wealthy these days. Most struggled for many years. The price of fish has jumped in the last eight years, because it is becoming so limited. Farmed fish have hurt them, but now people realize the difference in quality.

"Because I fish from a sailboat, others know who I am—it's so unusual. Other fishermen like it, but wouldn't do it. They fish in their slippers—towing the fish in and freezing them whole. They catch a lot more, but mine are worth three times more."

If you were envisioning Svornitch's boat as a cartoon rowboat with a single sail, liable to be swamped by the next big wave, try instead imagining a galleon capable of crossing the Atlantic, or a whaling boat from Nantucket. It's a tidy but sophisticated ship, with two sails and a freezer. Paul Svornich and shipwright Diana Talley built the albacore sloop as a commercial fishing sailboat with a fully battened main sail; it has logged over one hundred thousand miles. Modeled after an open Bermuda sloop from the mid-1800s, the *F/V Ocean* is made of fir with sawn locust frames. It has *ipe* wood floors, with stem and stern posts cut from the same selected log and fastened with iron. Dave Ullin, a Bainbridge local with great knowledge of boats and the sea, caulked it.

"There was a hippie movement in the sixties, which I fell for lock, stock, and barrel," says Paul. "I got the opportunity to sail to the South Pacific, and got a sense of a bigger mother. I love the ocean. Sailing deepens a personal relationship with the sea, and with God."

Paul's voice changed as he described his experiences at sea. I listened in the dark to see if Lorraine, who was recovering from a long illness, would say anything. She seldom speaks. He went on.

"I like dancing with the sea, with nature, rather than plowing straight through using fuel. My engine uses biodiesel. I use that because the engine is prone to stack fires. The biodiesel doesn't do that. There are also fewer carcinogens in the exhaust. It's way better fuel—it smells like French fries, soybeans, and other fats.

"I went tuna fishing out of San Diego to learn how the gear ran. I found myself looking at Sea Grant, which has lots of research on how the Japanese fish for it. I also looked at the National Marine Fisheries Service in La Jolla. They gave specific reports on catches, a lot of information that is not available now."

I asked him if he had seen effects from the meltdown of the three nuclear reactors at Fukushima in 2011 on West Coast albacore.

"An analysis in the summer of 2012 showed a footprint from Fukushima of both long- and short-lived radiation. Both were found in fish at higher levels than naturally occur, up to 1 percent of the danger level for humans. We would have to eat four thousand pounds to reach that level.

"We already suffer from 'naturally occurring radiation' left over from the weapons testing of the fifties and sixties. We are bathing in the stuff that probably did not exist before."

Can we sustain ourselves on Bainbridge? I asked him, the same question I had asked the Rapadas and many others.

"Of course we can. Scale down your consumption. [People dependent on fossil fuels] will become dinosaurs. I wish the bureaucracy would get out of the way. I would like to see a community of mixed housing around farms, closer to nature. We are so far removed from it.

"We need the controls, we need the regulations, but we don't really get it. We need them just like we need police. There is a plane above that where we would not need them."

Paul quoted Dave Ullin, a well-known figure around town who lives close to the land and sea, as saying we need two acres per person to sustain ourselves. Land on the island is expensive, he explained, because the wealthy do not produce anything. Forty percent of our production goes to paying interest, he added. The ratio of people to land came up again: How much land does it take to feed a single person?

The Bainbridge Island to which these immigrant families came was split into ethnic groups, with the Japanese living in their own village, Yama, at Blakely Harbor. But when harvesttime came around, everyone worked. Author Suzanne Selfors, a fifth-generation Bainbridge islander, remembers picking berries with her best friend for extra money in the summers, and how their parents canned food in a late-summer frenzy. She is a descendant of Alfred Welfare, a British sea captain who settled on the island in 1868. Her father's family, the Selfors, were all Bering Sea fishermen of Norwegian ancestry.

But I'll never need to know this, you are thinking. I live in a nice house with a good grocery store down the street. I've got canned goods and a propane tank. Let's leave canning and fishing to people like Doreen Rapada and Paul Svornitch, who know what they are doing. This is what the Japanese Americans thought in 1942 before they were uprooted and sent to camps far from their farms on the island.

IT COULD HAPPEN TO YOU

Lilly (Kitamoto) Kodama and Kay (Sakai) Nakao were seven and twenty-two, respectively, when they were uprooted from their lives on Bainbridge Island and sent "straight to Manzanar," according to Lilly, simply for being part of the West Coast Japanese American community. Their mothers were thirty-four and forty-six, respectively. The families stayed at Manzanar, in the Owens Valley of California, for eleven months before being sent on to Minidoka, a camp constructed on a barren plain outside of Hunt, Idaho.

The families took famously "only what they could carry," which did not include cooking utensils.

"Our first meal," said Lilly, "was Army fare. It was served in a metal container you opened. It turned into a dish and cup with metal utensils. They put the food in a buffet line."

"At first," said Kay, "there was no Japanese food, then we got rice. There was no soy sauce or any condiments at first."

"They served this yucky green stuff—canned spinach," Lilly remembered. "I just couldn't eat it. But we had to sit there until we had cleared our plates, because of my mom."

Was there anything you liked? I asked. Lilly and Kay looked at each other. "Vienna sausage was another thing I didn't like," said Lilly.

"I can't remember anything I liked," added Kay. "We were served Jell-O, but it was next to hot food on our plates, so it melted. At first we had paper plates. Later, we got real china."

That change was due to people like the Reverend Emory Andrews of the Seattle Japanese Baptist Church. The church had put many of the belongings of the internees in storage, and soon the reverend began to make regular visits to Minidoka in the Blue Box—a pickup truck with a square enclosure on the back that resembled a very square bus. Later, he moved his entire family to Twin Falls, Idaho, in order to continue serving his and the Reverend Kihachi Hirakawa's congregation from Bainbridge Island, since Hirakawa, too, was incarcerated.

"The good thing," said Kay, "is we could eat with our families."

There was a camp nutritionist, a Japanese woman who was also a dietician. "We called her the nutrition mafia," said Kay.

"They served chunky cottage cheese—I refused to eat that, too," said Lilly. "We never ate cottage cheese before the war."

Once settled in the camp in Idaho, the imprisoned families planted huge gardens.

"There was heat and lots of water," added Kay. "The watermelons were delicious," she remembers.

As a child Lilly, now in her eighties, assumed that all the families in the camp had roots in farming before they came to the United States, "but it was not true. Some left good positions to come here." Most Japanese immigrants at the time were from southern Japan, an area especially hard-hit by famine conditions.

She remembers one man who, before internment, had wanted to become a doctor. "He did an emergency appendectomy on someone on the island."

The camp diaries of Arthur Kleinkopf, an administrator who worked as an assistant school superintendent, were recently transcribed and made available to the Bainbridge Island Historical Society through the National Park Service. Mixed in with his complaints about the bureaucracy are frequent notations on the food that was served in the camp, and an increasing emphasis on requiring the Japanese Americans to grow their own food. Kleinkopf, who had a dry wit, was generally sympathetic to the camp internees. All of the excerpts that follow are from 1943, when the internees from Bainbridge arrived at Minidoka, although he kept a diary before and after that time.

February 26

One hundred seventy-seven evacuees from the Manzanar Relocation Center in California arrived. They were former residents of Bainbridge Island. Banners of welcome were flown and a delegation was out to greet them as they came in the gate.

Kleinkopf, whose wife also worked at the camp, took all of his meals there, and frequently recorded what was served.

March 8

An impossible concoction of ground spiced meat and eggs was served for lunch. Took two bowls of soup and saved the meat dish for the garbage. There's great waste of food here because of food preparations that many people can't eat.

Sometimes I found it hard to tell if the food was really bad, or simply unfamiliar to the people who prepared and ate it.

"We did not feel the Depression because we were poor," said Kay, of their time before Minidoka. This was something my own parents had said as well. "But at the camp, they served 'Depression Era' cuts of meat: tongue, lamb stew, liver. Cheap cuts we hadn't eaten before."

"My mother's good friend worked at the mess hall, and told me it was lamb stew. I got sick," said Lilly.

"It was all in your head," Kay responded. The Japanese Americans did not raise sheep, and were unfamiliar with the meat. "I'll tell you what I did not like: a type of canned smelt laid out on a cookie sheet and dried. Terribly dry."

The staff had their own, separate, mess hall where Kleinkopf would have eaten most of his meals. Everyone—teachers, internees, and general staff—was expected to pay a small amount, twenty-five or thirty-five cents, for each meal.

Minidoka received water via a canal from the Snake River. This project was completed just before the families from Bainbridge arrived. The canal was both a boon and a heartache, as several young people drowned in its swift-moving waters.

May 11

It seems that summer is here at last. As I look down along the banks of the canal, I can count scores of people—men, women, and children—fishing. Some of the men have even built shacks out of rock and sagebrush near the banks of the canal where they spend the entire day, and, if permission is given, part of the night. They do not catch enough to pay for the time they spend but, after all, what is time to them. This seems to be about the only diversion that many of these people have. They are good fisherman because they actually catch fish out of this canal, which is not supposed to be a fishing stream. The only fish that get into the canal are those that happen to come from the backwater of the dam when the gates are opened to fill the canal.

Kay worked at the hospital, and as she came home from work each evening, people asked her which mess halls had the best food that night, since she came into contact with people from all over the camp. They would go there until made to return to their assigned halls.

April 6

The residents have petitioned the Project Steward [the government euphemism for the internment camp was "project"] to serve more salmon and halibut and less link cod. The cod is terrific. One needs a gas mask. Forty-five cents per day per person is the amount allotted for buying food for the evacuees and this does not permit the buying of the better foods. The milk situation is still bad. One-half cup per meal is allowed the children under twelve years of age, elderly people, invalids, and pregnant mothers.

While many women worked as servers in the mess halls, the chefs were all men. "Some had restaurants before the war," said Kay. "It was part of their jobs to cook in the camps, so they received salaries." Salaries for Japanese American cooks in the camps were capped at $19 a month, while a comparable job held by a white person was paid $150. The chefs had to work with what they had, which posed challenges. Often, as part of the mysterious process by which food was sent to the camps, large quantities of a single item would arrive, sometimes spoiled by the time it reached them.

"At meals, we had to eat or starve. No snacks."

Residents were not supposed to cook in their living quarters, but with help from outside visitors, that began to change.

"My mother sent me to the laundry to wash rice," said Lilly, "which she cooked on a pot-bellied stove."

"We were not allowed hotplates," said Kay, "but we got one."

May 15

According to the head of the public works division, 100 percent of the equipment for that division is in the garage at the present time. This individual is very much concerned because recent instructions from Washington have set the value of food to be raised on the farms at the Minidoka Relocation Center this year at $253,000. Many of the Japanese who had knowledge of farming methods have

relocated so that many of those who are now working on the farms
know little or nothing about farm work. This increases the difficulty
of raising the desired amount of food.

I have to pause, here, for a little irony. At any given time, Minidoka housed between eight thousand and nine thousand people,
including the fifty-four families from Bainbridge Island who had
been taken by force from their farms during wartime and relocated
to an undeveloped desert area, where they were expected to raise not
only their own food, but additional food for the "war effort."

There was a great deal of resentment against the internees from
the nearby communities. While those forced to live at the camps
occasionally received passes to go shopping at nearby Hunt, Idaho,
shopkeepers there would often refuse to sell to them, or to provide
other services such as haircuts. There were rumors in Hunt that
shortages of certain items, such as sugar, were caused by individuals
from the camps buying up supplies. The resentment against Minidoka was extended to Anglo Americans who worked there as well.

Incarcerated Japanese American schoolchildren in Minidoka
were put to work both after school and during their scheduled physical education classes, in order to meet the food quota. Over three
hundred Minidoka high school students were put to work on camp
jobs, mostly farming, and given work-study credit for it. Those of college age who had been pulled out of school to be incarcerated were
given positions as teaching assistants. Forums were held at the dining halls to instruct people on growing victory gardens and farming.
"Great emphasis is being placed on the growing of farm crops and
garden vegetables," according to Kleinkopf.

The land was so dusty and barren that people dug up and trans-
planted sagebrush to serve as decorative plants near their housing
as it was cleared from farming areas. Children brought nickels and
dimes to their teachers in order to pay for flower seed packets that
Kleinkopf and his wife bought for them in Twin Falls. These too were
planted near the barracks.

In June 1943, farm animals, including pigs and chickens, were brought to Minidoka, in hopes of supplying the mess halls with meat. That month, the first produce from the gardens, seventeen baskets of radishes, was harvested.

Meanwhile back on Bainbridge Island, Filipino caretakers ran the farms owned by interned Japanese Americans, most often those they had worked for, either seasonally or full-time, before the war. They also brought supplies to the internees when they could. Because the Filipino farmworkers could continue to work for regular wages—many were employed in the shipyard on Bainbridge Island— some of the Filipino families were able to save enough money to buy farms from the Japanese families during this time.

"Just before the war," said Lilly, "we had earned enough to build our own homes, but then had to sell everything. Felix Narte took care of our home. [In Minidoka,] my mother and aunts all had infants with diapers. Narte brought a washing machine to them. Felix was like my mother's brother."

The temperatures at Minidoka were so extreme that, even in early July, it got "so cold that it is necessary to build a fire in the rooms," according to Kleinkopf. If the classrooms felt that cold during the day, it probably felt even colder in the uninsulated housing units that internees tried to sleep in at night.

Nevertheless, gardening was emphasized as a school activity, and nearly every barrack had a garden of vegetables and flowers around it. Many of the pupils and teachers still had much to learn about gardening. One student teacher asked for the potato plants and was surprised to learn that one planted a potato and not a seedling.

While the canal from the Snake River brought water to the camp, the irrigation ditches into the farmed areas had not yet been completed. Internees came up with a variety of ingenious ways to move water into the gardens and to furnish the barracks using materials from the surrounding landscape.

By June 21, 1943, the camp population was close to eight thousand, with 1,376 on indefinite leave to work in jobs that were not considered security risks, and 948 on seasonal work leave to perform agricultural work outside the camps. Presumably, those on work leave were older than high school age, and either fit enough to do agricultural work, or had skills such as accounting that could be applied elsewhere. With the labor shortage caused by the deployment of so many Anglo men, women in the general population were also put to work in unprecedented numbers. Three hundred acres of vegetables had been planted in the camp, with more planned. Four hundred chickens were on the chicken farm, and ninety feeder pigs on the pig farm. One hundred bushels of radishes had been produced so far. A complaint was made that many people who worked on the vegetable farm only worked until they had eaten all they wanted, then filled their pockets and went home.

At a dinner party for his teaching assistants, Kleinkopf was introduced to what he called "osushi":

July 9

Mrs. Kleinkopf and I sat down to one of the most unusual and most attractive luncheons that I have ever seen. The student teachers had bought young chickens from the man who hauls away the garbage and the cook in Dining Hall 32 had prepared them for eating. In addition to the fried chicken there was potato salad, ice cream, coca cola, and a rare Japanese dish called "osushi." It is made of seaweed, rice, dried mushrooms, eel, spinach and egg omelette all rolled together like a jelly roll. There was a second kind of "osushi" made from rice rolls prepared with a vinegar and sugar solution and then rolled in shredded shrimp. It looks beautiful although I don't care for the taste of either form.

Even with the temperature extremes of the high desert, dust storms, and brush fires, by August the fields maintained by the high school students had produced ten thousand pounds of peas, and there were ten thousand chickens on the chicken ranch.

By September, the gardens were lush. One of the elementary

school teachers knew how to preserve food, and began teaching her sixth grade students how to can and use a pressure cooker. Her students had their own garden plot, and had raised their own vegetables.

"This is certainly an excellent learning situation to follow the summer victory garden," noted Kleinkopf.

A "harvest vacation" was declared during October, so that the high school students and their Japanese American teachers could help bring in the farm crops. Many of the students were also allowed to earn money by working in the potato and sugar beet fields of southern Idaho. There was such a shortage of labor both in Minidoka and in the general area on privately-owned farms, that the "vacation" was later extended to November 1.

Throughout their stay, internees proved to be resourceful in their quest for familiar, palatable food. Some foraged for native plants familiar from home, and cultivated them for their nutritional and medicinal uses. "We used to soak and eat fiddlehead ferns *(warabi),*" said Kay. "They grew in Japan."

"We also ate *fuki,*" added Lilly, "a big green plant with a hollow stem. It is similar to rhubarb, and grows well in wet areas."

November 8

Mr. Stafford has several pounds of gobo seed in his possession. Gobo is a Japanese delicacy. To us it has always been known as burdock. The roots of this plant are used for food by the Japanese. It is cooked and served in various ways. It may be made into a stew, a pudding, or again it may be boiled then fried brown and served very much as potatoes would be served. I am told that many Japanese think that the gobo plant contains rejuvenating powers. (Maybe Ponce de Leon missed something!) The Japanese people have insisted for a long [time] that a crop of gobo be raised on the Project farms. This plant grows wild along the banks of the canal so Mr. Stafford sent a group of men to collect the seed. . . . Next spring several acres of gobo will be planted.

Kleinkopf included in his diary information from the camp's farm report for 1943, showing the kind and amount of crops produced in the Minidoka farms. These included potatoes, green and dry onions, squash, cabbage, watermelon, turnips, peas, green beans, sweet corn, green peppers, cantaloupe, celery, cucumber, eggplant, lettuce, and broccoli for a total of 2,221,512 pounds by December 14, 1943. Four acres of cauliflower were totally destroyed by insects. Much of the lettuce, Napa cabbage, and turnip crops suffered from lack of water, and the cabbage and broccoli were partially destroyed by insects.

Kleinkopf also made a note of the New Year's celebrations in the camps. "The evacuees make greater plans for celebrating New Year's than they do for Christmas. They have a three-day celebration: the day before New Year's, New Year's Day, and the day after." This celebration remains familiar to people on Bainbridge Island today as Mochi-tsuki.

GO WEST

Starting with the indigenous people, ethnic and religious groups in the United States have regularly been rounded up, incarcerated, or driven out of town by advancing waves of European immigrants. While the Americas have long acted as a refuge for those fleeing persecution in Europe, other groups found persecution here as well.

One of these is the Church of Latter Day Saints (LDS), whose founder, Joseph Smith, was killed by a mob in Illinois in 1844. The survivors moved west to establish themselves in Salt Lake City and then throughout the world. Since then the group has thrived and grown, in part because of their emphasis on planning, highly structured group endeavor, and individual preparedness. This duality in approach, the strong individual and the supportive group, includes the church's attitude toward food policies. In 2008, an LDS church was built on Bainbridge Island, although members had lived on the island for at least three decades, and had been organized as a "ward"—the LDS term for a congregation—since 1991. LDS members, often called Mormons, are encouraged to "prepare every needful thing . . . so that, should adversity come, we may care for ourselves and our neighbors and support bishops as they care for others," according to the official church website. "We encourage members worldwide to prepare for adversity in life by having a basic supply of food and water and some money savings." Specific directions suggest that members try to have a three-month supply of the foods that are part of their normal, daily diet.

Church guidelines also encourage people to store water, and to gradually build, in addition to the three-month supply, a supply of foods like grains and beans that will last "a long time, and that you can use to stay alive." How long is a "long time"? "These items can last thirty years or more when properly packaged and stored in a cool, dry place. A portion of these items may be rotated in your three-month supply."

Doing all this is not mandatory. But the official church website implies that taking responsibility for stockpiling these supplies "builds the character of the individual."

Utah, home to LDS headquarters, calls itself the Beehive State—church members hope, like bees, to be prepared for any contingency by working cooperatively. In part because of the violence its members have been subjected to in the past, the church looks both optimistically and practically to the future. A "provident living coordinator" for each ward tries to help members become "more self reliant" for the "trials we may have in our lives" through emergency preparedness and food storage.

A Mormon friend told me that in recent times, the expectations for the amount of food that families are expected to keep has been relaxed from one year's worth. If a family moves, rather than take all of their stored food with them, they usually give it away, then have to acquire it all again. Advances in food packaging means that stored food can last a long time, my friend explained, so families try to keep enough food to last for three months or so, without having to refresh it so often.

Speaking as someone who grew up in earthquake country, I know that keeping an emergency supply of food and water is not a bad idea. Though it's true that after a severe disaster, a source of power is probably the first thing we would miss, that would quickly be followed by freshwater, and shortly after that, food.

EATING AS A JEWISH ACT

During an interview with one of the farmers on Bainbridge, Betsey Wittick, I was struck by her use of the word "ceremony" in discussing the consumption of food. Food was meaningful to her if it had a story, if she could trace it from the ground to the table, if it was grown and served by people she knew. My spouse and I sometimes attend fund-raising dinners on Bainbridge where the history of each item of food is carefully recited before the food is served. This is to emphasize its local origins, and the care that was taken in planting, harvesting, preparing and serving it to us.

Mark Glickman, the former rabbi at Kol Shalom, the small Reform synagogue on Bainbridge Island, had a different story about food. He is not especially interested in the origins of the food he consumes. Nor is he obsessed with the minutiae of the rules and regulations in the Torah, or their interpretation through the ages in rabbinic literature. As a Reform rabbi, he is flexible in his approach—he used to drive from east of Seattle on Shabbat to serve our congregation.

In *Being God's Partner*, Jeffrey K. Salkin notes that "more than one hundred commandments in the Torah address economics, but only twenty-four form the basis of traditional Jewish dietary practice."

"When we say the prayer, 'Blessed are you Adonai, who brings forth food'—we are telling a story about the food. We could praise the baker, or the trucker, or anyone else who helped produce it, but we thank God," Glickman said. "The food comes from God, through the ground and onto our plate. We raise eating above the gluttony that has become part of our modern lives by telling a story. The prayer opens our eyes to the connection God has established with us."

"The modern eating process," he says, "harkens back to the laws of sacrifice. The home is still treated as a sanctuary, and the table is the altar, or *mikdash m'at*, little sanctuary. *Mikdash* is from the root of *kadosh*, which means devoted. The practice of Judaism is meant to evoke an earlier time, an idealized time, when the Temple was still standing."

I noted that in his book, *The Omnivore's Dilemma,* Michael Pollan said that the directions for Jewish sacrifice made a point of rotating the priests who performed the ritual, so that they would not become inured to the killing.

"Yes," Glickman said. "If you read the laws, there seems to be an awareness of the importance of taking away a life. We are allowed to do it, but it was a big deal.

"When I was studying in Israel, some Bedouins took us on a camel safari into the Sinai during Pesach (Passover). We asked to eat, and we stopped at an encampment. They brought us a goat, and we were encouraged to pet it, play with it, talk to it. The Bedouins held its head and said some prayers. They sent up smoke, and used a clean knife to slaughter it.

"I imagine that is very much what it was like when there were sacrifices in the Temple," he said. "There is a similar sense in the Torah.

"Adam and Eve were not allowed to eat meat. Only with Noah did we receive permission to eat meat, as a way to release our aggression. It's not ideal, but it's better than taking it out on each other."

"Really?" I asked. "I've never heard that."

"I made that last part up," he confessed.

Anthropologist Spencer Wells has a different take on that. In *Pandora's Seed,* he cites research showing that hunter/gatherer societies are less aggressive than agrarian societies. Since the sample of hunter/gatherers left on the planet is fairly small, his conclusions seem a bit tenuous. Yet I can see that, once someone has planted some land, watered and weeded it, and spent all spring shooing off the crows, he or she is going to get aggressive if someone tries to take the land or the food. Wells claims that there were always enough resources for hunter/gatherer groups, since they require very little in the way of material goods, and that dependence on cultivating food leads to shortages.

I'm going to speculate that in addition, hunter/gatherers quickly shed any members of the group who are not productive or cannot keep moving, while fixed-in-place, agrarian societies are able to keep the elderly and ailing alive even if they are not contributing directly to food production or acquisition. So I suppose on a strictly survival level, that is the trade-off: grandparents and war, or travel and less conflict. Perhaps the indigenous people of the Northwest tried to practice a combination of the two, with a mode of transportation—canoe—that accommodates the elderly, as well as garden plots that were tended seasonally, and food-gathering territories that were established by both war and negotiation among neighbors.

The directions in Torah for planting, gathering, and leaving a portion of the fields for gleaners to harvest, as well as the strict laws about what meat can be eaten and how it must be slaughtered and prepared, with as little fear and pain as possible, all point to a settled society, one fixed in place and dependent on domesticated crops and animals. The festivals of Pesach, Sukkot, and Shavuot were all once agricultural celebrations. An animal that has been hunted is not likely to die without fear or pain.

The significance of taking a life, even that of an animal at close quarters, seems widely shared. Pollan talks about the profound guilt he felt after his initial elation at shooting a boar in Northern California. Bainbridge Island resident Stephen Hubbard said he once killed one of his sheep in the traditional way, by slitting its throat with a knife.

"It died instantly, it bled out almost immediately once the carotid artery was opened. But holding it like that, yeah, that's getting close to your food." He now has professionals who come to the farm to slaughter and dress his sheep. During hunting season, the mobile butcher is in big demand, and can come on short notice to Hubbard's farm, Chateau Poulet, as I witnessed.

"Animal sacrifices ended permanently after the destruction of the second Temple," Glickman said. "There was no sacrifice during the fifty years after the destruction of the first Temple and the building of the second. You can only have sacrifice if there is a Temple. The idea is that when the Messiah comes, they will rebuild the Temple and start sacrifices again. We rabbis will be out of a job, because the priests, the Kohanim, will take over. At that time, who'll need rabbis?"

Glickman referred me to a book by David Kraemer called *Jewish Eating and Identity through the Ages*. "The Hebrew word for sacrifice is *korbanot*—the root is [from the word for] drawing near. When Jews eat today, they are harkening back to the *korbanot*, the rituals for drawing nearer to God. They do it by telling a story, especially during Passover.

"When we eat the bitter herbs, we recall the plagues in Egypt. When we eat *mazzot*, we reexperience the repression under the Egyptians. We taste the sweetness of freedom, the bitter tears. We enter the story, reexperience the lives of our people. It provides a way to transcend time and space and to touch eternity.

"This sometimes happens through song and other means." Glickman recalled hearing a woman sing who had attended the same synagogue in suburban Chicago. "That song took me back immediately, it brought back a flood of memory and emotions. Food can do that, too. But we bless God, not the food. It is symbolic, pointing to something beyond itself.

"In my father's childhood, there were three kinds of bread: wheat, rye, and *goyashawhitebread*. That's how they said it, all one word. My uncle, who was a Reform rabbi, had a farm in Illinois. We were not kosher at all.

"In college, I got more religious. I started to refrain from pork, shellfish, and cheeseburgers. My approach became 'I don't eat it unless I do,' because in Boston, I would eat lobster. Now, I order fish instead. I no longer feel like I am missing anything. It has attained the 'ick' factor."

This seemed to be an important concept in Judaism, the "ick" factor. As a friend of mine in California, a Conservative Jew, says, "We don't eat any of those creepy crawly things." Pollan talks about the ick factor as a basic human survival skill, one that keeps us from eating spoiled meat or things that taste or smell bad.

Glickman sees the laws of kashrut, or kosher food, as coming directly out of Middle Eastern customs. In kashrut rules, fish that have fins and scales may be eaten, as may animals that meet certain criteria. Rules for halal food in Islam are very similar. Both religions prohibit pork. My own parents maintained that the Biblical rules concerning eating were mostly for health reasons. When I told Glickman that, he disagreed.

"If that were true," said Glickman, "pork would be kosher, and schmaltz [chicken fat] would not be. There are people who think this should be the basis for kosher—that healthy food should be kosher, unhealthy food should be unkosher. There is lots of unhealthy kosher food, lots of healthy food that is not."

I recalled my father describing a butcher who had trichinosis, in which a parasite carried by pork is inhaled as tiny eggs by people, then worms hatch and exit through the skin. The man's arms and hands were covered in scars. As a child, that seemed to me like a perfectly reasonable excuse for not eating pork, kosher or not, and I still don't eat it. I'm told that cooking pork well kills the parasite.

In Torah, animals without cloven hooves or cud are not considered kosher, or permissible to eat. Camels and pigs are not kosher, because they do not have rumens, and so do not chew their cud. The camel is not prohibited in Islam, because making camels off-limits was seen as too much of a hardship for those crossing the desert—the last resort before starvation is to eat one's camel. The pig is especially disdained because from the outside, it looks like it has a rumen. Only when it is butchered can we see that it is an omnivore, not a ruminant. Humans, I discovered through Pollan, cannot digest grass, one of the few things we cannot eat directly. A rumen is what distinguishes us from grazing animals. By eating these animals, we "convert" pasture to something from which humans can draw nutrition.

I have my own theory about pork. I suspect that pork was originally prohibited because it cannot be differentiated from human flesh on a plate. German cannibal Armin Meiwes agrees. He is serving a life sentence for killing a man and eating more than twenty kilos of him. In the first television interview after his arrest, Meiwes described how the meat tasted of pork and how he prepared an elaborate meal of human steak in a green pepper sauce with croquettes and Brussels sprouts. But then, Meiwes insists he is a normal guy. The rabbi refused to comment.

Kraemer says you can only tell a Jew by what he doesn't eat. Food is certainly cultural. Most Jews in the United States are Ashkenazi, of Eastern European or German ancestry. There are only two Sephardic congregations in the area, both in Seattle, and I have often thought that their potlucks would have more in common with the food I grew up with than do the potlucks served on the long tables at Kol Shalom. One of the ways that people trace Jewish ancestry in the Southwest, like mine, is through traditional Sephardic food. *Pan de semita* (flatbread), *capirotada* (bread pudding), and the use of certain spices can be traced back to recipes brought over to the New World from Spain by Jews fleeing the Inquisition.

"Prayers and thoughtfulness about food is what makes eating into a Jewish act," Glickman said. "If I say a prayer, it makes the meal meaningful to me. It places the act of eating in the context of the sacred. It also places it into a social and cultural context that means, 'I am eating as a Jewish person.'"

What I am grasping for is the connection between ourselves and the land. Does the way that we worship have to do with how we think of the land? I think so. If the land is here for us to exploit, and nothing more, then our politicians are doing their duty. If we have steward-ship over the land, are responsible for it and everything on it, then all of us need to take responsibility for it on a daily basis. If someone else is hurting it, then we must stop them. If it is not our problem, then we can just look the other way and hope that there is clean air, water, and food as long as we need it.

A young friend, Leonard Stein, reminded me that every seven years, the fields and orchards in Israel are left fallow for one year, a practice called *shemitah*. Participants put up signs that invite the public to enter and help themselves. "It's a Shabbat for the land," said Stein.

This allows the trees and fields to rest and renew themselves, and probably comes from the same observations of the land that were practiced in Mesoamerica and elsewhere, where lands were once held in common by a village or settlement, and the fields were alternately worked, rested, and burned: if left fallow for a time, the land will heal itself, and be ready to yield more to human partners.

The corollary to all these practices is that a person who is starving should eat whatever it takes to stay alive. I have seen Jewish friends go hungry at events that did not offer kosher meals, but anyone who starves to death because kosher food is not available is violating Jewish law. Like the Muslim crossing the desert, choosing life is a mandate. Regardless of varying cultural and religious mandates and proscriptions, this, I suspect, is the bottom line for all religious food practices, Christian, Muslim, Jewish, Mormon, Hindu, Bud-dhist, or indigenous—eat well, eat carefully, eat gratefully, but most of all, eat to stay alive.

WHAT HAVE WE ALWAYS KNOWN?

What have we always known? Many of the people who now live on Bainbridge came out of starvation circumstances, severely restricted food environments, or have a cultural memory that includes times of both feast and famine. The people I talked to suggest that we:

- Scale down our consumption.
- *Mottainai*, Japanese for "Do not eat wastefully"—something Kay and Lilly were often told by their mothers.
- Pay attention to our environment—it might save our lives.
- Remember we are all—people, trees, land, animals—in this together.
- Always be prepared (for the worst).
- Know that it could happen to us (even when we least expect it).

Yet as we will see in the next chapters, most people don't have more than a day's worth of food in their homes, and have only a vague idea of where their food comes from. Under what circumstances do we lose these memories?

Haleets

There is a story I need to tell in this book, among all the others. It is the story of salmon, and without it, we really have no other stories. By we, I mean those of us who live in the Northwest—now, before, and later, when we are gone. The story of food in the Northwest is the story of salmon.

While Bainbridge Island does not include any major salmon streams, it attracts a few returning salmon, including steelhead, cutthroat trout, Coho, and chum salmon. These are all species that begin their wondrous cycle in the shallows, seeps, and protected wetlands of the island. Many of the streams have been dammed or diverted, and only in recent years has the city begun to repair culverts that would allow passage for returning salmon, or eliminate other barriers to them. The Bainbridge Island Land Trust recently conducted a stream survey, in which about one third of landowners adjacent or in close proximity to streams participated. The rest did not respond, or denied permission. Still, the survey allowed the land trust to begin addressing the loss of fish and food habitat on the island, a small speck in the greater order of things. However, the Sound is composed of such small specks.

Salmon is the miracle that happens every day, whether or not we see it. Loggers and builders and the Army Corps of Engineers have done their best to destroy it, but salmon is the lifeblood of this part of the world, the bright corpuscles traveling up and down the veins and arteries of rivers, whooshing in and out of Puget Sound like blood in a heart. We have told each other that "progress" is a good thing—damming the rivers, draining the swamps and estuaries, hardening the shores with bulkheads and breakwaters. But our hearts remember, and the fish—generation after generation—remember, and return each year in case we finally acknowledge them and let them in.

Others are watching, too. The most striking precontact artifact on Bainbridge Island is a boulder with petroglyphs carved into it, called Haleets (x̌alilc) or Xalelos (xʷaləlos). A collection of carved faces, their gaze shoots like an arrow across Agate Passage from Bainbridge to the heart of Suquamish. They never blink. The boulder, a "glacial erratic" left behind when the glaciers retreated, is sometimes called Figurehead Rock; no one knows how old the carvings are. Because the boulder is submerged at high tide, carbon dating and other methods are ineffective on it. Dan Leen, an archaeologist with a special interest in Northwest Coast petroglyphs, estimates the earliest designs at more than sixteen hundred years old.

According to Suquamish tribal historian Dennis Lewarch, photographs of the petroglyph date back to the 1890s. Anthropologist Thomas T. Waterman obtained information about the petroglyph from Suquamish informants around 1920. He also photographed and made a rubbing of it at that time. He noted that x̌al was the Lushootseed word for a basket design or handwriting. The Lushootseed name Xalilc refers to rock designs. In 1952, ethnographer Warren Snyder interviewed Suquamish elders, who called the petroglyph Xalelos, meaning "marked face."

There are several possible meanings to the carvings. The carvings include several facial images—one with some kind of headgear, possibly representing a headband or hat of cedar bark, another a star-like design representing a starfish, the sun, or some abstract concept.

Haleets is gradually wearing away, aided by barnacles. Individuals have attempted to clean it over the years, and have instead hastened the erosion by breaking off small pieces of the rock surface. Barnacle growth on the rock face, according to Lewarch, has increased dramatically in the past fifty years.

There was a time when honored Suquamish families maintained Haleets, removing barnacles on a regular basis. Lewarch is working with conservation specialists and the private property owner on Bainbridge to develop a program for careful removal of the barnacles, but for now, the rock is being left in place.

We, indigenous and newcomers alike, are beginning to reclaim much of the deep knowledge of place that has been worn away over the years.. In many cases, the old beliefs line up rather strongly with the desire to restore and regenerate the land in a way that will allow us to thrive without destroying everything around us. I will try to return to Haleet's long view now and then, just to see what we have made of the land since the carvings were engraved on the rock.

Whatever the specific intentions of the people who carved Haleets, it would not be there unless salmon had existed first. The story of the Suquamish, their friends and relations, and yes, their enemies and invaders, is the story of salmon. According to Upper Skagit storyteller Vi Hilbert, whom I interviewed many years ago, all storytelling is interactive. When the teller completes a story, the audience responds, "*Haboo!*" Which means, "We hear you!"

Ali (Alexandra Odin) at Tani Creek Farm.

– 2 –

To Market

OUR NEW HOME was right in town, on Twenty-first Street. I could walk to my elementary school, and my father could get to work quickly if he was called to substitute teach at the last minute. Our rented home was full of light, with built-in drawers and cupboards in the dining room that sparkled with glass insets. Behind the house was a brick patio, and behind that another yard, overrun with bamboo, and a garden shed.

We only lived there about a year. During that time, I made friends with an older brother and sister who lived down the block, and spent a lot of time in a crepe myrtle tree in front of the house. I'm sure the neighbors thought I was strange, but at least my mother knew where I was.

Dominating the backyard stood a shaggy black walnut tree, at least fifty years old. I used to eat those bitter black nuts until I was sick. At night the tree cast deep shadows across the yard when the moon shone brightly.

Rather than a basement, the house had a fruit cellar, with double doors that opened out over an earthy-smelling stairway into the gloom. It was still stocked with canned fruit from a previous owner. Basements of any sort were not common in Southern California, so it was all very mysterious to me. My father said that we could be safe here if there was a nuclear disaster. These were the days when we practiced for disasters by crouching in the hallways at school, our arms over our heads, away from windows, as though interior walls in an elementary school could protect us from a nuclear bomb.

Before the year was out, my father got a permanent teaching job at Franklin Junior High. With that, my family was able to buy a new house on the other side of the high school, on Sixteenth Avenue. It was on a huge corner lot, two blocks from the high school and on the eastern end of the bridge that led to the west side, where Franklin Junior High was located. It was not "four square acres," but it was large for a city lot. On the shady side of the house, hidden between flowering bushes, was a little loquat tree. In the backyard, my father made raised beds fronted with fiberglass, which my parents planted with herbs and flowers.

My father had graduated from high school in 1929. Since the age of seven, he had lived in the small farmworker's community of East Highlands, and gone to school in Redlands. His father, Celso, left the family when my father was small to return to Mexico, where he died shortly after from tuberculosis. My grandmother then married the man who built her house out of stone, but he died of cirrhosis of the liver during Prohibition when, according to my father, his stepfather would drink anything with alcohol in it. His death was a relief for my grandmother and my father, both of whom he beat regularly. My grandmother was not lucky in love, although she always struck me as a very practical person.

My father was the only Mexican to graduate from Redlands High School that year. His classmates had mostly dropped out of school after the required ninth grade to look for work. Every morning, a truck pulled up at the fork in the muddy road that marked East Highlands, to select pickers for the orange groves. In desperation one day, my father crawled onto one of the trucks, only to be turned out by the foreman. He was never chosen. My father remembers sneaking out to the orange groves one night to gorge on the fruit in order to stave off hunger pangs. This was dangerous, since the growers employed guards who beat anyone they caught stealing.

A son of one of the growers graduated in the same high school class as my father, and witnessed the humiliation he endured in trying to find work. The grower's son told his father, a trustee of Redlands College, who offered my father admission to the school, free of tuition. My father could attend classes for credit as long as he could keep body and soul together. A variety of tactics on my father's part, accompanied by acts of both cruelty and mercy toward him, got my father through Redlands College, now Redlands University.

One year my father got hired to pick cantaloupe. All he had was his one pair of street shoes, and his feet grew sore and blistered down the insides from walking in the narrow irrigation ditches.

Another summer he hitchhiked north. His uncle had gotten enough cash together to buy property and start his own truck farm, and my father worked for him. I doubt that it is still in the family, but "Alcala Farm," outside Hanford, California, still shows up on maps.

From his undergraduate work, my father moved on to the Pacific School of Religion, located at that time in Stockton. He was ordained as a Methodist minister in 1939, but he had always been interested in education as a vocation.

My father's early experience as a failed farmworker sharpened his sense of thrift, if not his common sense, and he continued to cultivate herbs or fruit trees or vegetables wherever we lived. This seemed to be true of other Mexican families, while the Anglo homes I visited preferred ornamental plants. Later, in retirement, my father fantasized about raising catfish in a series of pipes and basins that he set up in the backyard. It would never have occurred to him to research what it took to farm fish, he just enjoyed pretending that he could.

We moved to the Sixteenth Avenue house when I was seven years old. San Bernardino was "redlined," meaning that real estate agents would only sell to people of color in certain neighborhoods. Our house was on the very edge of a white neighborhood, but we had purchased it from another Mexican family. Across the bridge were heavily brown and African American neighborhoods.

In the back stood a tall, sturdy tangerine tree. My father cut it back severely several times without harming it. Bright orange tangerines of a huge size grew every year around December, prompting passing students to try to get into the yard and steal them. If I saw them, I let them in. The tangerines were unbelievably sour, and I figured if word got out that they were inedible, people would leave them alone. That worked until the next brilliant person decided that she would steal fruit.

In the very back, my father planted two white fig trees, mere sticks that he stuck in the ground. No one else believed those little pieces of wood would turn into trees. But sure enough, as he watered and tended them, they put on leaves and pale green fruit. The secret of the fig is that it is not a true fruit, but an infructescence, harboring the flowers and seeds within. These desert trees grew vigorously in our little oasis, and were pruned back each year only to grow leaves and fruit again.

My parents grew herbs for both cooking and medicinal uses: *yerba buena, rutha, cola de caballo*, oregano. Menstrual cramps could be soothed with *te de rutha*, or rue. *Yerba buena* (mint) or *te de canela* (cinnamon) was always brewing in a pot on the back of the stove, waiting to be heated up. These are both comfort teas, good for a midday break. Both of my parents thought it natural to use home-grown herbs as medicines. Years later my father said that his grandmother had been a *curandera*, a trained healer. My mother's mother was half Opata Indian and half Irish, so she may have inherited some knowledge from her own mother, or learned it in the various Mexican communities she lived in over the years. Mostly, I think poor people of that time and place knew how to treat minor illnesses without resorting to doctors. The landscape was legible to them, in that they could name the trees and plants that grew well in the area, and understood their uses.

My mother grew up in a preacher's family that moved constantly as her father was assigned to one congregation after another across northern Mexico and the southwestern United States. With each move, my grandmother gained a new baby, until she had given birth thirteen times and accumulated eleven living children. My Uncle Eduardo was the last, and he remembers that when he wanted to nurse, he would bring his mother a book so that she would sit down and read and nurse him. This was probably the sum of my grandmother's education, but at least she could read.

At some point, my mother's family was given a lamb, which became my uncle's pet. This of course, came to a bad end when the lamb ended up on the dinner table. My uncle ate none of it, and did not eat lamb for the rest of his life.

In such a large family, the children specialized. My Aunts Esther and Rosa Fe were good translators, a constant task in a bilingual ministry. My Aunt Julieta became a wonderful cook, as were two of her sisters-in-law, Arcelia and Julia. My mother, however, was the piano player and chauffeur. Her relationship with food was strictly as fuel, and our meals were tasty, but predictable. Each Sunday, my mother prepared a midday supper of beef pot roast, potatoes, and carrots. We ate this all week with flour tortillas and the occasional salad. Sometimes she made Spanish rice to go with it. Other times, she cooked pinto beans. At that time, the uncooked beans had to be spread on the kitchen table and sorted out from the pebbles that got packaged up with them. I remember pulling each bean toward me, leaving the dry little rocks behind, then sweeping aside the clean ones to be rinsed before they went into the pot. Our Sunday suppers might be followed by Jell-O with canned fruit in it. If we had company after church, lunch might be followed by ice cream.

In the 1960s, food in the United States was influenced by what was considered a scientific approach to eating. In the aftermath of World War II, we were told that canned fruits and vegetables contained more nutritional value than fresh food. We tried things like Tang and Space Sticks, both inspired by the space race between the United States and Russia. There was also something called Instant

Breakfast that was stirred into a glass of milk. I can't remember if it was used to gain or lose weight. Maybe both.

Both of my parents loved milk, while I found more than the amount I put on my cereal hard to digest, although I did not understand that. All I knew was that it gave me a stomachache that might last all day. Because I was thin, I was constantly encouraged to drink it.

My mother loved milk in spite of the fact that as a teenager, she had contracted typhoid from drinking milk fresh from a cow. All her hair fell out, and she had a vision of the angels bowing down to greet her. She was in bed for so long, that she had to relearn how to walk. Years later, she still remembered how good that milk tasted. She was sad when our local dairy discontinued home delivery. Fresh milk had been a big luxury for her. The dairy advertised itself as having "contented cows," and because it was local, we could drive by and see if the cows looked contented or not.

In summer, my father bought cases of Shasta soft drinks in cans. I seem to recall "blackberry" as a favorite flavor. Mostly, the sodas tasted good because San Bernardino was often over 100 degrees in the summer. My parents did not drink alcohol, and considered it one of the biggest dangers to humankind. There were no sugarless sodas. If my mother bought beef with a marrowbone, both of my parents wanted the marrow fat from inside the bone, to spread on a warm tortilla. Sometimes my father stopped at a bakery before coming home from work to pick up day-old sweet rolls at half price.

What I mean to say is that my family had an elemental relationship with food. There was never an attempt at "high" food or "low" food. There was food, not too much, and we ate it. Both of my parents had grown up in near-starvation circumstances. As a result, their taste in food ran to the high caloric: sweet, fat, cheap, and easy to prepare. At the time, there was little emphasis in popular culture on nutritional eating—three glasses of milk a day were recommended for children, to build bones. Other than that, I don't think the charts on daily vitamin intake had been invented.

In contrast to this very practical relationship with food, we spent part of every summer in Chihuahua, Mexico, with my aunt, uncle, and their five children. This was a loud, joyful household, and food was served in abundance. My Aunt Julieta spent much of her time in the kitchen, sometimes with a hired helper, in order to keep up with the demands of her family.

Julieta was friends with the various vendors who came to her door, who knew she would always buy something. And some of the cooked food went back out the door as charity, mostly to the Tarahumara (Raramuri) indigenous people who came to visit. I remember an entire porcelain plate laden with steaming food disappearing into someone's open bag. When my aunt saw me looking skeptically after her plate, she said, "Oh, she'll bring it back. I know her."

My aunt's world revolved around her five children and her kitchen. Everything else that mattered, all that she needed, came to her. My uncle left the management of the house to my aunt and her bottomless apron pockets full of *plata*, money, and went off to work every day as director of a private school, La Palmora. Chihuahua is where we were treated to fruits and vegetables not available in the United States, popsicles made from fresh mango or pineapple or coconut milk, and food served on both a regional and seasonal basis. The United States had already narrowed the availability of food to only those things that appealed to some general notion of an American diet, all year round. As a fifth grader, I challenged the results of a standardized test that offered multiple choices to a question about breakfast. Both the other Mexican kid in class and I chose "beans and eggs," which is a typical Mexican breakfast, and it was marked incorrect. The principal ended up throwing out the answer for everyone.

Outside the house on La Calle de la Llave, the street of the key, we sometimes went to restaurants. There was a hotel that served delicious food, and a famous restaurant called El Caballo Bayo, which specialized in beef. Northern Mexico is all about beef and flour tortillas—both cattle and wheat are tough enough to survive the desert climate. Although we associate the corn tortilla with Mexico, corn takes a lot of water, and is not the best grain crop in the north.

At home in San Bernardino, my mother gave piano lessons to little girls, and at someone's suggestion, began holding recitals for them each spring. I think this was mostly an excuse for them to wear frilly dresses, and for their mothers, many of whom knew each other, to get together socially. These were white women from a better part of town, and my mother was always nervous about whether or not the house was clean enough for them, and whether or not the rest of us were presentable. In junior high, I was in school with some of her students.

When I was in high school, I began to make cookies and cakes for these recitals. This was sort of fun, and people really seemed to like it. I still use one recipe that I got out of a copy of my mother's *McCall's* magazine. A whole orange goes into "Orange Kiss-Me Cake," peel and all. As I learned then, desserts transcend social differences— everyone loves sweets. In this case, they helped to bridge the divide between my family's culture and economic standing and those of my mother's students.

This was the first time I took any real interest in what the kitchen was used for, other than getting in and out for breakfast as fast as possible. For most of high school, I had to catch a bus three or four blocks away at 5:45 A.M. to the north end of town. San Bernardino High School, which was two blocks away, was being remodeled during that time from the gracious hacienda style my sisters had known, with open breezeways, to a series of closed boxes with no windows that were dependent on air conditioning. It had probably been years since anyone in downtown San Bernardino had smelled an orange blossom on the breeze, but the new design did make us safe from those Santa Ana winds made famous by Joan Didion in "Dreamers of the Golden Dream," the essay that helped make me a writer. Safe, at least, until we walked outside.

John F. Kennedy, Robert Kennedy, the journalist Ruben Salazar, and Martin Luther King were all assassinated during my childhood.

Unemployment in San Bernardino was around 14 percent, and local men considered themselves lucky to get jobs at Kaiser Steel. These already difficult circumstances were followed by race riots when I was in high school. At school, we were distinctly separated into three groups—brown, black, and white students—and sometimes sent home on separate buses. The American public had grown sick of the war in Vietnam, and drugs became readily available. I didn't use any, but some of my friends found relief in them. Two ran away from home, from all of us, during that time.

I was anxious to leave, and by some miracle, was accepted to Stanford University. I was completely unprepared for the experience, but determined to find a way to succeed. Like other immigrants who left their homes to face the unknown, I was willing to hop into the fire in order to escape the frying pan.

SWEET LIFE

Bainbridge Island curls like a fist of rock around Eagle Harbor on the western edge of Puget Sound, thirty-five minutes from downtown Seattle by ferry. Over half the island's working population commutes to Seattle every day on a Jumbo Mark II ferry, either the *Tacoma* or the *Wenatchee*. The ferries resemble floating airports, they are so large and stable, each capable of carrying twenty-five hundred passengers and two hundred vehicles at a time.

One must be patient to live on an island. Once in awhile the placid waters of Puget Sound are rough enough that a ferry is cancelled, and people must wait for the next one. Or the boat is held at the island to wait for an ambulance taking a critical case to one of the hospitals in Seattle. Otherwise, they must be airlifted by helicopter.

Off the northwest corner of Bainbridge is the short Agate Pass Bridge, constructed in 1950, that leads to the Kitsap Peninsula and all points west. I have joked that, if the bridge closed, ferries stopped, and we were completely cut off from the mainland, Bainbridge Island, with its population of about twenty-three thousand, could live off locally made white wine and goat cheese for quite awhile. Every April the farmers market reopens, and we have our choice of ... goat cheese, honey, and a few vegetables. The truth is, our growing season is short, and there are just some things that won't grow here in quantity.

But also, members of the farmers market protect their own interests. Products sold there must be grown or made within Kitsap County, a largely rural area west of Seattle that includes Bainbridge, and participants must be approved by the market's board. At one point, the owner of an old produce stand near the highway tried to sell fruits and vegetables that had been grown in Eastern Washington, but members of the farmers market board got it shut down as a violation of their regulations.

As a result, most of our produce is still grown off the island, purchased through the locally owned Town & Country Market or a Safeway store. Once, Bainbridge was famous for its strawberries, but the Marshall strawberry's susceptibility to rot, followed by the forced internment of Japanese American farmers during World War II, ended their production. By the fall, a greater variety of produce is available, but as Americans, we are used to having seasonal products year-round: lettuce, tomatoes, broccoli, avocadoes, citrus fruits, things that grow in limited quantities or not at all in our cool, wet climate. "There are no seasons in the American supermarket," as the movie *Food, Inc.* put it.

Bob and Nancy Fortner, whom I first knew as booksellers, began selling honey, soap, skin care products, and preserves, all produced at their Sweetlife Farm, at the farmers market. Their website proclaims that "Sweetlife Farm is a 'cottage' business (just the two of us); we value quality over quantity, and urge you to purchase as things appeal to you, understanding that everything is a 'limited edition,' and may not be available again."

Or, as Nancy put it in our conversation, "We try to grow enough to feed ourselves and make value-added products," all in their state-inspected, certified commercial kitchen.

This is not the first transformation for the Fortners. They first met as medical professionals at the William Beaumont Army Medical Center in El Paso. They married and moved to the Bay Area, where they lived in a house high in the Santa Cruz Mountains, at La Honda, and Bob was a kidney specialist at El Camino Hospital in Mountain View. Bob and Nancy moved to Bob's native Washington State in 1992, and Bob continued to practice medicine part-time, until becoming disillusioned with the profession.

"The changing ethics of the medical profession," he said, "contributed to the fragmentation of medical care." As doctor's groups reorganized as businesses, he felt patients took second place: "When the pie gets smaller, the table manners change."

Sweetlife Farm is located on one of the highest points on the island, around three hundred feet above sea level. It often snows here when it does not snow at my house, which is only about a hundred feet above the cold waters of Eagle Harbor. In the winter, the steep, gabled roofs shelter the entrances to their Arts and Crafts–style home, and to the building that now houses their commercial kitchen and showroom. For "Christmas in the Country," an island-wide event that encourages shoppers to travel from one venue to another, "buying local," the Fortners always host several artists whose wares complement their own seasonal products, such as "Cocoa Local" and Nancy's meticulously wrapped gift soaps.

"The evolution of none of this was planned," Bob said. "There are early decisions, early influences under which you fall." One was the writings of Helen and Scott Nearing. In 1954 the Nearings published *Living the Good Life.* Bob and Nancy discovered it when they were starting out in the 1970s. The book advocates a "back to the land" lifestyle, and describes how the Nearings grew most of their food on a farm in Vermont. The book recounts how, after Scott Nearing was kicked out of academia for being a Communist during the Depression, the two of them were able to sustain themselves with almost nothing purchased from the outside, while leaving half of the year free to travel and promulgate their ideas. "Such a handbook," says the preface, "is needed for the many individuals and families, tied to city jobs and dwellings, who yearn to make their dreams of the good life a reality."

A follow-up book "by that frugal housewife" Helen Nearing, *Simple Food for the Good Life* (1980), includes recipes and a description of the kind of food they grew and ate, such as "Casseroled Carrots" and "Buckwheat Crunchies."

The Fortners did much of the work themselves in building their present house, with its view across a small pond to a natural stream, backed by hundred-year-old Douglas firs. Every time I go over there, it seems, a new structure has been added. At the last Christmas in the Country, a new wood-fired oven occupied its own shingled building, covered in tiny Christmas lights. A florist was exhibiting in there, and I worried for the first time that Sweetlife Farm was beginning to resemble those commercial gardens that rely as much on tourists as on regular customers. Was this a proprietary feeling? If it seems that way, it is because the Fortners have cultivated that feeling in a great many people. I think of the Fortners' house as the island's living room. Although Bainbridge Island is a small town, it is a big island, the size of Manhattan, and we residents do not cross paths that often. By providing a place for intentional gathering, either for work or play, the Fortners have strengthened the fabric of our community.

I decided that if there is ever a major emergency, such as the bridge washing away and the ferry service shutting down indefinitely, I would make my way to the Fortners'. I'm not sure how they feel about that. But I know that if I showed up under those circumstances, they would put me right to work. I have never seen either of them idle.

I continued to think about those ideas, the what-ifs implied by people trying to become independent of the grocery store for their food. I have another friend, Marilyn Holt, who with her husband Cliff Wind, runs a farm off the island in Kitsap County.

On a Thursday morning, Nancy and I followed the directions to Holt Ranch. Bob had already left for a sustainable farming meeting in Port Townsend. Forty-five minutes later, Marilyn, Cliff, and their three dogs welcomed us inside. We gathered around their dining room table. The oilcloth had a rooster design, and Marilyn served strong coffee.

The current farmhouse was built around 1900. It is the second house on the spot, and the third on the property. The first was at the top of a small rise, partly underground. A new house was built when the spring ran dry, but its location, near a creek, means that it always feels damp inside. Marilyn's great-grandfather, Frederick Walker, bought the almost thirty acres in 1892 from the homesteaders, a Mr. and Mrs. Cooksey.

Cliff retired in 2011 after working for the U.S. Postal Service since 1977. Marilyn had worked as a technical writer and was also a certified management consultant. From 1999 to 2000 she served as the chief financial officer of an e-book company. She still has a consulting company, Holt Capital, and says she might return to it if she needs to. I know Marilyn as one of the founders of Clarion West, a science fiction writers workshop, and I think she has the sort of authoritative air that would make young software developers pay attention. Now, both she and Cliff work full-time on the farm.

The two realized that at some point decisions would need to be made about the farm. In late 1998 or early 1999, it became obvious, Marilyn said, that her father needed help. Her mother had died in 1982, and Marilyn is an only child. When Marilyn took over, she was simply considering which five acres to sell in order to pay for his care. He had Alzheimer's and MRSA—methicillin-resistant *Staphylococcus aureus,* a bacterial infection common in hospitals. The cost for his care was "amazing."

"I didn't think I'd get to keep it," she says of the farm.

Marilyn and Cliff have one permanent part-time employee, and in the summer hire teenagers to work part-time. Because farm work is hard labor, a different set of employment rules, as well as wages, apply for hiring young people. For example, no one under sixteen can drive any of their farm equipment. This is not true in most states, where young teens or even children can drive farm equipment as long as it remains on the farm.

"I'm a huge 'right to farm' advocate," Marilyn says, meaning that she opposes regulations that restrict farming near high density areas. In communities like Bainbridge, this can be an issue as housing developments begin to impinge on agricultural areas, or cities try to conform to the statewide Growth Management Act of 1990, which mandates planning by each municipality for increased density. It does not look like an issue at Marilyn's farm, which is surrounded by other small farms and by houses on multiacre lots. Still, if one of their neighbors decided to subdivide their property into residential lots and build houses, there could be complaints about the odors associated with raising cattle, or the noise of farm equipment. This became an issue on Bainbridge Island, when a pond of effluence from pig-raising overflowed and contaminated nearby areas.

At the same time, more urbanized areas are loosening these laws a bit, allowing households to keep chickens and other small livestock such as goats, and to replace lawns with edible plants.

I asked Marilyn what seeds she had bought for the coming season: lettuce, broccoli, onions, garlic, beets, and carrots, she says, as well as bok choy, kohlrabi, potatoes, beans, and corn. They plan to put seven acres in crops, and keep twenty in pasture for the cattle. A lot of the vegetables will start under plastic.

"We do a lot out of books," says Cliff.

Marilyn agrees, "The knowledge has been lost. We need to find it in books." Among others, they consult books written by a pair of farmers in Maine who use unheated greenhouses. Writers Barbara Damrosch and Eliot Coleman run their Four Season Farm as an experimental market garden in Harborside, Maine, that produces vegetables year-round. The photos on their website show clean, spacious greenhouses, with wide rows of orderly vegetables, and enough vertical space to grow corn. It looks like something out of the space movie *Silent Running,* in which refugees from Earth farm in unnaturally perfect rows on their spaceship.

Like the Fortners, the Holts farm full-time. More than full-time. At first, Marilyn and Cliff focused on hay and cattle. About six years ago, Holt Ranch started its Abundantly Green community supported agriculture (CSA) program, in which subscribers pay at the beginning of each season to receive a weekly share of produce. Holt Ranch begins its CSA season in April, and continues through October. The CSA model has grown increasingly popular across the country over the last twenty years. The advantage to farmers is that they receive cash up front. Consumers receive fresh, locally grown produce, and form a relationship with a specific farm and its products. Abundantly Green subscribers can also opt to receive beef from Holt Ranch, which is organic but not certified, in order to save on cost. More recently, Cliff and Marilyn invested in a WSDA/ USDA-compliant processing trailer, and offer processed chicken as well as eggs. They also buy from other farmers to supply pork and additional produce.

Cliff and Marilyn sell at the Poulsbo Farmers Market, and distribute their CSA shares in Poulsbo, Bremerton, and at the farm. When we all go outside, Cliff and Marilyn show off a bright yellow cart built by her cousin for use at the market. It has bins and drawers that open out to display the vegetables. The farmers market is Cliff's realm. He staffs the market stall during the season, and distributes the CSA shares, a rotating variety of vegetables as the season progresses, to participating families.

I asked one of the hypothetical questions that sent me on this quest: If there was a food emergency, and I showed up and wanted to work for food, what would they have me do?

"We can all do something," Marilyn said. "Weed. I would expect you to learn how to field dress." This means, to slaughter an animal and divide the meat into its appropriate parts for consumption. I could also learn basic gardening, she said: loosening the soil, harvesting vegetables, seed saving. Marilyn, it turns out, cannot touch the ground: she is allergic to mold, as well as much of the produce that they grow, such as legumes. She described putting a bean into her mouth before having to spit it out, as her throat began to swell.

Marilyn told me that her mother used to read to her from Chairman Mao's *Little Red Book* and tell her to keep the farm for when the revolution came. This made me wish I could have interviewed Marilyn's mother. Her fiercely independent spirit, rolling with the changes in consumer demands and government regulations, is still evident in Marilyn. After discussing her departed parents, Marilyn noted that she and Cliff, now in their early sixties, are the national average age for farmers in the United States.

We pulled on our mud boots and went outside in the drizzle. I was the only one using an umbrella. We walked by a large barn, built from a Sears kit around 1930. It occurred to me that the beautiful weathered planks on the barn would probably be worth more than the building itself, if sold to a young family on Bainbridge; they would probably use it for flooring, proudly pointing out the flaws in the wood.

Another outbuilding contained cold storage units for their produce in the summer. This building looked relatively new, and Cliff and Marilyn seemed very happy with it. The extra storage will enable them to harvest food for their CSA shares ahead of time and to prepare the boxes on the spot. We passed an area full of old tractors and their attachments, the sorts of farm vehicles that preceded combines. The farm is the kind of place my husband would call "Implement City" when we lived in western Colorado—farmers have no way of disposing of outdated or obsolete equipment, so it usually just rusts in piles around the property.

Cliff, a thin man with a long, graying ponytail, pulled up a stray kohlrabi from the previous season and, with a wizard's flourish, gave us a little presentation on this root vegetable. Cliff never expected to end up a farmer, but he likes the interaction with CSA shareholders, "interesting folks doing this for different reasons." Often, their share-holders do not know how to prepare specific vegetables. As he told us about the kohlrabi, I saw what a great math and science teacher he would have made, his first aspiration. He told us the best way to eat it is steamed, mashed, and served like mashed potatoes. I've been to potlucks with Cliff and Marilyn, and Cliff likes to try new things. He once brought an exotic fruit and dared the other guests to guess what it was. I guessed durian, but it was another knobby, aromatic fruit, jackfruit.

We walked up a rise to the site of the original farmhouse. The stumps of old hazelnut trees mark the spot, which looks south across open land to dark forest beyond, and is flanked on the east by firs and pines. It's a beautiful setting, and I wondered what it had looked like to Marilyn's great-grandfather. Under cultivation, Marilyn said, their land can yield one thousand dollars' worth of produce per acre a week. All I saw was damp pasture where the cattle grazed north of us, mud where we stood. I wondered if, given their overhead, this was sustainable. I asked Cliff and Marilyn how they envision their farm in thirty years. Will it still be a farm? "I hope so," said Marilyn. "Yes, I see it as still being a farm." Marilyn has faith that, as long as people know how to work the land, there will be sustainable agri-culture.

On Bainbridge, there is a man who grows wine grapes and talks a lot about *terroir*, a French term for the characteristics of a specific piece of land. Supposedly, these characteristics are reflected in any-thing grown on it, and the savvy farmer will work to enhance these flavors in his or her crops. Cliff and Marilyn have invested in the *terroir* of Holt Ranch, and believe that specific knowledge can and will be passed on to others.

Driving back to Bainbridge, I realized that the practical questions I had come with—how many acres, which elevations, how many days of sunlight—were not as important as the question I thought might be the most frivolous: If I were desperate, what could I do to earn food? I wasn't thinking of a Cormac McCarthy scenario, like *The Road*, where people resort to cannibalism due to some unnamed global cataclysm. I was concerned about something like a breakdown in transportation, since almost all of our food is shipped or trucked in.

The most important factor in the equation turns out to be not acreage or elevation or sunlight, but simply labor: the more hours that human beings work on a farm, the more it can produce. Child labor laws were originally written to protect children in industrial settings, but agricultural exemptions were made to allow families to farm together, and to loosely regulate harvesting, fishing, and the types of seasonal processing that include a whole community.

Nowadays, it is still the children of migrant workers who suffer the brunt of agriculture's low wages and of the constant uprooting that precludes success in school and a chance at a better life. Dependence on labor also means that couples like Cliff and Marilyn, who have no children of their own, are constantly hiring and training young people to perform work necessary for the success of their farm.

"We have not solved the problem of living," wrote the Nearings. "Far from it. But our experience convinces us that no family group possessing a normal share of vigor, energy, purpose, imagination and determination need to continue to wear the yoke of competitive, acquisitive, predatory culture."

Marilyn and Cliff, Nancy and Bob have not solved the problem of living. But if they succeed in finding and maintaining the sweet life, we will all benefit. There is always earth. And around here, there is always water. As long as people preserve the knowledge of growing food, we will be able to eat. As humans, we will continue to divide the pie many ways, probably keeping the biggest pieces for ourselves.

LAUGHING CROW

Betsey Wittick met me at a purple, open-sided shed on the eastern edge of Laughing Crow Farm on Bainbridge Island. Her four acres are part of a larger area set aside for farming on Day Road. Betsey received a master's degree in horticulture from Cornell, took a bicycle trip across the country, and stopped when she got to Bainbridge Island. She fell in love with the West Coast and says she was very lucky that in 1984, Junkoh Harui, the late owner of the Bainbridge Island Nursery, gave her a job. The Haruis had been among the interned Japanese Americans who, after the war, returned to Bainbridge.

Now Betsey stood and talked with me as she polished bell peppers for market the next day. It was very windy. Sallie Maron joined us a little later. Sallie is one of the cofounders of Sound Food, a group organized to facilitate access to local farm products. I described the concept of a food oasis, a place of abundance where growing food will continue to be sustainable during climate change, and asked Betsey if she thought we lived on one.

"We don't really know what will happen with climate change. It may be warmer, it may be wetter. I think there will be more variability," said Betsey. Industrial agriculture developed, according to author Fred Kirschenmann, she said, during a few hundred years of climate stability, but now the climate is fluctuating. Farmers can't invest in large-scale industry and equipment unless they know that the crops they are cultivating will be viable in the long run. By contrast, before industrial agriculture, there was greater diversity—you didn't put all your eggs in one basket.

"Now, we need agriculture to be more local. Some think, 'Technology will save us!' but infrastructure takes awhile to evolve. We need to be more resourceful in how we raise food."

Who are your role models? I asked. Your heroes?

Betsey answered without hesitation: "Judy Wicks and David Suzuki."

Betsey saw Judy Wicks speak at the conference of Business Alliances for Local Living Economies in Vancouver. There were a lot of people there from *Yes!* magazine, she said, a Bainbridge Island–based publication about local sustainability.

Wicks is a business entrepreneur from Philadelphia, said Betsey. She started as a waitress, lost her job, and began to sell coffee and scones out of the downstairs of the brownstone she rented. That evolved into a restaurant, and Judy got involved in local equity and local food issues. She saw a movement toward social justice everywhere except in restaurants, so she raised wages in hers. Wicks began to buy local chicken and beef from the Amish, then pork. She got into distribution when she helped an Amish farmer buy a bigger truck. Then Wicks began loaning money to other locally sourced and sustainable restaurants. She ran her restaurant for twenty-five years, all the while starting and funding other people's projects along the way.

"She kept finding fun ways to introduce people to the idea of social justice and local food," Betsey said. I haven't danced with a tomato yet, as featured at one of Wicks's fund-raising parties, but we have begun to see more events of this kind on Bainbridge, as people like Sallie and Betsey search for ways to engage the general public with the importance of local food and its producers.

David Suzuki, Betsey's other hero, is a Canadian scientist. He is interested in how we use local resources in the economy. He has a number of videos on YouTube, and started a foundation called The Sacred Balance that describes how humans fit into the planet's ecosystem. He argues that humans need to be in touch with nature at a local level in order for our economies to thrive.

"He's funny and right on with how I feel about stuff," Betsey told me.

Suzuki, a geneticist by training, got into this because he audited a class on economics. Anyone who has sat through a class based on Keynesian economics knows that the charts used to graph economic success or failure are oddly clean and devoid of on-the-ground reality. This is what is supposed to make them scientifically correct, their dissociation from anecdotal evidence. To Suzuki, the economics professor was leaving "all sorts of variables out of the equation," because factors such as culture, climate, and local conditions are not included in the standard economic model. "Suzuki told his wife that he would be quiet in the class," Betsey said, "but his hand was raised before he even knew it" to challenge the model. That is when he knew he had to get involved in how we think about sustainability and economics.

I asked Betsey whether or not we could grow wheat on the island. She said that some people were growing wheat in Sequim and Chimacum, areas farther west of Bainbridge, both slightly warmer and drier. Because of the rise of monoculture farming, in which farms raise only one crop at a time, we have lost the varieties of wheat that would grow here, she said. The seed companies cultivate and distribute only seeds that can be grown by the majority of farmers nationally, and the maritime Northwest is not a big wheat-growing region. However, we can, she told me, grow wheat, corn, and rye—Betsey herself has grown triticale, a hybrid of wheat and rye. In fact, Betsey turned out to be the person who had grown the grain and baked the bread served at the Slow Food dinner that the Fortners hosted for ethnobotanist Gary Paul Nabhan. "You need a combine for wheat, to thresh and harvest it, unless you want to throw it in the air and winnow it by hand." This did not seem to interest Betsey. However, Washington State University continues to experiment with wheat varieties—they may yet find a variety of wheat, or another grain, that would thrive on Bainbridge.

If we needed to support the population of Bainbridge with food we grew on it, I asked Betsey and Sallie, what is the first thing we would miss?

"Trees," Betsey answered. "We would have to cut a lot of the trees down" in order to have the room for crops, as well as the sunlight.

"A lot more people would have to be involved in growing food," she added. "We would have to eat a lot more seasonally, and the diet would change. We would have to shift our way of living."

"The first thing I would really miss is coffee," said Sallie. "But we might be able to grow some things in greenhouses."

"We would miss olive oil," added Betsey, "and would need to use animal fats to substitute. We would need handpresses to extract oil from sunflower seeds. The fat from a cow or pig is better."

As we mulled these ideas over—where our food comes from, how we can connect people more closely with their food and environment—Betsey said, "I'm not 100 percent a purist, but some of the best meals [I've eaten] were grown by me or people I know. It is ceremonial food, a meal with a story." This began to remind me of Rabbi Glickman's description of the Jewish relationship with food. We are grateful for it, and we create ceremonies around gratitude. We like to have a story around our food.

As Betsey points out, industrial food "packagers are beginning to take advantage" of our desire for a personal connection. I have noticed this in the grocery store—the down-home name, the slightly crude drawing of farm folk enjoying the sunshine with their happy cows. It's true, this packaging does remind me of the supposedly happy cows that supplied the milk of my childhood. Michael Pollan has dubbed this form of packaging and advertising "supermarket pastoral."

"The true story is when you know the person who grew the food," said Betsey "If people begin to grow their own food, even if less is bought from the farmers market, it would be worth it" to her for people to understand the complete process of growing food.

Sallie and another farm advocate, Carolyn Goodwin, started Sound Food, a nonprofit and a website, in 2007. "Sound Food is made up of people who love local food," said Betsey, "and support local food.

It tastes better. They want to find a way to support local farmers by telling the story, and bringing food to where people are."

Sallie and Carolyn created the first comprehensive map of local food on Bainbridge Island, so that consumers could go straight to the farmers. "We wanted to do a green map," said Sallie. "There wasn't one for food, to connect farmers with consumers. We wondered, how do we find where things are?"

Sound Food also came up with an ingenious method for getting local food directly to busy commuters. During the farmers market season, they set up a table at the ferry terminal every Wednesday. People got off the ferry, handed five dollars to Sallie or another volunteer, and took home a bag of fresh greens or other vegetables. "It ties in with how we are as a society right now," said Betsey, meaning that people are pressed for time. "It took a lot of coordination." But the ferry terminal stand was too dependent on a few volunteers to be sustainable.

"Then we realized we could put a map on the website," said Sallie, "but how would people know it was there?" First, they decided they needed to draw attention to the site by showcasing farmers. "We used the idea of breaking bread. It is a historic symbol, breaking bread together." Betsey and her recipes are also often featured.

"Second," Sallie continued, "we wanted to look at the whole food system—from distribution, to convenience, to cost. Ecotrust out of Oregon has created an online program called FoodHub through which restaurants can order food from local producers. It took awhile for us to get started with it, but now restaurateurs can locally source their menus" by going to FoodHub, seeing what is available, and placing an order.

In an effort to reach out to other farmers, Betsey joined the local chapter of the Grange, originally established in 1915. Betsey and Sallie laughed as they exchanged stories about the old and new Grange, and the reaction when Betsey and other women farmers began to join. The old-timers, once they recovered from their shock, brought out their sashes and badges, and insisted on "a lot of ritual."

One reason the women joined the Grange is that it has its own state and federal lobbyists, and still offers home and farm insurance. Historically, the Grange has always welcomed women farmers as full members, not relegating them to "auxiliary" organizations as many fraternal organizations do. In fact, it was once one of the most radically liberal institutions in both the United States and Washington State.

Although the Grange's statutes did not forbid minorities from joining, the Japanese American and Filipino American farmers on the island were not allowed to join the local Grange prior to World War II. After the war ended and those who had been interned were freed, only a few Japanese farmers returned to farming full-time. Because the Grange offered a good farm insurance policy, one of the Japanese farmers asked to join, but was turned down. "They wouldn't let us in there," he said. "After serving two years [in the military] they turned us and the Filipinos down." Sadly, that farmer was Akio Suyematsu, who went on to mentor many non-Japanese farmers. He expresses his anger and frustration in an oral history interview that is part of the Densho Digital Archive, an online collection of historical documents and interviews concerning the Japanese American experience. Later, Akio was invited to join the Grange, but was too angry to do so. "I got stomped on that one too much."

Nevertheless, Sallie said that "the Grange helped Lilly Kodama's mother grow raspberries when her husband died." A Filipino American was president of the Grange when Sallie joined.

The Bainbridge Grange hall, an eighty-year-old building, was recently refurbished and made available for community events. However, paid membership remains at seven or eight, according to current president Brian Stahl, so the Grange does not enjoy the power it once did on the island.

"Farmers live at poverty level," said Betsey, "no insurance, no retirement. The produce brought from California is grown with subsidies, on the backs of Hispanic people."

Sallie agreed. "The incredible cheapness [of industrial produce] is because of subsidies. The lack of logic is amazing. People want to pay the least for what they get, and get paid the most for what they do." I think we are all programmed to operate that way, even at the expense of others.

FARMERS ARE ALWAYS BUSY

Brian MacWhorter is a mountain of a man. Not only is he tall and broad, but he was covered in dirt when I first met him in the produce section of our grocery store. The following week, I called Brian, who grumbled that farmers are always busy, but agreed to meet me at Day Road Farm.

Day Road Farm was originally part of the Suyematsu Farm, purchased in 1928 in American-born Akio Suyematsu's name by his parents. Now leased to several farmers and farming concerns, it is protected as agricultural land by the City of Bainbridge. Every time I talked to people about growing food on Bainbridge, they referred me to Brian. "He is the premiere farmer on Bainbridge," said Bob Fortner of Sweetlife Farm. "He probably has the most acreage under cultivation, both on the island and elsewhere in Kitsap County."

At Day Road, Brian began to direct his helpers, three young women, including his daughter, to move a pile of compost from in front of the greenhouse. They also began loading flats of starts to be taken to another farm property, the site of the original Nakata Farm, now called Middlefield Farm, a translation of *nakata*. As far as I know, everyone else still calls it the Nakata Farm—or rather, the Nakata property, since it has lain fallow for most of living memory. But then, Bainbridge is the sort of place where people give driving directions according to landmarks that no longer exist, like the old strawberry plant, or the Texaco station that once stood at the intersection of Highway 305 and Winslow Way. The starts were for sunflowers, greens, and squash. I asked if the sunflowers were for seeds or flowers. Flowers, he said.

Brian greeted a nearby worker in Spanish and introduced him to me as Nacho. They proceeded to have a discussion in English about arugula. Brian directed the women to spread the compost and roto-till it. A good farmer knows how to delegate efficiently.

Brian grew up on a small family farm in Pennsylvania, "where Washington crossed the Delaware. I loved it." Brian was an orphan from Ireland adopted by an American family. He always liked the outdoors, he said. Upon returning from Vietnam in the early 1970s, he moved to Oregon to attend the University of Oregon, where he studied pre-med on the GI Bill. In 1974, while still a student, he built a house on an organic farm near Eugene and became one of the first organic farmers in the country.

After graduation, Brian was broke and wanted to teach, but there were no jobs. He moved to a commune and lived there for four or five years. That is when he started Butler Green Organics with broth-ers Dave and Tom Lively. Later, the group teamed up with a broker who connected them with organic fruit grower Joe Gabriel. Then a big company bought the business. Renamed "Organically Grown," the group produced over fifty million dollars' worth of organic veg-etables in a recent year, according to Brian.

Nineteen eighty-four was a bad year for farming, so Brian and his partner, Amy, went to Hawai'i. Brian "just relaxed," while Amy worked as a nurse in Honolulu. Eventually, Brian leased some prop-erty and started a "beautiful farm" in Kona. The couple returned to Oregon to marry. They also intended to visit friends in Federal Way, Washington, who had offered Brian a job in the solar energy busi-ness. On the way they stopped on Bainbridge to camp at Fay Bain-bridge State Park, and Brian ended up renting a farm on Lovgren Road. Their first daughter, Alana, was born at this time. They began to live six months a year in Hawai'i, and six on Bainbridge. That was twenty-six years ago.

Brian began to sell at the Bainbridge farmers market. "A hand-ful of people sold in front of Bainbridge Bakers" at that time, he told me. The market moved around before coming to rest on the green between the Bainbridge Performing Arts playhouse and city hall, in a space built specifically for that purpose.

When their second daughter was born, the family tried to make a living by farming full-time on Bainbridge, but were unable to do so. Farmers need to own or lease enough land to pay them back for their labor, both in food to eat and in surplus to sell. This is an age-old problem. Many farmers have second jobs. Brian began working as a cook, which he says "forged a new connection" for him with local chefs. He learned that chefs feel responsible for what people eat, and are willing to pay more to provide good food. "Some just use the concepts of 'local' and 'organic' for marketing purposes, but others are really committed," he discovered.

"This is a maritime climate, the best climate in the world," Brian said. "This is rain forest weather, with thirty-two to thirty-six inches of rain a year on Bainbridge." He grows lettuces, brassicas (that's the broccoli family), beets, carrots, leeks, and chards. He wouldn't try to grow tomatoes outside, but he says that with greenhouses, it is possible to grow anything that will grow in the continental United States almost year-round. He uses high tunnels, which are unheated greenhouses, but says that regular greenhouses have the best temperature control.

During my visit in mid-June, Brian was starting a winter garden with kale. "You want things full grown in the fall," he said, "because they don't grow much in the winter." The trick is how to provide consistency, quality, and dependability. "Then the restaurants will be willing to support you." Here, Brian stopped to give some directions concerning a wheelbarrow.

Brian has met farmer Eliot Coleman, author of some of the books used by Marilyn Holt and Cliff Wind, whom I interviewed earlier. Brian says he has been farming ten years longer than Eliot, and came to many of the same conclusions on his own, in particular that crops can be grown in unheated tunnels and greenhouses for maximum yield almost year-round. "I don't read as much as I should," Brian said, but he has learned through trial and error. "People can read," he said, "but that doesn't mean they get it. I've seen it, done it, now I'm teaching it."

Brian sees himself as one of Akio Suyematsu's heirs. Akio went out of his way to help people get into farming on Bainbridge. He had most of the equipment, and knew how to fumigate the fields against soil-dwelling pests for other farmers.

As for the Middlefield property, which the family has turned over to Brian to farm, "I don't know what to do on the Nakata property. It's marginal." The land was overfarmed fifty years ago, he said, so he is growing things that do not need much water: beans, squash, and sunflowers. "Maybe that is a good place for more greenhouses," Brian muses out loud. He will be raising organic produce especially for the Nakata family's grocery store chain, Town & Country.

"The organic produce business has gone up 20 percent a year for the last twenty years. Now it is a billion dollar business, and big money is moving in," said Brian, meaning the mega companies such as Monsanto and Tyson. "Eventually, all produce might be organic. There is a push on one side to radiate all food. There is another group that reads and understands all the problems, and is trying to eat right."

I mentioned that one of the factors in my interest in food has been my own health. "I've dropped thirty pounds," he told me. Brian won't tell his age, but said that he was about to have a "big" birthday. Brian had stayed up celebrating the night before with his friend Mario Perez, who sells fishing nets all over the Spanish-speaking world. Nacho, who was still toiling out front, is Mario's brother, and has worked for Brian for thirteen or fourteen years. Nacho and Mario are from a town outside of San Blas that is called "the golden valley," in Nayarit, Mexico. It is an area five to ten miles inland from the Pacific coast, a good growing area. Brian, thinking ahead, would like to start an orchard there.

In fact, Brian already has a farm in Nayarit, purchased with Mario. The farm is located in the town of Lodemarcos, whose name roughly translates as "of the boundaries" or "near the border." It is outside Sayulita, a winter destination for tourists of means from the Northwest. I've never been there, but Brian and his family began to go as a cheaper alternative to Hawai'i. There are lots of gringos and Canadians there, he said, who have formed an organization called Amigos de Lodemarcos. Here, they would be called Friends of the Farm.

Back in Bainbridge, Butler Green Farms serves over two hundred CSA subscribers. They now also provide "animal protein": pigs, cows, lambs, chickens. The thing that is missing, and that's tough to grow on Bainbridge, is grain. The commune in Oregon where Brian was first introduced to farming grew everything it needed, Brian said, and only traded labor for cooking oil and kerosene.

Right now, he said, "there is too much variety, choice in the stores." Farming this way caters to a wide range of tastes, but uses the land inefficiently. I asked if the island could grow enough food to feed its population of twenty-three thousand. He started doing some calculations in his head . . . how much acreage, how many people. He figured he could probably raise food for one thousand people on the thirty acres he is farming now. Two hundred families could live on the produce of thirty acres, he said, if they grew things that could be stored, such as corn and beans, and grew two or three crops per year. This is much more optimistic than what the other farmers I talked to offered. But on the commune in Oregon, Brian said, they traded for prunes, wheat, and filberts. They grew dry corn and beans on the farm. "Yes, it would be possible to sustain Bainbridge," he decided. The statistics I've since looked up show that Bainbridge has 1.3 people per acre, though of course not all of that is arable land.

At times, Brian said, farming and selling produce on the island has been too political. "Every other person on the island is a lawyer, but they want to engage in the only way they know how." To me, this implied that farmers do things a different way, negotiate for land and retail space in a different language than lawyers, who speak the language of Keynesian economics and of real estate. It seemed as though Brian was pointing out that farmers have a different value system, one that values land not for its maximum monetary worth, but for its worth in potential food.

Brian realizes that for agriculture to succeed on Bainbridge, all these various factions must work together. Since he grows food for a local supermarket, he is a pioneer for this new order, directly crossing the gap between farm economics and retail economics.

"I go into the schools and talk about my work," he tells me. "We do the math and there are lots of young kids who do seem to get it. It's really a cool thing. I am getting back to where I wanted to teach. I wanted to be a biology teacher, maybe math. This spring, I worked with some kids at Wilkes Elementary School." They grew starts and had a plant sale. "We did some algebra to figure out a farm-related problem. They got it."

A little after 10 A.M., Brian took me out in the fields in a golf cart to meet Akio Suyematsu. We left the cart on an unpaved lane and walked down a laser-straight row of raspberry plants that were about five feet tall. Brian pointed to some tiny weeds as we walked. "Akio would consider that too weedy."

Akio, at ninety, was as diminutive as Brian is large, dressed in a baseball cap and a woolly vest against the morning chill, where he worked with a single-pronged hoe to root out weeds. He had misplaced his hearing aids. He said he had left them on the dashboard of his truck, but could not find them. Brian said he would look for them, leaving me on purpose with Akio, who would otherwise have insisted that I talk to Brian instead.

"I don't know anything," he said as if on cue. "I have this work to do. Ask Brian."

But Brian was gone.

The raspberries were Meeker, and the bushes were just about Akio's height. I asked if it would ever be possible to grow strawberries on the island again.

"No," he said, "too many diseases." Strawberries are susceptible to black rot, especially the tender Marshall strawberries. This made them unpredictable as a crop, and after the Japanese Americans who had specialized in growing them were sent away, their cultivation was dropped. Akio has been farming all of his life, interrupted only by his time in the internment camps and then the Army during World War II. He never married, and was one of the few Japanese Americans who continued to farm on the island after returning. Most of the other returning Japanese American families sold their land for development, or developed it themselves. They returned to the island owing back taxes, heavily in debt, and without capital to invest in seeds or equipment in order to start over. Others were warned off by friends that the tension on the island made it dangerous to return, so they settled in other towns like Moses Lake in Eastern Washington.

I asked him if the soil on the island was good. He could not hear me. From experience with my father, I know that I sound like a mosquito to older men without their hearing aids. Down the lane, a man was working with a weed eater, which did not help our communication. I reached down and picked up a handful of rich dirt, held it out, and asked if it was any good. "No," he said. "Bainbridge has terrible soil. But I have been amending *this* soil for years. Every year, after the harvest is in, I put down a layer of goat manure, then this much (he showed me about four inches with his hands) compost." East of the field where we stood was a compost pile about fifteen feet high.

I asked Akio if it would be possible to grow enough food on Bainbridge to feed its population of twenty-three thousand people.

After a moment's thought, he said yes. "We cannot grow wheat, but we can grow corn." The chill, overcast morning did not seem to bother him at all.

I said thank you and goodbye, and made my way down the row, its dark soil studded with tiny rocks. Akio Suyematsu, born in October 1921, passed away in 2012 at the age of ninety-two. He was fiercely tied to the land, and able to work on it until nearly the end of his life.

AFTER THE WAR

Bainbridge continues to be home to a thriving number of Japanese American elders who were sent to the camps as children or young adults, but returned to rebuild their lives. Others stayed in the communities farther inland where they were relocated during the war, or went to live with relatives outside the area.

The most famous returnee is Fumiko Nishinaka Hayashida, because of the iconic photo of her holding a sleeping daughter as she is being taken from her home. She passed away at the age of 103.

Wayne and Judy Nakata live within walking distance of my house in a snug, heavily decorated condominium that must offer a great view of the fireworks over Eagle Harbor every Fourth of July. Wayne was born in 1940 and sent to the internment camps with his family when he about two years old. Because he has always been interested in the history of the island, several people referred me to him.

There was a "good relationship" between the Japanese families and the Filipino families who took care of their properties, he told me. A man Wayne knew only as Vidalion was a Filipino bachelor who took care of the Nakata property, the land that Brian MacWhorter now works. "We were able to come back because of the Filipino families. We had a reason to come back. Others wouldn't, or couldn't."

The Nakatas' closest neighbors, said Wayne, were the Moji family, who lived at Weaver Road and Moji Lane. Nick and Dan Bucsit, Filipino brothers, worked for the Mojis, and Dan was one of the five builders of the Filipino Hall. The Mojis also owned property at Meadowmeer, which is now a large, upscale neighborhood with its own golf course, a few miles north of downtown Winslow. Wayne shared a sad story about the Moji family: when they were being taken away to the camps, their dog first tried to jump in the truck with them, then refused to eat after they were gone, until it died.

What happened to other Japanese American farm families?

I asked. The Sakais, Wayne said, kept the property at Bainbridge Island Gardens, but couldn't start the business back up again, "financially, physically, and emotionally." The Kitamotos kept their property. The Takamoto family was the first to come back.

"I don't know any who lost their properties, unless they wanted to," Wayne said. I thought, silently, of the stories I'd heard of mismanagement, of other islanders taking advantage of unpaid back taxes in order to acquire Japanese American properties for next to nothing. Wayne deflects the question, referring me to those who were older when internment happened. "Ask Lilly. She was my brother's age. This is the difference between me and people like Lilly." On an island, I realized, a certain amount of amnesia is required in order to move forward, to remain a community in balance with both the past and the future.

"My first memories were of Manzanar. The Sierra Nevada was so spectacular, that view of the mountains is imprinted on my memory. I was there from the ages of two to five. My Dad's folks lived with us, and my grandmother babysat. Dad worked as a meat-cutter, and my mom as a domestic. *Bon odori* dances were held once a month." For Wayne, internment was "like an extended summer camp. We got out in March or April [of 1945]. Dad called Walt Woodward [the Bainbridge newspaper editor who had very publicly defended the rights of Japanese Americans] to see what it was like on Bainbridge.

"'It's a little iffy still,' said Woodward."

Instead of returning to the island, Wayne's family went to Moses Lake in Eastern Washington, where other Japanese American families had been allowed to settle. Wayne's father Masaaki, who went by John, worked on a cattle ranch as a cowhand through the summer until the fall of 1945. He then checked with Woodward again, and the family returned to Bainbridge in time for Wayne to start at McDonald School (now Captain John Blakely Elementary School).

How many Nakatas went to Minidoka? I asked. "There were four sons and three daughters," Wayne turned to his wife for affirmation. "The daughters were all married by then and went elsewhere with their families. About nine people came back from Minidoka."

"Before the war, my father had a meat market. When T&C [Town & Country Market] started after the war, my father and his brother Mo merged their two business interests." They also had a third partner in the venture, Ed Loveritch, a high school classmate of Croatian ancestry.

"I grew up in the store," Wayne said. "I was a senior in 1957 when T&C opened. That's where I started with the company. When we started T&C, we were all related, including Ed Loveritch's family. The family atmosphere has been retained. We were a close-knit community."

"There were adjustments after the war in order to start over. My dad's parents lived with us after that. I didn't realize, until later, that I picked up so much of my memory from my grandfather Jitsuzo. We had to be self-sustaining. Most Japanese families had enough property to grow vegetables. Ours was the property at Weaver and Wyatt [Roads], where you see the low-rise building. My grandfather got hold of the grinding stones for making tofu. My job was to pour soybeans into the hole at the top of the stone, and catch the runoff to make *okara*, a tofu by-product. We were able to make it right in our backyard. I thought that was cool."

The owners of the property before the Nakatas, the Sumioshi family, had planted Bing cherry trees around the house. Their land once held the neighborhood's original strawberry processing plant, and covered a total of fifteen acres. When strawberry production exceeded the capacity of the plant, processing moved to Seattle, then back to an expanded plant on Weaver Road within easy access of the farm. During the 1920s and 1930s, berries were "cold-packed," in wooden drums on ice for shipping. As home freezers became more widely available, the idea of frozen foods took hold.

"After the war, we all had to scramble. Some families had no money, but had land." I realized that even the Japanese American families who had managed to retain their land—either because their Filipino farmhands acted as caretakers or other non-Japanese neighbors held it in trust—still lacked any income to speak of while living in the camps. What little they were paid for their labor there was used to buy the meals they were served in the cafeterias, meals made from the produce they had grown.

"My grandpa had a small, twelve-foot boat, and we would fish for perch near the old cannery. We would go down there just to have fun and fish."

Sometimes Wayne, who was seven or eight by then, would go with his grandfather to Blakely Rock (a small island offshore) to catch octopus. "Octopus was a delicacy, but I wasn't crazy about it then." His grandfather had a system. "He would put bluestone [copper sulfate] at the end of a metal pole in a little bag, tie it at the end of the rod, fish under the rocks, hook them and bring them out. We had to wash them really good. It was a real treat to get them, but we can't do that now. Bluestone is highly toxic and illegal."

"We harvested seaweed, *nodi,* and used pea poles to dry it. We used it as we needed it." Orchards, planted by various immigrant families, took up more of the land before the war, providing fruit for eating and canning. Today, neglected apple trees stand along the edges that separate groomed yards from the second-growth forest that is reclaiming land, bursting into unappreciated bloom and dropping their fruit for the birds. I pass one every day that grows next to a bank building. In the fall, its apples fall and roll downhill into a busy thoroughfare, gently reminding us of what came before.

Can people grow rice here? I asked Wayne.

"I don't know if anyone has tried. I doubt they could get the production needed to be worth it. It's cheaper to buy one-hundred-pound sacks in Seattle."

Could we grow soybeans?

"I guess so. When I was a teen, a Japanese food truck would come from Seattle and visit each family in a big van. We would buy Japanese food from him. Before the war, there was a Japanese community in Blakely that had a store. It provided for that community."

This would have been the town of Yama at Blakely Harbor, which was founded during the height of the timber industry in the 1880s, and had a population of around three hundred at its peak in the early twentieth century. Abandoned and overgrown since 1924, Yama is now being excavated by student archaeologists from Olympic Community College in cooperation with the Bainbridge Island Historical Society.

Postwar, there were no Japanese products available.

"My grandfather was a second son in Japan, meaning he inherited nothing. The economy in southwest Japan was horrific. There were bad storms. A friend of his settled in Tacoma, so he heard about the area by word of mouth. There were also advertisements in Japanese magazines." Wayne tapped the top of a small, three-legged table his grandfather had made of ironwood in the internment camp. I had seen this stool in many photographs. "A lot of good things happened because of him." Wayne showed me the symbols inlaid into the tabletop: two cherry blossoms for Japan, the characters for "Manzanar," and a star. "In Japan, a star doesn't mean anything. He included it because he loved this country. The original barber pole he put up in 1906 had stars at the top and the bottom for the same reason. They mean the U.S.A."

"My mother's parents, who stayed in Japan, were educators." His grandparents' generation, the Issei, were very troubled by the internment, Wayne recalled. Just before the family left for the camps, "all the customers came and paid their tabs at the Eagle Harbor Market. This was a key part of how the family felt. We had close friends on the island, so we were able to come back. We knew we had the community support." This dynamic was dramatized in David Guterson's novel *Snow Falling on Cedars,* published in 1994. The book portrays the murder trial of a Japanese American in the 1950s that stirs up old resentments and hostilities that have lingered since World War II.

Executive Order 9066 continues to have ramifications for the people of the island. "What the Woodwards did was so significant," added Judy, referring to the newspaper editor and his family, who openly opposed the executive order. "They could have been shot" as collaborators.

"Our cousins remember different things than we do," Kay and Lilly agreed. "But some stories are too good to disregard, even if they aren't true." They both laughed.

After the Kitamotos were forced to leave for the camps, six Filipino workers moved from the bunkhouse into the main farmhouse on the Kitamoto property, and worked the farm while the family was gone. "After the war," said Lilly, "my mother [Shigeko Nishinaka Kitamoto] started growing vegetables to sell, and started saving for me to go to college. My father saved money for Frank [her older brother, who became a dentist on Bainbridge Island]. She knew that he would not save for me."

"We ate the wormy ones," said Lilly, "things we couldn't sell."

"Even if we gave things to friends, we gave the best," recalled Kay.

"We saved the squished raspberries for jam," Lilly said. "One of my daughters works in the food industry. She chops everything fast and leaves good stuff on the rind."

"Same with my daughter-in-law," said Kay.

"I cringe to say anything to my daughter."

"Don't eat anything wastefully, we were always told," said Kay. "*Mottainai.* My daughter now says a lot of things I said to her." Both laughed. "That's just the way we were brought up."

Both admit to old-fashioned eating habits, and a tendency to hoard food. This sounded familiar. I took care of my father in his last years, and I was always finding saltines and little packages of jam in his belongings, squirreled away after his meals at the local retirement center.

"We love white bread. Wonderbread or Langendorf, with a slice of baloney and mayo. I like it," said Lilly.

Kay, who is in her nineties, worked at the local supermarket, Town & Country, for twenty-five years. She likes Olympia and Rainier beers.

"We are Costco buffs," says Kay. "What am I doing with all this food?" My parents, too, loved food wholesalers.

"I was going through my cupboards and found all these cans with old expiration dates," said Lilly. "Like soup that was given out as samples at Costco. Joe [her husband] didn't like it. It had dumplings in it."

"It became kind of a habit," said Kay. "On the farm, we kept cans because we couldn't get to the store easily."

"We have boxes of elbow macaroni."

"I keep a freezer downstairs. It is full of berries people have given me," said Kay. "The refrigerator in the garage is for when I get meat or fish from people. But most of my freezer is full of kitchen jams. My refrigerator stopped working, so I got the smallest I could from Schmidt's, but it was too small."

"I blame my memory for getting overstocked," said Lilly. "If Joe goes with me to Costco, he say, 'We gotta get this.' We also have too many paper products."

"Right now I have three balsamic vinegars, and sesame oil," said Kay. "But mostly freezer jam. I make two batches at a time and give it all away—raspberry, boysenberry, sometimes strawberries."

"I don't can as much as I used to," said Lilly. "I used to make dill pickles. Now I get them from Kay. I do pies more than anything. I love wild huckleberry, loganberry, and wild blackberry."

T & C

Rick Pedersen wears a windbreaker and baseball cap in Town & Country's signature dark-green. He is store director of Bainbridge Island's Town & Country Market, the flagship of six in the greater Seattle area. Rick Pedersen is a team player.

Town & Country moved to its present location in 1957. It had been

preceded by two small grocery stores. When the original partners—
Mo and John Nakata, and Ed Loveritch—opened Town & Country,
it must have seemed huge at the time. Its most famous feature is the
signboard on Winslow Way. Originally erected to advertise specials,
the signboard was long ago turned over to announce special events,
now limited to nonprofits. The permanent lettering on the "Town
& Country" sign is close to the "Sahara" typeface on my computer,
a flowing, pseudo-Arabic script, and is hopelessly, unfashionably
retro.

I asked Rick if he grew up expecting to become a grocer. He
paused for a minute. "Once I knew I was not going to be a professional ball player . . ." It turns out that his father was a grocer in Fern-
dale, Washington, north of Seattle. Rick first worked in the Shoreline
store, then came to the Bainbridge store in 1998.

Between two thousand and four thousand customers visit Town
& Country each day, spending an average of twenty-five dollars each.
This includes people who buy lunch there every day, and day trip-
pers from Seattle who ride the ferry as tourists. Rick estimates that
about 25 percent of the food revenue at Town & Country comes from
products sourced in Washington, Oregon, and Idaho. He says that
the store charges less for local products, and so must sell more. As a
rule, the farther the food comes, the more expensive it is.

"Take wine, for example. It's a big local business, compared to
ten years ago. However, the recent change in the euro makes it more
reasonable to buy imports. It affects how people shop."

If a product is available both locally and from somewhere else, I
asked, how do they decide whether or not to carry it?

"First is integrity." The store must learn all about how and where
the product is produced. A director of food safety works on behalf of
all six stores. He inspects licensed commercial kitchens, and verifies
that organic produce is in fact grown organically.

"We used to buy products out of the trunks of people's cars," Rick
said, "but not anymore."

"Then there is supply." If a producer cannot consistently and reliably supply a product to the stores, they cannot carry it. Shoppers might like something and want more, but if it is not available, it leads to customer dissatisfaction. I have, in the past, requested items that suddenly disappeared from the shelves, only to be told that they could not carry it consistently, because supplies were unreliable. My husband thinks I am a sort of canary in the coalmine for certain products, since that seems to happen to me fairly frequently. They did, however, begin to carry the enchilada sauce I like, Las Palmas, shortly after we moved here and I requested it. It is still stocked, which means it is readily available from the manufacturer and that other shoppers like it as well.

"Finally, there is distribution." Town & Country must be able to transport the products to its six stores on a regular basis. So supply must be reliable. "Or customers will purchase something, then not be able to get it next time they come in."

Recently, Bob Fortner began to produce his own tonic for mixed drinks under the label "Dr. Bob's Tonic." Town & Country agreed to carry it if he could ramp up production to meet the needs of all six stores. He will need to contract out the bottling and labeling for his product in order to produce enough.

I ask how marketing decisions are made, like the "Big Board Buys," specials that started at Town & Country a couple of years ago. These are often dairy or meat products, perishables that must be moved quickly. "T&C has a corporate staff of marketing specialists," Rick said. "They look for the best value, great taste, and price. They look for products at the peak of perfection."

A few days later, I met Vern and Rick Nakata in a small, upstairs boardroom across the parking lot from the store. Gene was late. All three cousins are now in their early sixties, and all wore some piece of clothing with the Town & Country logo on it—a vest, a cap, or a shirt, all in the khaki or forest-green that marks a Town & Country employee from down the block. Vern, Rick, and Gene are the third generation of the Nakata family, both on the island and in the grocery business. Wayne Nakata is an older cousin to Rick and Gene, while Vern is his younger brother.

T&C, as the store is called familiarly by locals, is about four blocks from my house, and I often take a midday break from writing to walk into town and pick up a few groceries. Carrying them uphill back to my house serves as my exercise. Town & Country owns an important piece of downtown Bainbridge Island. About twenty years ago the whole island was incorporated as the City of Bainbridge Island, but the old downtown is still called Winslow. At one point, the owners of Town & Country considered trading some of its land to the post office in exchange for the adjacent property, where the post office currently stands, so the market could remodel and expand.

Instead, the market was rebuilt where it stood, staying open even during construction. During this operation, groceries were shifted from one location to another as the store morphed and strained to serve us, to keep the employees working, and to sprout modern freezers, ovens, and seating for coffee drinkers. Every visit was a new adventure, as customers plunged into the aisles to triumphantly emerge with that one item they had failed to find on their last visit.

I asked Vern and Rick if they had always thought they would go into the grocery business.

"No," Rick said. "It just happened, because it was so easy. I was studying electrical engineering, but I had my doubts if I was really qualified to do something with it. I got my degree at the University of Washington, but I stayed here. "

"Rick was my role model," Vern joked. "We wanted to go to college and get degrees, but we were not motivated to get real jobs. We both went to OCC [Olympic Community College] for two years. I continued at Seattle University and got a degree in math. Like Rick, I didn't think I could compete to get a job."

I realized later that they had both graduated from college during a local recession called the "Boeing Bust" during the 1970s, famously remembered by the billboard someone erected that read, "Will the last person to leave Seattle please turn out the lights?"

The family store was a warm and supportive environment. The social element was important, said Vern. It was "just a really happening place in the community, a fun environment."

"Gene is probably talking to someone right now," said Vern—we were still waiting for him to join us. "We were encouraged, not restricted, to go into the family business." In other words, they never felt obliged to join the business, but were not excluded from it, either.

Vern's title is point of sale manager. Rick's is frozen food lead. They seem embarrassed by the idea of job titles. Their style of management is collegial; they are in it together with all the other employees.

Despite the Nakatas' casual style, the management of a grocery business is highly competitive, and can call for a quick and drastic response if any aspect of the business—supply, transportation, distribution, marketing, or competition—changes. Although the T&C board is made up of family members, the decisions they make are crucial to the success of a lot of people.

Married couple Mo (Momoichi) and Sa Nakata, and Mo's brother John Nakata were the founders of Town & Country, in partnership with Ed Loveritch, whose parents had immigrated from the island of Lošinj, part of Croatia. Mo and John's parents, Jitsuzo and Shima, had immigrated from Japan in 1899 and 1906. In the 1880s, Port Blakely Lumber Mill on Bainbridge was the largest, highest-producing sawmill in the world, attracting workers from all over. Jitsuzo and Shima Nakata arrived in the wake of that boom and opened a barbershop, then a bathhouse, followed by a laundry service, all adjacent to each other, and close to where I now live. A new building stands at the spot, with a plaque on the front saying it is the original site of the Eagle Harbor Market, a later Nakata family business, and the precursor to T&C. "Even though they barely spoke English, they anticipated what people would need," Vern said. Home deliveries were made by rowboat or horse and buggy.

Jitsuzo and Shima had ten children, three of whom died early. The children hauled water for the bathhouse. The family struggled financially, and to augment their income, Jitsuzo bought a strawberry farm from another Japanese American family in 1924. A friend's son signed the legal papers, since immigrants were not allowed to own land in the United States at the time.

Ed Loveritch, a childhood friend, picked strawberries alongside the Nakata boys. His parents, Tom and Christina, had purchased the Winslow Dock Grocery Store in 1921. Income for the Nakata family continued to decline with the onset of the Depression, and in 1928, when the family officially took possession of the farm through their oldest, American-born son, Masaaki, his father took him aside and encouraged him to ask for a job at the Eagle Harbor meat market next to the bathhouse. The owner, Charley Bremer, had trouble pronouncing Masaaki, so he called him John. In 1935 John Nakata bought the Eagle Harbor Market from Bremer.

As Wayne had told me when I spoke with him, "It was my grandfather who told my dad one day, after the Depression, that the money was not in the businesses the family had started: a barbershop, then a laundry, then a bathhouse in 1924. He saw that strawberries were a hot market, and bought property in 1924. By the middle thirties my dad was worried. My grandfather saw that the future was groceries."

The family managed to persevere through the Depression, and John Nakata paid off the mortgage on the farm through income from the market. This trait—to achieve through patience and perseverance—is called *gaman* in Japanese, and runs in the family. John Nakata tore down the old bathhouse and barbershop in 1940 to build a new, expanded Eagle Harbor Market. It had a chicken coop in back for their "Friday fryer" special. Gross sales were about fifty dollars a week.

One year later, on December 7, 1941, the Japanese navy bombed
Pearl Harbor, and only weeks later most of the Nakata family was
ordered to Manzanar. Although several families, including the
Loveritches, offered to help with the business, John decided it was best
to sell. His brother Mo Nakata went into the all-Nisei 442nd Infantry
Regiment, the same regiment that Akio Suyematsu served in, where
Mo was wounded and awarded a Bronze Star and a Purple Heart.

On January 2, 1945, the U.S. government rescinded the exclusion
order as unconstitutional, and Japanese American families were allowed to return home. There was little work on Bainbridge at the
time, so the Nakata brothers and their friend Ed Loveritch wrapped
guidelines onto fishing poles for a local business, Sage Fly Rods,
which still sells poles today. One day, Mo said that they could not do
this forever, and proposed that he, John, and Ed lease a then-vacant
store, the Bainbridge Gardens building, at the center of the island.
John bowed out because he thought there would not be enough business for three partners. Other stores followed the Bainbridge Gardens venture, until a group of businessmen decided that Bainbridge
needed a supermarket downtown as the area's commercial anchor.
They approached Ed and Mo to lease the store, and this time John
Nakata joined them.

When I moved to Bainbridge in 1995, Mo and Sa's son Don Nakata
was running the business, which by now had several stores in the
Puget Sound area. When Don Nakata passed away suddenly while
on vacation, his brother Larry was being groomed to take over the
company, but it happened a little sooner than expected. Both Don
and Larry were older cousins to the three I interviewed. The family realized, at that point, that the margin of profit was extremely
narrow. Larry made the six stores profitable by reworking them
to serve a high-end clientele, complete with delicatessen counters,
salad bars, and a wide choice of imported goods such as chocolate,

olive oil, and wine. A lavishly illustrated corporate history, *Town & Country Markets: Nourishing the Quality of Life*, by Russ Banham, tells story after story of customer service through the years, including Ed Loveritch taking the ferry to another store to buy a product requested by a customer.

I asked what legacy the three cousins had inherited from the founders, Mo and John Nakata and Ed Loveritch. "We continue in their tradition." Gene said. "We all worked with them. It's not any great philosophical thing, just their work ethic."

There was some discussion at this point because, really, they were all very small when their grandfather Mo Nakata was at the store. They may have worked at the store since they were children, but Gene, the oldest, was only three years old when their grandfather Mo Nakata passed away in 1955. But Ed Loveritch, a former basketball star at the University of Washington and a charismatic character, was there for a long time after that. They also learned a great deal from those in their own generation. "Don was a great philosopher," Gene said about his older cousin. "He took it to the next level in terms of thinking about being sensitive to what the customers needed." Larry has continued to refine this approach. In other words, the cousins felt as though they had all worked with their grandfather—the family tradition has been so consistent.

I asked about the rise of organic products, and the subsequent call for more local produce. "The eighties were when people got interested in organics. Margaret Clark was ahead of her time," Vern said. He was working in produce then. Margaret had moved from California, where she had become "disheartened" with her sociology work in Indian affairs; on Bainbridge she became an evangelist for fresh, organic food. "At the time," Vern said, "we struggled to maintain a corner as organics." Margaret is the person who brought Brian MacWhorter in as a source for organic produce. When it was determined that he could meet the three main criteria Rick Pedersen had outlined for me—integrity, supply, and distribution—Brian was contracted to supply organic produce for the stores. Margaret herself eventually left Bainbridge to become a science and conservation specialist at the National Tropical Botanical Garden in Hawai'i.

I asked the Nakatas what would happen if the island were cut off from outside supplies of food. They have researched the question, and found that few islanders keep more than a day's worth of food in their homes, and often shop daily at the market. This surprised me, but T&C did an assessment in anticipation of Y2K, as the year 2000 was called in the period leading up to it. At that time, there was some speculation that the computers on which we have all become so dependent would not be able to handle the change in the first digit of the year, and all of our systems would crash. "Y2K made people talk about emergencies," Vern said. "We brought in a trailer/tractor rig with extra supplies."

The store, too, would be out of food within one day if off-island supplies were cut off. I remembered being snowed in for three days our first December, no power, with my stepdaughters and their husbands, who were big eaters. Every day my husband and I would put on backpacks and walk to the market to see what supplies had made it through. T&C has emergency generators, but cannot keep all the cold cases going. They were serving fish chowder and other warm treats every day just to use the food. Some families had no way to heat or cook, or even to get water, so this was a boon to them.

"We got those things called MREs," Gene said, in preparation for Y2K. These "meals ready to eat," standard field fare for military personnel, are known for their indefinite shelf-life. "The sodium content was unbelievable."

A woman came into Central Market, in Poulsbo, they recalled, and bought four hundred dollars worth of MREs in late 1999. In March 2000, she wanted to return them. "We could not take them back," Gene said.

Disaster aside, I asked if they thought interest in local produce would continue.

"I think so," said Gene. "We now use signage that says 'Northwest Produce.' We are looking into growing strawberries again. It is part of the Nakata family history. For over fifty years, we have worked on relationships with local farmers, distributors, and salespeople. At least for these stores, the demand for local produce won't go away."

There is also a Safeway store on Bainbridge, which caters to a different clientele. I get my prescriptions filled at Safeway, which opened on the island in 1990, and noticed recently that its Hispanic/Latino foods aisle keeps expanding. I don't think there are more Latinos living on the island, but there are more working here, often as gardeners or restaurant servers. Everything is very shiny at Safeway, with wide aisles and too much air-conditioning. No one ever approaches you on the floor to ask if you need help. I used to try to shop at both stores to save a little money, but Safeway eventually dropped most of the products that I purchased there, substituting store brands. But I can still buy huge cans of menudo or *albondigas* soup.

Costco is my husband's favorite place to shop, and he will be a hard sell on eating locally or seasonally as long as he can drive another ten miles and get what he likes. I usually do not accompany him on these trips. I find standing around on concrete floors to watch overweight people purchase pallet-loads of food depressing. I understand that Wal-Mart is even worse. But I have to agree that the quality and prices at Costco are excellent. Who cares where we buy Kleenex or club soda? And then it feels so easy to pick up, say, some "fresh-caught" salmon at $9.99 a pound, although who knows how it was caught or where. It's easy to get sucked into the "bigger is better and cheaper" way of life.

In keeping with its organic and sustainable efforts, T&C instated a "bring your own bags" policy early on, and still gives customers five cents back for every bag they bring. Their environmental sustainability coordinator, Tony Tenofrio, has gradually trained the employees to be more environmentally aware. All of the employees will eventually attend his half-day presentations, which includes a showing of the animated documentary, *The Story of Stuff.* Rick told me that after attending the presentation, "now I'm more conscious of environmental things."

"Without disrespecting people," Gene said, the presentation "makes you think about it."

The store makes other sustainability efforts. They have started a composting program: all green waste is put through a grinder and sent to the Bare Rose Emu Ranch. The emu ranch, in turn, sells manure to farmers and gardeners. If someone is raising chickens and asks for scraps to feed them, the store will provide trimmings. The Bloedel Reserve, a famous private garden on the island, recently asked for romaine lettuce to feed the swans. The store has saved between $160,000 and $170,000 a year since putting these practices into effect.

As for customer education, "we try to give out the facts so people have choices," Vern said. "But we can't eliminate a lot of the food. We are a store of choice." This reminds me of the way Vern, Gene, and Rick's generation was invited, but not forced, into store management—it was their choice as well. "If people have questions, we answer them or refer them to someone who has the answers."

"We attempt to buy products that are not genetically modified," Gene said. "But even at T&C, we lose a little of where it comes from. People want to reestablish that trust." He is referring to trust in the story of the food as farmer Betsey Wittick described it—where it came from, who grew it, and who prepared it.

The vegetables that Brian MacWhorter grows for Town & Country, grown organically in greenhouses, are priced at a premium. But there it is; just like the contented cows of my childhood, you can go over to Wyatt Way and look at where they grow on the old Nakata farm, now Middlefield Farm. In this case, the distance the produce needs to be transported is not reflected in a lower price, but we all want T&C to succeed as both a local retailer and a local producer.

It's all about what Gene calls "the trust issue." "[The customers] know they will get quality stuff. The next generation will stay here, and is used to shopping at our store since they were children with their mothers. The boundary of the island is a big plus for us."

T&C does not sell at the farmers market, where both Brian and Betsey sell their own produce, so it is not perceived as a rival for their customers.

After interviewing the Nakata cousins, I learned the difference between "farm to table," and "factory organic" from Michael Pollan's *The Omnivore's Dilemma*. Farm to table is food grown and sold locally, often at farmers markets. Most of the Northwest food that is sold at Town & Country, with the exception of the vegetables grown by Brian MacWhorter, is factory organic. This is food grown on a scale to serve stores like T&C, as well as other chains that specialize in upscale organic products, such as Whole Foods.

I checked the labels of a couple of the products that I buy on a regular basis from Town & Country, and they are definitely factory organic. Pollan describes the growing and harvesting of "organic greens" sold by Earthbound Farms. They are grown in raised beds in California, cut with special machines, and packaged in the fields, using huge refrigerated systems where workers sort the greens and put them into individual containers. When you think about the amount of energy used to produce baby greens on such a scale, the notion of "green" comes into question.

One day at T&C, I bought some organic chicken that was a much better price than usual, which is around eight dollars a pound. Only upon unwrapping it did I find that it came from Iowa. It was about as tasteless as one would expect, frozen for its trip to Washington State. Now I know to look on the very bottom of the package, as well as on the label on top, for "Northwest chicken."

Another product I buy, soup by Pacific Natural Foods, comes from Oregon, a little closer to home than Iowa. This is a processed food, sold in rectangular cartons. Still, they must keep up high, consistent, and organic production in order to meet T&C's criteria, and in order for T&C to make its profit margin at the stores on Bainbridge and in the Puget Sound region.

Every grocery store now carries some "organic" products, usually factory organic. The farmers I talked to on Bainbridge dismiss this type of food as a small step above conventionally grown produce, since it uses so many resources in transportation and preservation. Customers, say the farmers, don't know the story of this food, only what the labels say. But factory organic farmers would argue that just removing acres from conventional farming, with its heavy use of pesticides, is a boon to the environment. Growers of factory organic spend a lot of resources lobbying to keep the definition of organic vague, in order to accommodate the widest range of produce under the label.

On a small, local level, Nancy Fortner's value-added products include preserves and powdered cocoa in cans, but nothing substantial. When we lived in Western Colorado, I kept a spacious kitchen garden and canned tomatoes, corn, and one or two other things. I didn't mind it then, but growing and canning require a lot of time and work. If people are to eat locally, this is a necessary step. We need to get used to seeing mundane products like corn and green beans in jars with local labels on the shelves. Before and during World War II, people canned food at home as a matter of course, but after the war, commercial production of canned food picked up and displaced the need for most people to continue this labor-intensive practice.

Another approach is to eat seasonally. That means eating only what is growing or available at the time. No lettuce in the winter, and no tomatoes before mid- to late summer. People used to keep fresh and preserved foods in root cellars in order to have food year-round. Was I ready for this? We don't have a cellar.

HITCHCOCK

I met Brendan McGill on a Tuesday just after noon, when he typically arrives at his restaurant, Hitchcock, in downtown Winslow on Bainbridge Island. The restaurant business is a young man's job. "He's the one with all the tattoos," my friends said before I visited. Brendan shook my hand. He is compact, thirty-something, with a crinkly smile. A veteran of several Seattle restaurants, he has also worked in restaurants in France, Italy, and Spain.

Hitchcock is not open for lunch, only dinners and brunch on weekends. It was dark inside. Member of his staff chatted quietly while he stood at the bar doing payroll. He slipped out for a moment to go to the bank and get the checks printed, and before they left or started to prep for that evening, most had set their schedules with Brendan for the week. The entire time that we talked, Brendan took deliveries and directed staff, all with aplomb. Persephone Farm delivered greens, and Elysian Beer dropped off a few cases. Each delivery person required a check that Brendan wrote out on the spot. Hitchcock emphasizes locally grown food, and the word is out that he will buy from foragers, so people like Preston Onkst of Wild West bring him fresh fish, mushrooms, whatever they can.

Brendan described Preston as a "fantastic middleman. I'd much rather pay him the mark-up than a retailer." Preston and the other foragers aren't corporations, just "a couple of humans." Brendan clearly relishes this interaction with the suppliers, the interaction between "a couple of humans" rather than with a large corporation. More importantly, he trusts these people, and is happy to do repeat business with them.

I asked Brendan if he had been one of those kids who took over his parents' kitchen at the age of eight and started cooking. "No," he says, "I was not a prodigy chef. I started cooking for my roommates when I moved out of my parent's house at seventeen. I was working in a restaurant, trying to figure it all out."

I ask if either of his parents were chefs. Brendan grew up in Fairbanks, Alaska. His parents had "a fantastic kitchen garden." He used to go fishing with his father and brothers and bring home "ninety salmon . . . I grew up surrounded by examples of good food."

At the time, his father was a cabinetmaker, and his mother a schoolteacher. His father underwent vocational retraining, and has taught sixth grade for twenty years; his mother is now a school administrator. Both of his parents are fluent in Spanish. "My father lived in Argentina as a kid, and my mother lived in Mexico City for a couple of years." They have a second home in Ecuador.

The restaurant is named for his wife's family: her grandparents, Malvina and Carl Hitchcock, homesteaded on Bainbridge, and his father-in-law, who died suddenly, was also Carl Hitchcock. A black-and-white Hitchcock family photo decorates each booth in the restaurant. Brendan remembers digging clams at Neah Bay with his in-laws.

Brendan did not reconfigure the restaurant when he bought it, and uses the wood-fired pizza oven at the back to finish his meats. When he was considering the space he was surprised, when talking to farmers, that no other restaurant on the island specialized in the farm-to-table concept. Today, several restaurants on the island emphasize their local food connections, but try to distinguish themselves with other features.

"As a restaurant," he says, Hitchcock is "a future concept." It is "totally different than any other organizational system I've worked with," said Brendan. In Seattle, he calls suppliers once a week and takes deliveries the next day. Here on Bainbridge, if he decides one night that he needs more produce, he has to call "three farmers, two gardeners, and a forager." In other words, it's a lot more work, and he needs to be flexible. "The menu changes every day." He showed me the Saturday and Sunday menus, and said they run out of duck pâté by Sunday because it takes three days to make. The restaurant is pricey for Bainbridge, though not for Seattle.

The concept, however, seems to be working. Brendan was named *Food and Wine* magazine's "People's Best New Chef" in 2013.

"What's nice is that it shows you are on their radar," Brendan said. The award is by "people's choice," in other words, anyone can vote. To be eligible, chefs must be running kitchens that are no more than five years old—McGill was among one hundred chefs from across the country chosen to compete.

For all of his restaurant positioning, Brendan is mostly interested in local food. "If you read *The Omnivore's Dilemma* or *Fast Food Nation,* it changes the way you view food." After spending time cooking in Southwest France, Spain, and Italy, he realized the value of cooking and eating locally. "I couldn't buy an orange in summer in Valencia," he said. "Stupid American—I wanted to taste a Valencia orange, and it was summer. After that, it became ridiculous to have asparagus on the menu in fall."

"I don't want a vegetable from Chile on the menu. It just doesn't make sense at all. I want to eat real food, buy food from a human."

Brendan reminisced about shopping in the *mercados* of Latin America, where a variety of foods are on display, direct from suppliers. In Ecuador, he said, there are little old ladies who act as "fixers," and will take you through the market, bargaining and purchasing on your behalf. He told me that, even though he knew Spanish from Spain, he had to learn "kitchen Spanish" to talk to Mexican workers here. More and more, even in Chinese restaurants, I have noticed Mexicans in the kitchen. Most of our food is not only grown and harvested by Mexicans, but prepared by them, too. I see round-faced Yucatecan boys coming to work on Saturday mornings, or on their way back to the ferry mid-afternoon, after the lunch rush on Bainbridge has ended.

Brendan originally had a consulting business in Seattle called Saint Mac. It acted in part as a catering company, but "mostly as a consultant to other chefs who liked what I do." Dan Barber of Blue Hill Farms in New York State, he says, has his own delivery system for two restaurants. Brendan sees that as a viable alternative to ordering from the big companies, more responsive to the market and day-to-day needs.

"Community is important in a place like this," he says. "In Seattle, I can't get a delivery of Hood Canal clams" except from big companies.

I ask about the economics of food, something that had puzzled me since I began this exploration. Why is a locally grown tomato so much more expensive than one trucked in from California?

"It's a lifestyle difference," he said. "For someone to have a first world lifestyle and sell you tomatoes, pay for the farmers market stall, the truck, et cetera, they have to charge four dollars a pound. In the supermarket, you are buying a tomato grown in a giant field, tomatoes as far as you can see, all tomatoes, or canning tomatoes. They employ questionably paid workers. The tomatoes are picked unripe, put in a warehouse pumped full of CO_2, put in a truck, and distributed through Con Agra or Charlie's Produce. The tomatoes are cheap, and have wax on them. They are cheap because the growers can consolidate their costs. The whole system is propelled by petroleum."

Brendan was just getting warmed up. "Why is a burger at home more expensive than at McDonald's?" he asked. "Because they cheat, and because of the quantity."

Brendan admires the business acumen of people like Tom Douglas, who runs five or six restaurants in Seattle, each with a different emphasis, such as Greek food, seafood, or pizza. "I made a business model [for Hitchcock], and have blown those projections out of the water," says Brendan. "If I can tighten up costs, I will make a profit."

Another important focus at Hitchcock is on the servers. Brendan wants them knowledgeable about the food and wine, but to be unobtrusive otherwise. He worked at a bar while a student at the Art Institute of Seattle. It was during the early days of the first dot-com boom, when people were living high and fast, ordering Cristal (the iconic three-hundred-dollar-a-bottle super-luxury bubbly celebrated in hip-hop anthems). In that setting, all he did was offer drinks, and the atmosphere did the rest. This was in direct contrast to his experience working in hotel restaurants in Alaska that catered to tourists from the cruise ships. There, he was expected to spend a lot of time describing the food and interacting with the customers.

During the first months Hitchcock was open, everyone had something to say—about the décor, the location, the food, said Brendan. Diners would point out that they had eaten in restaurants in Europe.

"You can't outsnob me," said Brendan, "I've worked in first-rate restaurants all over the world. You either enjoy it or you don't."

"People also make suggestions along the lines of, 'If you are going to make it out here . . .'"

But most people just say thanks.

Who eats here? I asked. I've eaten at Hitchcock a couple of times. The food is excellent, but not inexpensive. We don't eat out that much: my husband and I tend to save it for when we travel or entertain guests. Also, the restaurants on Bainbridge are always packed, so as a rule, you need a reservation.

"Local residents and Seattle destination diners. There is some Poulsbo and Silverdale action, but Bainbridge Island is not the center of action for the county. People don't wander in," he says. "We keep our overhead low, the landscaping simple." By landscaping, he seems to mean the décor.

"We see Seattle customers referred from the concierges at the W Hotel, among others." He says he has done a couple of big concierge dinners, which is how restaurants get referrals.

Brendan's biggest challenge right now is to get his costs down. He is trying to make friends, he said, while not pricing himself out of the market. They serve fresh pasta daily, and house-made charcuterie. More recently, he opened a deli adjacent to the restaurant that serves sandwiches to order, ready to be enjoyed outside on small tables. It is very popular, and usually has two to five people enjoying lunch, plus more drinking coffee.

"We are getting good blog stuff," he says. "It's a big network, more like a family."

At one point, Brendan apprenticed with Joseba Jimenez de Jimenez at his original restaurant in Seattle, Harvest Vine. Joseba "was a pioneer in Seattle" for fresh, local food, and Brendan considers him a mentor. "If he wanted to serve pimientos, he would go to Spain, find the seeds, then find the right microclimate in California, have a farmer grow the seeds for him, and FedEx the peppers to him."

Because Brendan buys from foragers, he receives a constant stream of notes and phone calls. He showed me one: "ten lbs. tomatoes, vine ripe," with a phone number.

He said that a lot of people with kitchen gardens start to think they like the idea of being in the produce business, and so get a UBI (universal business identification) number so that they can sell to people like Brendan. "I trade gift certificates for mushrooms," Brendan says, "that people find while out walking their dogs."

But as the manager of Town & Country pointed out, customers need high quality, quantity, reliability, and dependable delivery. After a couple of weeks of rising at dawn to search out mushrooms and make deliveries, most people are happy to stay in bed. Like the farmers market, foraging for a restaurant attracts a certain type of romantic, people romanced by the idea of fresh food and vegetables.

Diners are "still not thinking all the way within the season." Even knowing that he serves local food, he says, people are surprised that he does not serve decaf espresso, or carry artificial sweeteners such as Nutrasweet or Splenda. He does serve coffee, however, so this is more about Brendan's standards for food quality than about local production or seasonality.

I asked him what he wished would grow on Bainbridge. Brendan sighed. "For the sake of this restaurant," he said, "olives and citrus."

"But I don't want to bring a mango, a date, or a fig in here," he said. "If I have to cook with tropical fruit, I will open a restaurant in Maui."

Brendan was the first restaurant owner I ever talked to who seemed acutely attuned to when and where the food he prepared came from. I had talked to other people trying to serve "fresh, local" food, but none in such a hands-on manner. Brendan relies on people directly connected to the land or sea. He trusts them to bring him fresh food grown or foraged on the island or nearby. He seems able to move freely across that divide between farming and land, and prepared food and restaurants.

Haleets

Although the adult salmon have done their best to lay and fertilize the eggs in a protected setting, only a few will thrive undisturbed and undiscovered. Each embryo has enough yolk and oxygen to survive for awhile, but as it grows, it needs more room. Finally it breaks the confines of the soft shell, but remains attached to the yolk sac. This little creature is called an alevin. It continues to live under the gravel until the soft shell is completely absorbed. It is virtually impossible to see in the wild.

The Suquamish, as close allies and relatives with the Duwamish, fished the Duwamish River and gathered shellfish along the many protected beaches of Puget Sound.

The tribes made a forced transition from communally owned territories to private land ownership. In the case of the Suquamish, a reservation was set aside just off of Bainbridge Island, across Agate Passage on the Kitsap Peninsula in the 1800s. They lost all of their clamming and fishing rights on Bainbridge Island. Bureau of Indian Affairs agents then allowed private speculators to subdivide and sell off much of the reservation, in most cases keeping all of the profit and forcing members of the Suquamish tribe off land they thought had been deeded to them. Only recently has the tribe gradually begun buying back many of the checkerboard inholdings on its land, reconstituting a larger body of land on which it has rebuilt a tribal center, a casino, a new museum, and facilities for common use. Old Man House remains silent and covered in small brush and trees. It is the place best suited for viewing Haleets. I don't know if there are ever plans to build there again.

As Ed Carriere, a Suquamish tribe member, told me, "I have a tree farm—eighty acres. We recently harvested sixty-year-old firs. I also have a horse ranch. My property is interesting because in 1890, allotments were given out from Indian Trust land. All of Indianola was trust land."

In traditional Suquamish life, trading was a matter of negotiating—and of necessity. Tucked safely alongside their parents during long winters at Old Man House, children learned the stories, the oral maps, the ceremonies that smoothed the way between neighboring tribes. They learned how to weave specialized baskets for a wide range of uses, how to carve wooden utensils, and watched fishing nets repaired.

I once worked with a Samo'an woman whose parents had both held high positions in traditional Samo'an society. They spent long hours in discussions with other chiefs. The youngest of ten children, Veronica sat at her mother's back and listened to the ceremonial conduct of official business. She learned the words, gestures, foods, and stories that accompanied negotiations, entertainments, marriages and divorces, the settlement of disputes and territories. I imagine the Suquamish conducting business the same way, gathered around the open pit fire, their children taking it all in.

One of the carvings at the right end of Haleets might be a figure wearing a traditional cedar hat. Might this have been a sign of commerce? Get your good cedar hat here? Probably not. It might be a portrait of a protective spirit, however, or an ancestor who had passed from the realm of the everyday to that of the mythic. It might have been someone with good trading stories, who had ventured far so that he or she could return to the safety of the long house and share goods and stories with the children, snug in their goat- and dog-hair blankets. Winter was for stories.

Madrona School has a farm annex where students grow and cook vegetables in an outdoor kitchen.

−3−

School Me

THE SUMMER AFTER MY FRESHMAN YEAR, I was sure I could get a decent job in San Bernardino. I would return and conquer with my one year of college education. Maybe at the library, maybe as an assistant teacher at a summer school program. Everywhere I applied, I was turned away. Unemployment in San Bernardino was around 14 percent in 1973. My ex-boyfriend from high school, who had gone off to attend Harvard, got a job as a garbage collector, which paid a lot of money. I was just a girl, at a time when anyone female was "just a girl." No one wanted a temporary worker.

The rest of the summer I worked the floor of a department store for $1.20 an hour. When the youth pastor from our church went through the store one day and talked to three of us who worked there, the store security hustled around and questioned us to make sure he was not a union organizer. We wished he had been. I took peanut butter sandwiches on Shepherd's Boy bread to work with me to save money. Although I lived at home with my parents, I barely saved five hundred dollars from an entire summer of work.

The summer after my sophomore year, I got hired to work at the U.S. Department of Health, Education, and Welfare, a conglomeration of agencies that no longer exists. I worked in Washington, D.C., the following summer as well, which led to my first job out of college.

These visits were my first to the East Coast. I still earned so little that I would take fifteen dollars in cash to the grocery store to stay within my weekly budget. I lived mostly on Spanish rice and the occasional piece of chicken with tortillas. Canned refried beans were also cheap and easy to fix. Interns and summer employees in Washington went to the receptions and parties held by diplomats, journalists, and lobbyists in order to get enough to eat, unless they were independently wealthy, or had indulgent parents. At the time, people drank a lot (think *Mad Men,* but in the 1970s). I did not drink at all at that time, so I would put two ice cubes in a glass in order to be left alone. Otherwise, partygoers felt compelled to make sure I had a drink in my hand, although I was still under the legal drinking age most of this time.

That first summer, I was appalled at the food in the District's grocery stores—it was pricey and mediocre compared to what I was used to in California. I remember standing in the produce section of a store in Georgetown one day, looking at the wilted lettuce and scrawny tomatoes that passed for fresh food. Nancy Kissinger was standing there, too, and we just shook our heads at the choices.

Midway through the summer, it was apparent that someone in the house I shared with six or seven other Stanford women was stealing food from the others. When it was discovered that no one was stealing my food—a few modest cans in one of the cupboards, a little rice—one woman accused me of being the thief. In fact, I had sometimes made a spontaneous dinner for the others with my meager cache, so suspicion quickly moved on. But that was a clue as to who was actually stealing the food, someone who thought kindly enough of me to not steal from me. Either that, or she hated what I ate. I think the disappearing food stopped after that.

My conclusion, at that time, was that no real food grew on the East Coast—I figured that they must be dependent on the West for anything fresh. Recently, a friend said she grew up in New Jersey, and they had access to abundant fresh food in the summer from the local farmers. There must have been farms near Washington D.C., but I guess that food did not make it into the inner city. Or it went straight to the chefs at the many restaurants in town, leaving home cooks to fend for themselves.

Another year I lived near the Adams Morgan section of town, a center for Latin Americans, and I discovered what Latino/as ate on the East Coast—black beans and rice, yucca, sauces that included coconut milk, and other delicious combinations that were new to me. I had never eaten black beans before, only pinto beans. Now they show up in Mexican restaurants all over the United States. The restaurants in Adams Morgan were much less expensive than those in Georgetown, and I was able to eat out once in awhile, as well as to purchase fresh produce and goods at the bodegas with which to experiment.

One evening I was taken to a French restaurant that served artichokes. Although California probably grows all the artichokes in the United States, I had never tasted one before. It was not something my parents ate, and they were not served at Stanford. I asked about it, and the waiter carefully explained how they are eaten. It was delicious.

Washington also had a French Vietnamese restaurant called Germaine's that was all the rage at that time. I ate there once, and it was fantastic, although I had little idea what I was eating, combinations of sweet and sour, florals, maybe tamarind—flavors I had never tasted before. I remember the crisp delicacy of vegetables that were not overdone, sauces light enough to let the flavors of the vegetables shine through. That was before Vietnamese restaurants dotted the landscape. Or at least they do in the Northwest.

I did not drink much coffee at that time. When I was growing up, my mother made only instant coffee for herself in the morning, but made coffee in a percolator if there was company. In that case, I would drink what was left over and it did not keep me awake at night. In Mexico, our cousins were allowed to drink coffee with a lot of hot milk added to it. This was also really good.

The coffee served in Washington tasted like dirty dishwater, whether it was made in an office or a fancy restaurant. I would pour it into a Styrofoam cup just to warm my hands. However, I began to date a man who ground his own coffee, something I had never seen before, much less tasted.

NORTH DAKOTA

My sister Aida grew up to become, among other things, a farmer's wife in North Dakota. No one would have predicted it. In 1979, her father-in-law suffered a heart attack, and she and her husband moved to North Dakota to help out. After a year or two it became clear that this was a permanent job.

Farming in North Dakota resembles farming on Bainbridge Island only in that, at some point, seeds are put into the ground and plants emerge. Scott and Aida farm twenty-eight hundred acres with two or three people and a combine. Sometimes they hire an extra hand. They grow pinto and soybeans, corn, wheat, and other grains for the commodities markets. A local co-op helps them engage in "forward contracting." That's when the farmer sells his grain before it has actually grown. The bushels must be delivered on time, and, as she tells me, "If you don't have it, you end up paying. That's why farmers diversify their crops, so that if one hasn't produced, hopefully, you can count on one of the other commodities to do well." Some is held back and sold on the open market. If the crop is a failure, they owe money back to the big companies that purchased their grain futures, although they take out crop insurance. "Don't you watch the Hefty Brothers?" my sister asked. "They have a television program called *Ag PhD.*" I don't think I convinced her that the stations in Seattle don't carry it.

In *The Omnivore's Dilemma*, Michael Pollan describes this type of farming as too large and specialized to be considered subsistence, too small to take many losses. It's also very reliant on industrial chemicals. My sister and her husband once believed that, without the use of chemicals, we could not produce the amount of food now available. They embraced the use of chemicals and genetically modified seed as the only way to ensure success, although they were quick to point out that not all the crops they grew were genetically modified.

The idea that without chemicals we could not produce enough food was how pesticides and herbicides were first sold to farmers after World War II, when the chemical companies needed to find new markets for their goods. Realizing that the extension agents paid by the U.S. government to provide agricultural information to farmers were the perfect conduits, chemical companies concentrated on supplying these agents with brochures, and sometimes samples, of the chemicals to share with their clients. This trend intensified in the Green Revolution of the late 1950s and early 1960s when, hailed as a way to cure world hunger, treating plants and soil with heavy doses of chemicals became routine practice.

It was just a matter of time before the same companies began engineering seeds to make sturdy, disease-resistant hybrids, and finally, herbicide-resistant corn and wheat strains that could be patented. According to Farm Aid, a nonprofit organization that supports family farms, "A handful of corporations control our food system from farm to fork. This concentration of power leaves eaters with fewer options to support good food from family farmers, while pushing droves of family farms out of business."

Their website goes on to say that four companies control most of the beef industry, four control most of the chicken industry, and four others control most of the pork industry. As for seeds, four companies control over half of the market worldwide, and Monsanto controls almost all of the genetically engineered crops, amounting to "over 85 percent of U.S. corn acreage and 91 percent of U.S. soybean acreage." These genetically engineered corn and soybeans are what my sister and her husband grow. They really don't have any choice if they expect to grow enough to make a profit, and to sell to the markets for their products, which are usually cereal and animal feed companies.

NAFTA

What about the farmers on Bainbridge who think they can feed us? And what about the farmers in other parts of the world?

By the time the World Trade Organization held its meeting in Seattle in 1999, people turned out in droves to express their anger at what they perceived as undercut wages, lost jobs, anti-union practices, and trading agreements that seemed to further divide the rich and the poor. The protests included some violence, mostly perpetrated by anarchists who would like to bring all of these organizations—multinational corporations, trade unions, and what President Eisenhower once called the military-industrial complex— down and start over. In my opinion, starting over like that isn't likely, at least not without a lot of bloodshed, and that is not something I would like to see happen. But others turned out to express their frustration with organizations that were supposed to protect the interests of "the people," not just those of big corporations, including the World Trade Organization, which describes itself as "the only global international organization dealing with the rules of trade between nations." WTO provided the forum in which the terms of NAFTA were hammered out.

Tomatoes and avocados in the winter are about Mexico's only revenge for the North American Free Trade Agreement (NAFTA), which was signed in 1992 and went into effect in 1994. NAFTA eliminated tariffs between the United States, Canada, and Mexico, thus removing any advantage Mexican farmers might have had in selling food to their own people. American corn producers flooded the market, simultaneously raising prices for consumers, and making it impossible for small, local farmers to compete.

NAFTA was presented as a way for farmers to compete in a global market, but after tariffs were removed, only the gladiators were left standing. Mostly, it means that Big Agro from the United States has been able to dominate markets in Latin America.

In this environment of free trade, only those who can produce enough quantity for a global market have a chance. Remember the requirements for selling food products through Town & Country? Consistent, high quality, dependable, and with enough quantity to supply all of their stores? Imagine that at a global level. I'm sure NAFTA looked great on paper, but by putting so many people out of work, it may contribute to the illicit drug trade that so many are now caught up in, whether as willing participants or as victims.

All of this high-minded regulation, meant, at some level, to improve people's lives, left local producers in the dust years ago. When I listen to people's stories on Bainbridge, I see many good ideas that went awry somewhere, and usually to the detriment of the small, local farmer. For example, the Holt Ranch started out as a dairy, along with over seventy other dairies in Kitsap County, in a climate in which being closer to the consumer was once an advantage. Between the 1950s and early 1970s, farming in Kitsap County declined by 71 percent. After new requirements for standardized inspections, pasteurization, and refrigerated trucking were instated in the early 1970s—all available only to those with the capital to afford them— the dairy business was consolidated into a few companies. Once slaughterhouses were made subject to U.S. Department of Agriculture (USDA) inspections, in part thanks to literary works like Upton Sinclair's *The Jungle,* which drew attention to the appalling conditions of big meat operations, smaller producers could not compete.

Regulating food eliminated most producers, concentrating food production into the hands of a few corporate giants. Most food consumed in the Pacific Northwest is now brought in from Central California and Eastern Washington. And we are lucky to live that close to the sources, because the rest of the country receives its food from the same places.

But it is safe food, you say. It has been inspected, processed in clean rooms, and labeled as to its source of origin. This is true. I trust the food I buy at my grocery store. But in general, the increasing use of hormones and antibiotics on livestock, as well as the increased use of pesticides on fruits and vegetables, has led us to the next phase of our existence, in which we suffer from illnesses and medical conditions that were once rare.

EDUCULTURE

Fifty years after I was first told to chase a pheasant out of a cornfield in Devore Heights, I walked through another cornfield getting ready to harvest on Bainbridge Island.

The previous week, Jonathan Garfunkel, director of EduCulture, had encouraged me to come join the harvest at Day Road Farm. The day itself dawned cold and wet, the first steady rain of fall. I kept checking my email to see if the harvest had been cancelled, but by 8:30, it was clear that we were expected to show up.

I pulled out my slicker and ditch boots, purchased at Farmer Frank's outside of Paonia, Colorado, many years ago. Because I always have trouble with hoods, and knowing that an umbrella would be ridiculous, I took my canvas sun hat, hoping it would remain waterproof for awhile.

By the time I got to Day Road Farm, where Karen Selvar's corn was ready to be picked, a preschool class had already invaded the fields. Helped along by their parents, grandparents, and teachers at a ratio of about one to one, they had made serious inroads through the tall, dry stalks, filling bushel baskets with green ears of corn. Fortunately, I had also brought my leather work gloves. This made the work easy: grab an ear, push down, and twist. Behind us, pumpkins ripened in another field, and crows flew overhead now and then just to see what we were up to.

The preschool that was harvesting that day is my neighbor on Cave Avenue. None of the children cared that it was raining, and a few ended the morning by jumping into a couple of big puddles that had formed on the dirt access road. The parents and grandparents smiled indulgently. Clearly, there were fresh clothes waiting back at the school. Jonathan Garfunkel did not pick corn, but helped to load up the truck, smiling the whole time.

By 11 A.M., the harvest of six hundred ears was complete. I filled about two bushels baskets myself. In the back of a truck, it didn't look like much. These would be shucked the following day and served on the cob as part of school lunches across the island on Wednesday.

EduCulture is a Bainbridge nonprofit that has brought farming into the local schools. Small plots of land have been made available to the students to plant and grow various foodstuffs, and the farmers I've been talking to—Betsey Wittick, Brian MacWhorter—as well as food suppliers like Gene Nakata, visit the classrooms to talk about the process of growing, processing, selling, and cooking the food we eat. EduCulture has gone to great pains to show how various parts of the school curriculum—math, science, and history—are addressed through this program.

The next month, students would harvest potatoes to be served in the schools. Eventually, Jonathan hopes that EduCulture will serve one locally grown food a month, weaving local food into the curriculum and diets of students throughout the school year. In addition, the schools pay the farmers for the food. The students at Wilkes Elementary School did most of the seeding and other work on this plot, as well as working on the Morales Farm directly south of the Day Road farms. The Morales Farm, now owned by the city, was once part of the farm that Doreen Almazan Rapada's father owned. Before that, it might have been owned by a Japanese or Anglo settler. Before that, it was forest, part of the intricate food system used by the Suquamish tribe. In the future, farm plots close to each of the elementary schools are planned, so that students will be able to walk to them as part of a math or history lesson, or just to see if the seeds have come up yet.

For me, keeping a little garden plot turned out to be a pleasure— an excuse to get away from my computer and get outside for a few minutes, where the birds could be alarmed by my presence. I can admire what little sunshine we have around here, and fuss over the state of my broccoli plants. I usually do this just before lunch so that I can cut the latest broccoli buds and eat them fresh, often with hummus. Growing food near where the students spent their days struck me as an excellent idea.

While EduCulture coordinates the program, it takes place with the help and cooperation of a patchwork of almost a dozen organizations and individuals. Jonathan laments the fact that more of the local restaurateurs don't buy directly from farmers.

"But isn't that what Sallie Maron and the FoodHub project, the online meet-up between suppliers and restaurants, was supposed to solve? Has that program been put into effect yet?" I asked.

"Well, it's not in person, which is what we really want," Jonathan answered. That's not what I had been hearing. FoodHub is kind of like speed dating between farmers and restaurants—it is meant to connect them quickly and efficiently. Farmers really are busy. But chefs really do like suppliers to show up at their doors and trade them food for money. In other words, there is, and always has been, a place for the middleman. Jon does not realize that he is a middleman, a facilitator between people who are very good at their jobs, but not necessarily good at marketing or distribution or all the things that grocers and restaurateurs demand of their suppliers. If no one wants to be that middle person, technology like FoodHub will have to suffice.

By showing children where food comes from, and showing them that they can be a part of this process, EduCulture introduces both kids and their parents to the food cycle as active participants.

ISLANDWOOD

IslandWood is another vision come true. In 1998, Paul and Debbi Brainerd, who made their money in software, purchased 255 acres of the Port Blakely Tree Farms, once part of a mighty logging company, to build IslandWood, a center for environmental education. Environmental education has been mandated in the Washington State public schools since 1990, but as with many legislative directives, no funding was included in the mandate. Debbi preceded their purchase with six months of research to confirm the need, then spent an additional two years of research and planning before forming an organization where teachers could bring their students to stay and play in the woods. The program is aimed specifically at fourth graders, who are considered to be the optimum age to learn about the outdoors—old enough to be a little independent, young enough to have it be a life-changing experience. IslandWood also now partners with the University of Washington's College of Education to offer a graduate course of study that leads to a master's degree in either teaching or education.

Especially at the beginning, the programs concentrated on kids from the inner city who might never have walked into the woods and spent time looking at plants and listening for animals. Now, fourth grade classes from all over the area can book a weekend at IslandWood, where eager student teachers will lead them through the woods. I hate to call this a natural environment, since every bit of Bainbridge has been logged, but the grounds of IslandWood provide an environment where nature has been allowed to reassert itself.

Small but elaborate dorms were built, as well as a great hall with a huge beam of wood of the sort that would once have been turned into a ship's keel, and a dining hall and kitchen with a full-time chef and helpers. The children eat "family style" in the dining hall, and must weigh their portions before and after they eat in order to become aware of the amount of waste they generate. The most popular feature by far are the cutaway composting toilets, where the children can watch their poop turned into a useful garden product. This ain't your mother's Girl Scout camp.

IslandWood, of course, has a mission statement, but its kitchen also has its own statement of values. The first goal listed is "to educate our staff, customers, and ourselves about the food experience and the effect it has on our global community." The rest of the statement is sprinkled with words like *authentic, socially responsible*, and *sustainable*. After eighteen years of operation, IslandWood has had many employees, so I am not sure if the kitchen staff got to generate those statements, or someone in public relations.

They do have an authentic chef, Jim White, and an authentic kitchen garden that the students get to visit. There is a sustainable farm liaison, Chris Agnew, and I also met a socially responsible garden educator named Jen Prodzinski.

A raven greeted me from high atop a Douglas fir when I pulled into IslandWood's parking lot. I had been here many times for community events, but had never gone past the great hall and the dining hall. In the first, a carving of a storyteller modeled on the late Vi taqʷšəblu? Hilbert, a Nooksack tribal member and one of the last fluent speakers of Lushootseed, greets visitors. I still cannot believe that Vi herself is gone. She was once a vibrant presence on the cultural landscape, an embodiment of what we have always known. The dining hall, in another building, backs up on a kitchen with a big picture window through which the students can watch the chefs work.

Jim White, a friendly guy, comes out to greet me. He sports the mandatory chef's tats on his arms. He has done the rounds of Seattle-area restaurants: Ruby's, the Bainbridge Island Bakery, and the ill-fated Wolfgang Puck's, which brought him out from New Jersey, where he worked at a country club, to take what he thought would be a stable position. "I thought they would take care of me." This turned out not to be the case, as Wolfgang Puck's suffered bad publicity over a prominently featured vintage poster that was considered racist by many in the Asian American community, and a subsequent boycott.

Unlike Brendan McGill at Hitchcock, Jim has cooked since he was little, and took his first cooking class at the age of ten. His stint at the Bainbridge Island Bakery, he thinks, made him a better cook in general, teaching him to pay attention to both the art and the science of cooking, the alchemy of transforming ingredients into food.

IslandWood now hosts special events, like weddings, high school reunions, and proms, so the kitchen is pretty busy. This not only generates income, but also provides Bainbridge with a much-needed large event facility. The special events allow the kitchen staff to "stretch out" their repertoire, because children tend to be less exploratory when trying new food. IslandWood recently hosted a wedding in which the groom was from Colombia, and Jim was able to get him to translate recipes from his mother and grandmother for use by the kitchen. The kitchen staff includes or has included people from Ethiopia, India, and Vietnam, which allows it to create food that is recognizable for visiting students. Seattle, where most students come from, is much more ethnically diverse than Bainbridge, although Bainbridge is becoming more diverse.

A big part of the kitchen's program is getting children to try new things. "Look at this beautiful thing that someone grew!" is the approach Jim encourages. IslandWood wants to help children to see that farming and cooking are manifestations of the same thing. They dig potatoes, then make gnocchi. They learn to create pot gardens (gardens in pots, not marijuana gardens) that can grow in small spaces.

"When we bring the produce in, they are so excited that they get to eat it." Sometimes, Jim says, their excitement inspires the parents to try new things as well.

But because IslandWood serves lots of meals to lots of kids, they have to stick to some predictable menu items. "We try to stay as close to home as possible for our sources, but for kids we have to have citrus and pineapple. People like to tell me what to do—all vegan, or no sugar." White has two young daughters, so he's fully aware of what even a chef's daughter will—and won't—eat.

Chris Agnew, the farm liaison, arranges for local produce from places like Butler Green Farms and Persephone Farm, but Charlie's Produce, a wholesaler, supplies the rest. "I know they use the best practices," says Jim.

Jim leads me out to the "garden classroom." Here, we find a beehive-shaped oven built out of cob, that is, mud and straw. It should stand for hundreds of years, says Jim. I'm not so sure. It is under a roof, I think to myself, so maybe it will not dissolve this coming winter.

Jim says it has taken some experimenting to use the oven well. The oven can sustain a temperature of 350 degrees for five hours, which "gives us time to make the best food." He tells me they've been able to make pizza. We have been waiting while a class goes through the greenhouse and kitchen garden. When they leave, Jim introduces me to Jen Prodzinski.

Jen Prodzinski has been a garden educator for IslandWood for a year, and a master gardener for Kitsap County for over twenty years. She doesn't look that old. Jen says that they try to make it a key message to the children that food comes from "light, air, water, and land."

Their "Soil to Snack" program encourages children to pick food, such as scarlet runner beans, that they will eat a short time later. They also get to take some seeds home—seed packets from Bainbridge Gardens, left over at the end of the season—to grow in container gardens.

I ask Jen about the seed saving program on Bainbridge. In 2014, the Bainbridge Public Library built a little shed and began a seed library. We were encouraged to "check out" seeds and plant them, return what we didn't use, and leave notes on the results. I checked out a commercial packet of cucumbers, which did not germinate. I did not hear much fanfare about the seed library the following season, but it is still alive and kicking. I really hope that the local farmers are saving and exchanging seeds, and keeping notes. I'm counting on them. When the big one comes, the ferry crashes, the bridge crumbles, and the sky falls, I expect there to be corn, triticale, squash, berries, and sunflowers that we can plant and use to save ourselves. In the meantime, by saving the best seeds each season, we can be sure to grow the strongest and most nutritious food for our climate.

According to Jen, the curriculum for the kids has three main messages: food comes from the soil, diversity is good, and kids can grow food at home.

This last item led to my next question. My son was a year ahead of the curve when IslandWood got started with its concentration on fourth graders, so he never went through any of their workshops. Even now, few of the children who live on Bainbridge go through the overnight program. Most of the schools that send children are in the greater Seattle area, where trees and open space are scarce. What, I wondered, do the children really take back with them? That there are a lot of trees on Bainbridge? That rich people can grow their own food? I guess a runner bean in a pot is a start, but what follow-up has been done to confirm a change in attitude by fourth-graders and their families?

When I wondered about that, both Jim and Jen referred me to a program that had recently affiliated with IslandWood. It is called Homewaters, and conducts environmental education and cleanup in the Seattle area. But when I reached Linda Versage, schools co-ordinator at Homewaters, she said that they did not work with kids who visit IslandWood. Even if they did, said Versage, it would be difficult to track the attitudes and outcomes of children who had been through the IslandWood program because of privacy concerns, and because children change schools. At that time, there had been no follow-up on the part of IslandWood to see if the program has, in fact, made a change in how children view their ability to produce food, or whether or not any of them have started gardens at home.

Once again, I was reminded that we live on an island. As a result, information can seem to reach a dead end where the road meets the ferry.

However, urban farming has received a lot of attention in the press recently, and regulations have been loosened so that people can keep chickens and farm the strips of city-owned property along the curbs in front of their houses. More industrious urban farmers are gaining permission to use lots owned by nonfarmers to grow food in exchange for sharing some of the produce.

This relates to another of my concerns in researching this book. The IslandWood kids come from a range of backgrounds far more diverse than those on Bainbridge Island, and far more reflective of the population of the state and the country. But very few of the people I talked to about farming on Bainbridge were people of color. The Nakatas are mostly out of the farming business with this generation, and into the retail business. Akio Suyematsu was the last of his generation to farm, and, with no descendants, he was the end of his family line. Karen Selvar and Brian MacWhorter gradually took over his work as he aged, and the land itself now belongs to the City of Bainbridge. The Filipino/First Nations people have mostly sold their land and gone into other occupations. Unless farmland is placed into a trust, it is taxed at the same rate as residential property. If it is placed in a trust, the taxes are waived, unless the land is later developed for housing, in which case the back taxes must be paid. Land on the island is expensive, since it is a desirable place to live, which encourages development. The only places being preserved as farms are those already in operation, often as public trusts, or on land purchased by wealthy philanthropists. Needless to say, all of them are white.

And even the existing farmers are not exactly reproducing. Farming has traditionally been a family occupation, since it is easy to pass land from one generation to the next through inheritance. But only one of the farmers I talked to has a child going into farming. Many of them have never had children. Although there are mixers held on a regular basis with farmers from other communities, farming in this day and age does not seem to be a very social occupation that encourages the establishment of families. It could be because the income is so low, and much of it must be invested back in the business in order for it to survive. Most of the farm interns I met were women. I also suspect that, especially in the Northwest, farming is a low-status job, in an environment where high status and high income are available in the software industry.

Even for the poor, farming is a low-status occupation. Many of the parents and grandparents worked on the land because they had no choice. They want their children to get an education and take indoor work. Of course, children from poor families are more likely to drop out of school before obtaining a high school diploma and to take dead-end, minimum wage jobs. Farming is also somewhat of a closed system. A young person living in the International District or the Central District of Seattle is not likely to have an opportunity to try out farming as an occupation. Who is going to drive them out to a farm in Snohomish or Kitsap County and say, "I will pay you to pick crops or weed onions for me?" In fact there is a program that introduces inner-city high school kids to farming. These are youth old enough to do farm work and a few have enthusiastically embraced the opportunity to get out in the country and hoe onions. The biggest hurdle for all of these kids is being able to afford land. Even selling organic vegetables at a farmers market for a premium, farmers earn very little cash.

In both Central California and Eastern Washington, programs have started that not only give young farmers a chance to try out the occupation, but also offer business classes and eventually loans for the purchase of land. Such programs may enable middle-class young people to enter the farming profession, as well as allow farm-workers to obtain both the financial aid and skills to buy their own land. One of the appeals of being a farmer is the idea of being your own boss. Of course, the market is your boss, the weather is your boss, and your own needs for food, clothing, and shelter are also your bosses. But owning a farm appeals to the entrepreneur who is willing to do hard physical labor, or who is already doing it for someone else.

AFTER THE WAR

When the Japanese Americans returned to Bainbridge, many continued family traditions that had been transported to the camps and back. Many things were lost in the transition. In an effort to assert their patriotism during World War II, families sometimes destroyed precious family heirlooms such as scrolls and kimonos, as "too

Japanese." Eventually, some traditions came back, helped by support and encouragement from islanders such as Gerald Elfendahl, unofficial historian of Bainbridge Island. One of these was the Mochi-tzuki tradition, which is now held at IslandWood, and brings old and young, Japanese and non-Japanese, to the beautiful grounds to celebrate.

Mochi-tzuki is held on the Lunar New Year. Sweet rice is steamed over a hot fire under pressure, and pounded with mallets to a doughy pulp in a stone basin. At IslandWood, the kitchen fills with volunteers from the Japanese American community, who shape the dough into little buns, serving them with soy sauce or sweet red bean paste. Anyone with clean hands can help.

Mochi-tzuki is a great midwinter activity, addressing all the senses. Visitors take turns wielding the mallets under the supervision of Shoichi Sugiyama, who bravely reaches in and turns the dough between strokes. The sound of the rhythmic pounding fills the courtyard as people trade off using the large wooden mallets in a stone bowl. Inside the great hall, Kokon Taiko of Seattle provide a drum show to the lucky people who stood in line to obtain the free tickets.

Started twenty-five years ago by a few island families, the event now draws over two thousand people. Many are families with children, and separate activities are set up in the art studio. Many mixed heritage families attend, here to remind their children that this is part of their inheritance, too.

In his Minidoka journal, Arthur Kleinkopf gave an account of the Mochi-tsuki celebration in Minidoka:

December 31, 1941

I observed three Japanese gentlemen pounding rice for rice cakes.
The first step in the preparation of the rice was the steaming process.
For this rice steaming they had secured a used oil drum, placed
it on some legs and built a fire under it. The drum was partially
filled with water above which were three trays containing rice to be

steamed. After the steaming, the rice was removed and placed in a hollowed stump which had been set in a cement foundation. Here three Japanese, each with a sledge or maul of wood, rhythmically swung and pounded the rice until it was the desired consistency for making into cakes. I thought each moment that someone of the three would receive a blow on the head but they seem to have a method of avoiding this. The rice was then made into various kinds of delicacies. This was usually done by the women who gathered around one of the long dining room tables; and while they chatted to each other they expertly patted and rolled the rice into the desired form.

Like many mid-winter celebrations, Mochi-tzuki revolves around food. It serves as a reminder that, although it is cold, spring is on its way. The last time I visited Islandwood for Mochi-tzuki, the winter had been still and dry, with sunbreaks through the gray clouds. Small birds foraged in the rustling leaves, and the fawns had lost their spots. Winter is the time to be grateful for what we have, stand with hands outstretched before a blazing fire, and tell stories. In the camps, far from home on Bainbridge Island, it was a way to commemorate the larger continuity of family and culture, and the changing of seasons. This too, would pass. Nowadays, it is used to share culture and stories with an even wider circle of people.

There is a memorial on Bainbridge dedicated to those who were taken away from their homes by armed soldiers and relocated to the camps in California and Idaho. The Bainbridge Island Japanese American Exclusion Memorial was recently incorporated into the National Parks System. The park is located in Eagledale, at the place where islanders were led onto boats that took them to Seattle. The dock is no longer there, but a long, undulating wall with plaques depicting Japanese American islanders at work and at play traces the path that they walked. It is a beautiful place for an ugly chapter of American history. The memorial is intended to school us in what can happen when we let war hysteria override our better selves. In this case, we sent our food producers to camps, making the remaining islanders subject to the whims and variables of a larger market. We have not recovered from that. There are plans to build a short pier there, maybe the kind of pier a boy like Wayne Nakata could fish from with his grandfather.

"*Nidoto nai yoni*," says the Japanese American Exclusion Memorial. Let it not happen again.

HUM

Most Saturdays, you can find Chuck Schafer at the Bainbridge Island Farmers Market. Chuck is an evangelist, a zealot who wants to convert you to what he found out about life. He doesn't sell anything, or even offer samples. He just brings some of his equipment and talks about the wonders of the apiary.

"Just like me, people are astonished to learn about bees."

Yet Chuck is surprisingly shy when it comes down to showing you his bees. I had to use all of my persuasive powers to get him to invite me over. The Schafers live high on a sunny hill at the south end of Bainbridge Island. I followed him there one day after the market, after helping load a centrifuge, trays from a hive with a bit of comb stuck to them, samples of pollen, and other large, heavy equipment onto the back of his truck. We entered the house through the back door, and I waited in his front room, where a pair of lovebirds hummed and beeped.

Chuck took me out the back door again and showed me a greenhouse overrun with beekeeping equipment. He extracted two sets of beekeeper's white overalls, and helped me get into a set meant for someone over six feet tall, Chuck's son. A sort of space helmet fit over my head, with a face veil that covered the neck and zipped onto the suit. Needless to say, the gloves were too big, but I had brought a set of cotton garden gloves.

When I made this appointment, I wasn't sure how macho we were going to be in approaching the bees, so I wore long pants and brought my own garden gloves and a long-sleeved white shirt. It turns out that Chuck is quite conservative when it comes to handling the bees. He always wears a beekeeper's suit and gloves, although he has switched from the unwieldy gloves that look left over from early NASA designs to blue stretchy gloves that give him more dexterity. He tried working without gloves once, but when a bee crawled across his hand, he automatically slapped it and got stung. "There are guys who work in tee shirts and shorts," he said, but Chuck is not one of them. "They get stung."

Chuck placed a small amount of tinder on a table in the back yard and set it on fire. He used pine needles. Some people prefer untreated burlap "or anything organic." When he had a tiny blaze, he transferred it to a bit of moss and placed it in the smoke box, closing it. Then he worked the bellows until puffs of aromatic smoke came out. "Some people sing to them," he said, "instead of using smoke."

Only then did we walk around to the front of the house, with its spectacular view of the water off of Fort Ward, now the domain of his bees. "If I move too fast," he said, "they get alarmed. But as long as I move at a slow, even pace, they are fine." I tried to remember that as I moved through the cloud of bees—slow, even pace.

Each hive is a Chinese puzzle box made of pine. Each contains framed screens, much like window screens, that can be lifted out individually to be examined, cleaned, or harvested.

My garden gloves worked fine, but as I lifted and set aside the sections of a hive at Chuck's direction, the cotton kept sticking to the shellac-like substance the bees use to glue things together. It's called propolis. I finally removed my gloves to take pictures with my cell phone.

Chuck directed me away from an area where I had been standing, because I was blocking the bees' path in and out of one of the three hives. Each hive contains seventy thousand to one hundred thousand bees. I realized that they have regular flyways, things to do. I had to think of myself from a bee's perspective. Chuck pointed to the frame I was holding. The bees always start working at the center, working outward in an oval. It looks like they are randomly crawling around, but I realized that each bee has its own subroutine that fits into the overall program of the hive, which is to hatch, grow, feed, and protect as many bees as possible. Each hive is about the size of my very first desktop computer, maybe a little bigger.

The bees are about a half-inch long, with the drones slightly larger. Chuck keeps Italian honey bees, known for their good nature and willingness to work with humans. They seemed very relaxed. If I looked closely, maybe I would see them holding tiny glasses of Chianti. And this was the best part, maybe the coolest thing that happened to me while researching this book: As I held the frames, turning them over to look at both sides, I realized that the bees knew a perfect stranger was handling them, and they allowed me to do it. It's like the Borg on *Star Trek*—if I am not interfering with the program, I am of no consequence.

Chuck had me pull out each section, and set the frame gently on edge as we paged through the hive like a book. The newer frames were on the ends, and were maintained by younger bees. These bees were a little shinier, moved a little faster. You could almost hear the drum and bass in their hum. Chuck was looking for the queen to show me when we came across an odd lump of wax on the end of a frame. With a putty knife, he scraped it off and held it in the palm of his glove. Just then, a large bee began to break out of it.

"Look at that! A new queen."

That? It looked like the rear end of a bee. Any bee. How could he tell? But as she emerged, we could see that the queen was slightly longer than the worker bees, but slender.

"That's what a virgin queen looks like. Once she starts to produce eggs, her abdomen will become wider." Uh-huh.

Chuck was really pleased. "I've never seen that happen before! Just because you came over to look at the bees." He explained that beekeepers try to mark the queens with a dot from a marker, but they always move too fast for him. He is also afraid he will squash it.

Meanwhile, the new queen walked around on the blue expanse of his glove, touching antenna with the other two or three bees that had ridden along on the bit of comb, telling them she was in charge.

"They're accepting her," he said. She dropped down to the hive below, and began her reign.

Soon she would fly away with the drones in pursuit and mate. Then she would start a new hive. "Probably on my neighbor's property," Chuck said, "and he'll be pissed." Chuck can then capture the queen and set her up in a new box hive, of which there are three right now. Her subjects will obediently follow.

Bees travel no more than two or three miles from their hives to collect pollen, and Chuck says there appear to be enough on the island to pollinate our fruits and vegetables. The only reason people move hives on Bainbridge is to get a particular flavor of honey. In other parts of the country, bees are brought in to pollinate the crops. Many fruits, vegetables, and spices, such as melons, cucumbers, apples, cherries, and most nuts, such as almonds, are dependent on honeybees for pollination. Beekeepers bring the hives in on trucks, leaving them on the edges of fields for a set amount of time, then move on to pollinate the next crop.

I remember seeing these mobile pollination operations in Western Colorado. At night, crop dusters swooped down over the fields near our house to spread chemicals. They said it was done at night to protect the honeybees, who would be in their hives then. All I know is, it made me throw up, so it probably didn't make the bees feel any better. Research points to pesticides as one of the causes of bee dieback. A class of pesticides that contain neonicotinoids causes the bees to lose their sense of direction, so that they cannot navigate the spaces between their colonies and the sources of pollen.

Bainbridge experienced a bee dieback along with the rest of the country in recent years, and beekeepers speculate on whether it was mites, a fungus, pesticides, or some other factor that caused entire hives to disappear. As a rule, beekeepers send off for a fresh batch of bees each spring, rather than trying to protect their earlier hives. Typically, commercial bees are raised in climates that do not freeze in the winter, and a queen, a few workers, and some food are packaged up and shipped to the wannabe beekeeper. The careful beekeeper can overwinter a hive with an adequate supply of honey, a healthy queen, enough winter bees—which have much longer lives than summer bees—and a hive protected from the weather until spring comes again.

Although there are fruit trees and other food sources for bees on Bainbridge, "it's all blackberries," says Chuck, "and then, not even native." He means that the bees prefer the Himalayan blackberries that will inherit the Bainbridge Island earth along with English ivy and Scotch broom, all invasive species crowding out the other low growth.

Plenty of insects besides bees are in the pollination game—wasps, birds, even small mammals that move through the tall weeds and collect pollen on their fur. I didn't realize until now that honeybees are from the Old World, brought to the Americas by Europeans, and called "the white man's flies" by Native Americans. Corn pollinates by wind, and there are other types of bees than honeybees that pollinate. But the plants that interest humans mostly depend on bees.

"When I started keeping honeybees, I thought my yard would be full of them. But if you look at this lavender," he said, pointed to a nearby bush, "it's about ten bumblebees to every honeybee." Chuck has deliberately added plants that bees are supposed to prefer, but the bees go where they will. He pointed downhill to a garden enclosed by a deer fence. "They told me to plant California bluebells for the bees, but the deer eat them, so now that big patch in the middle of my vegetables is for the bees." Out of season, the bluebells form an unattractive gray green clump in the middle of his edible greens.

The bees are mesmerizing, like Philip Glass music—repetition and variation too complex to comprehend, yet perfectly understandable. After my visit I realized how people can get hooked on beekeeping. When I described my visit to the bees to the next-door neighbor, he was ready to go in on a couple of hives with me. But I know that way lies danger—I could already see me constantly checking on the bees, fussing over them, wondering if the queen was comfortable and well-fed as she cranked out eggs deep in the hive. Bees do not sleep at night, I learned. Rather, they perform indoor work like constructing new cells, only stopping for the occasional catnap in their six- to eight-week lives.

Chuck worried about the new queen. She was emerging late in the season, and the bees might be reluctant to swarm and start a new hive. They would need to produce enough honey to carry them through the winter.

"Fall is when they get cranky," he said, "because they are more protective of their honey."

The bees are part of our gift economy. We do not compensate them for the honey, other than to provide hives in which they can build their combs. There are probably plenty of natural nesting sites on the island, although other people might try to destroy them. Another beekeeping friend recounted how he accidently took too much honey one fall. The next time he opened the hive, the bees rushed out and attacked him. Clearly, they know that the beekeepers are helping themselves to the honey, but tolerate it up to a point.

The bees reminded me again that there appears to be some pattern to how we relate to our food. I remember reading someplace that a beehive is, biologically, a single organism, like a jellyfish, in that all of the parts are necessary for it to thrive. Any single jellyfish is made up of individual polyps that can scatter and reform if they need to. But there seemed to be something more complicated than that going on, something having to do with an exchange between nature and people, or resources in versus resources out. How did this play out on an island? For one thing, our bees are not likely to leave, so everything they need to thrive must to be located here.

"People have been keeping bees forever," Chuck said, "but there's still a lot we don't know."

A WALK IN THE PARK

In the cool of a day predicted to get very hot, we walked through a gentle forest. Birds called and squirrels chittered at the small groups of visitors strolling the carefully groomed paths. My husband and I were in the Bloedel Reserve, started in 1950 by Preston Bloedel, son of timber baron Julius Harold Bloedel. Julius made a fortune harvesting the huge trees of the Northwest and turning them into lumber.

Preston taught school in California until called back by his father to work in the family business. He managed to retire in his fifties in order to devote himself to the reserve on Bainbridge, where he raised his children and lived with his wife, Virginia, in a Provençal-style home from 1951 until 1986. "The Reserve is a place that offers the visitor a variety of experiences of nature," says the brochure.

When my family moved to Bainbridge in 1995, the 150-acre reserve was open sporadically—one had to call ahead and make reservations, and we were turned away a couple of times with visitors who would not be able to come again. Only a few people were allowed to visit at a time, so as not to disrupt the experience of being close to nature. But in fact, the Bloedel Reserve is not a very natural place. In a style of garden that must hark back to European ideals, it is divided into several gardens, or rooms, that evoke different moods and emotions—the Meadow, the Mid Pond, the Moss Garden. Oddly, the most naturalistic is the most formal of these gardens, the one that surrounds a faux Japanese teahouse. Its scale, though still huge, has been toned down to be more in proportion to human beings, as opposed to the towering evergreens that mark our natural Northwest forests.

One can see how our idea of an "experience of nature" has changed over the years. The Bloedels saw nature as something too strong and rough to be experienced without the filter of another human sensibility. Nowadays, we buy expensive hiking boots and packs and go out looking for an "authentic" experience, one as unfiltered as possible. But the more human beings there are, the harder it gets to find nature that has remained unaltered by our presence. On Bainbridge, we are hours away from any uncut first growth, and even then only patches remain. Driving to them lost its luster for my husband and me pretty early, and the nearby parks and beaches began to substitute for the wilderness we had taken for granted in Western Colorado.

A garden offers a close-in experience—in both miles and time, not to mention gasoline—and one that can be shared with children or even city slickers. Bloedel is now open to the public on a regular basis, and offers just such a garden. Although its forests are second and third growth, there are still some impressive trees there—trees that the city would have taken down as unsafe or unnecessary. Soon, places like the Bloedel Reserve will have to substitute for an "authentic" experience. The logging companies worked hard to get every stick of commercially valuable wood out of our forests, and even today continue to chip away at environments that need peace and quiet in order to protect the complicated ecosystems within them. My vote would be to set aside part of the Bloedel Reserve for the long term, say one hundred years, and aim to regrow an old-growth forest for our grandchildren. Scientists have already determined that there are plants and animals that only live under old-growth conditions. Who knows what we are missing from our island ecosystem right now?

It's easy to say, "Oh, well. We used up all our resources. But we can get them from somewhere else." But this is somewhere else. People lived on this island for thousands of years without using up the resources. Yes, life was hard, and unmitigated nature can be evenhandedly cruel. But we can strike a balance. We can still build houses, but keep enough forest cover to recharge the aquifer. We can use power, but take it from a renewable source, like solar panels. We can walk more, and remember that we only choose to be slaves of time.

Modernization doesn't mean we have to use resources even faster; it means that we have the knowledge and tools to slow down our headlong rush to climate disaster.

GROCERIES-R-US

While we are trying to keep up as consumers, our suppliers and grocers are trying to remain schooled as well. In the same way that there are publications and blogs that help consumers keep tabs on food safety, cost, and availability, there are companies that write and research for an audience of food producers and retailers.

One of these is the Hartman Group, based in Bellevue, Washington. Started in 1989 by Harvey Hartman, the company follows consumer trends, from changing demographics to buzzwords, and provides this information to the producers and retailers who try to predict what we will pay to eat next.

Mostly this is geared toward figuring out how to market what the companies would like us to eat, but in order to do that, they must figure out the magic words that will prompt us to buy.

Hartman is thorough. In 2000, they hired their first PhD, a cultural anthropologist. The industry, still thinking in terms of marketing, found this strange. But the researchers who work for the company follow individuals around, watch them use their kitchens and eat, and provide data that go beyond what people will write on a survey.

For example, Hartman found that 48 percent of adult eating occurs between meals. They also found that, as societies have become more ethnically diverse, our overall food preferences are changing. This sort of information provides manufacturers with approaches to packaging, labeling, and marketing. Who would buy this? Where would you place it in a grocery store? Think about those shelves of breakfast bars in the cereal section: they are the result of some researcher noticing that breakfast is now eaten on the run.

Hartman also tests what certain phrases, such as "organic" and "gluten free," mean to consumers. Many of us complain about the vague nature of such terms, but marketers for big business would like to keep it that way, providing a big tent for as many products as possible. This pits profit against an informed consumer. As individuals, we probably cannot afford to hire our own food researchers, so we depend on local food producers and retailers who care about their product to keep us informed.

The trust factor is big here. Because the owners and managers of Town & Country live on the island, they have a personal stake in providing us with food that is attractive, nutritious, and will not harm us. This is true of our farmers, too. As for the packaged and imported foods that make up the bulk of our diets, we probably don't see those manufacturers on a daily basis.

Every day, lobbyists for various factions of the food industry make their rounds in Washington, D.C. There are approximately one thousand lobbyists representing 435 corporate clients alone, according to OpenSecrets.org, the website of the Center for Responsive Politics, a nonprofit that keeps track of lobbyists in Washington, D.C., and the money spent on lobbying elected officials. Their numbers come from the Senate Office of Public Records.

You can bet that small, local farmers do not make such an impression at our nation's capital, although the Granges do send people to lobby Congress. The microcosm of Washington, D.C., is a good place to consider the array of interests involved in food policy decisions—food growers, food processors, retailers, chemical companies, agricultural workers. Monsanto, for example, spent $4,330,000 on lobbyists in 2015 in Washington, D.C., while the United Farm Workers of America spent zero dollars, although it looks as though the Buena Vista Group might have worked on their behalf pro bono.

In addition, Monsanto contributed over nine hundred thousand dollars directly to candidates, either directly from the company, or through political action committees, in the two-year election cycle starting in 2014. Most of that money goes to Republican candidates.

Who represents the consumer? While nonprofit groups seem to outnumber citizens on Bainbridge Island, large portions of the U.S. population lack any advocacy on their behalf, much less advocates for healthy food. And even with the large number of self-interest groups on the island, their financial clout is miniscule. Private money started IslandWood, but public money needs to go to land use planning and enforcement, the purchase and maintenance of open space, and public education in order for private users and landowners to understand how important it is to assure the quality of our water and shoreline. We can support educational programs at the local level, but our elected representatives mostly hear from experts and paid professionals who have commercial interests at heart.

AMERICAN GROWN

Knowing where our food comes from needs to be part of all school curricula, and part of a national conversation that includes health, the environment, and international trade. In 2012, Michelle Obama, who has gingerly advocated for healthy eating and exercise for schoolchildren, published her first book, *American Grown: The Story of the White House Kitchen Garden and Gardens Across America.*

First ladies are expected to champion causes, but as we learned during the Clinton era of the 1990s, it can't be a cause that implies policy, such as a plan for affordable health care. Previous first ladies tried to Make America Beautiful, or Make America Read, or just wore clothes well.

Obama's original project was "Let's Move!" a plan to encourage schoolchildren across the country to get more exercise. One out of three children in the United States is considered overweight, and/or suffering from weight-related illnesses, such as diabetes. But as soon as she got started, Obama realized that diet and nutrition needed to be addressed at the same time. By starting a kitchen garden, Obama hoped, as she puts it in the book, to "begin a conversation about this issue—a conversation about the food we eat, the lives we lead, and how all of that affects our children."

Obama and her daughters visited Monticello, Thomas Jefferson's home, to collect seeds for the new garden she envisioned on the South Lawn of the White House. The book includes a sketch of that first garden Jefferson designed for the White House, along with maps of the Obamas' garden, which was first planted in 2009, then expanded to include more ground and more plants each season, including a berry patch, rhubarb, and a three sisters planting of corn, beans, and squash. It is the first food garden at the White House since Eleanor Roosevelt's victory garden during World War II, although the Carter White House kept an herb garden.

As with all new gardens and gardeners, mistakes were made, as well as adjustments, and there was lots of trial and error. Washington, D.C., has ferocious winters, monsoon springs, and punishing summers. There were also problems specific to the White House: several government agencies hold jurisdiction over the South Lawn, but Obama managed to co-opt the directors and get them moving and planting, too. The South Lawn now hosts its own honeybees, and the Obamas use White House honey for diplomatic gifts.

I'm sure the White House staff initially saw their involvement in the garden as yet another addition to their many tasks, but something else began to happen: the staff, whether kitchen-related or not, began to turn out in such large numbers to work on the garden that a strict schedule is now maintained to give everyone a chance. Garden-keeping is addictive, and the perfect antidote to office work. The garden now supplies much of the food served at the White House, and one third of the harvest goes to Miriam's Kitchen, a Washington, D.C., charity.

Obama's book, of course, ends with recipes, manageable dishes devised by the White House chefs—salads, soups, breads, and cookies that would tempt anyone to angle for an invitation to a White House dinner. Is this a policy-setting book? I hope so—let's bring food production closer to home. Just getting kids to move *outside* and plant a garden is a start.

American Grown includes a brief nod to Native people taking control of their health with an article on Native Hawai'ians bringing back indigenous foods. In the Northwest, a small movement is under way to bring back indigenous foods, as well as the lifeways and knowledge that make this food nourishing to both the body and the spirit. A friend let me know about a regular conference of people intent on doing just that.

OUR FOOD IS OUR MEDICINE

The high, vaulted ceiling and the back windows framed a view of Agate Passage and Bainbridge Island. Seen from the north, at

Suquamish, the island looks larger somehow. Maybe because the coastline is bowed out, rather than tucked in as at Eagle Harbor, where the ferry lands. If I had looked carefully, I suppose, I could have spotted Haleets. The room was filled with Northwest indigenous elders, some dressed in conical hats and button blankets with red and black designs, discussing ancient fish management methods that are still valid today. Sponsored by the Northwest Indian College in Bellingham, Washington, the Our Food Is Our Medicine conference is hosted by a different tribe each year. In 2014, it was held in Kiana Lodge at Suquamish. Native American food educators, scientists, and food activists gathered from the greater Puget Sound region to share food, traditions, and new information.

In another room, mostly women jostled each other to fill jars with medicinal herbs to create vinegars and infusions—tasting, smelling, comparing notes and experiences, sometimes bursting into raucous laughter as they shared stories about what people really want cured—constipation, impotence, and of course, pain. In a third, advocates for farmworkers and other food rights advocates testified about their ongoing experiences at area farms. A delegation from Oaxaca, Mexico, was in attendance.

What struck me about the fish management discussions was how simple and easy to implement the methods were: none required special materials or chemicals, or even much maintenance beyond repair and harvest. Marco Hatch, director of the National Indian Center for Marine Environmental Research and Education (NIC-MERE) and a member of the Samish tribe, was introduced by the organizer, La Belle Urbanec, a member of the Lummi tribe, and by an elder of the Suquamish tribe, and presented with a traditional conical hat made of cedar strips, which he immediately donned and wore throughout his presentation. First, he told an ancient story of how the Samish are linked to the sea by the maiden of Deception Pass, a famous story that roots the Samish people to a specific geographic place.

In a story much like that of Persephone and Demeter, except with a happier ending, when a member of the tribe fell in love with a sea dweller, the Samish formed an alliance with his people. Evidence of the pact can be seen in the restless waters between Fidalgo and Whidbey Islands, where the maiden's long, green hair can be seen waving in the water.

His affiliation with the tribal elders gave Hatch permission to tell the story in more detail than I have sketched here. With that foundation balancing his academic credentials, Hatch went on to describe how to build a clam garden, a raised area on the beach that protects clams from predators while allowing the circulation of water and nutrients. Shellfish benefit from human intervention, he said, and will substantially increase their numbers when provided with a protected environment. Clams thrive in what Hatch called the "Goldilocks" zone: too high on the beach and they dry out, too low and the starfish eat them.

These descriptions of the clam gardens and reef nets reminded me of my one visit to Hawai'i. Like Native people in Puget Sound, the ancient Hawaiians farmed fish by keeping them in large, shallow tide pools where they were easy to harvest. The high tides brought in food and nutrients, and took out waste produced by the fish. The fish in the pools were safe from bigger predators, and those that escaped helped to restock the nearby reefs. No antibiotics were used, and as far as I know, no artificial foods were fed to the fish, either. The Hawaiian Islands have hundreds of *loko i'a*, saltwater fishponds, that once supplied as much as two million pounds of fish a year, as well as providing other shoreline benefits. None of the ancient ponds have been restored, however, because the permitting process is so arduous. But people are raising fish in ponds built away from the shoreline.

Someone asked if there were now more red tides, and why people used to not worry about them. Butter clams, especially, are now often toxic. Marco explained that trimming away their siphons and gills can substantially lower the toxicity. Shellfish sold commercially are all tested before they go on the market, but foragers don't have those checks in place. While I would not think of collecting and eating shellfish during a red tide, it became clear that some of the people in the room were in the habit of doing so. Symptoms of poisoning from the neurotoxins in a red tide include diarrhea, loss of short-term memory, and paralysis.

"We used to feed it to the cat first," offered one person, to nervous laughter. That's one way to approach it. Still, the idea that people are often unable to harvest their local waters and safely consume the fish really bothers people. "It might poison our bodies," one elder said, "but it nourishes our souls. It is part of our *sche'lang'en*, 'way of life' in Lummi."

People, especially Native people, still consume fish from the Duwamish as well, it was pointed out, even though the river flowing through south Seattle to the Sound has been designated as a toxic waste site by the Environmental Protection Agency. While a major cleanup of the Duwamish River is under way, scientists doubt that people will ever be able to safely eat fish caught in it. "Don't eat crab, shellfish, or resident fish from the Lower Duwamish River," says a Washington State Department of Health advisory. This does not stop people, especially poor immigrant families and those who have fished and eaten from these waters all their lives, from catching and consuming these fish. "These are people with little or no income and people for whom fishing is a really important cultural practice," said B. J. Cummings of the Duwamish River Cleanup Coalition, a non-profit coalition of environmentalists, neighborhood groups, local businesses, and Duwamish tribal members.

Underlying all of the discussions at the conference was the awareness of the need to improve Native American health. Like me, many Natives suffer from metabolic syndrome, which includes a predisposition to diabetes and heart disease. Eating fresh local food, and just as importantly, participating in the active planting, fishing, and harvesting of that food, was the road to wellness advocated by all of the speakers.

In the farmworker rights sessions, the health of farmworkers exposed to pesticides was discussed. Ongoing difficulties with a local berry producer, Sakuma Brothers, have exacerbated ethnic differences between groups of pickers. This is all the sadder because the

Sakuma Brothers were berry farmers on Bainbridge before being sent to internment camps in Manzanar and Tule Lake, California. Upon their release, they continued farming in the Skagit Valley, as well as growing berries in Northern California.

The farmworker camps now used by the Sakumas, as well as camps in Mexico that belong to companies with contracts to supply grocery chains in the United States, resemble the camps once used to incarcerate Japanese Americans during World War II: long buildings nominally divided into small rooms, no or sporadic running water, high barbed wire fences to keep workers from leaving before the harvest is finished.

In between sessions, I chatted with some of the other attendees. This was the third year of Our Food Is Our Medicine. Some of the attendees I talked to were involved in elder care, while others worked with young people. I talked with an educator from Lummi, Shane Cordero, who would like to get legislation passed that would allow "sea to table" classroom involvement, in the way that EduCulture provides a "farm to table" program. This will take legislation on the state level. People were filming some of the sessions, so the information shared in person could be disseminated to a wider audience. It won't have the generous, spontaneous sharing between elders, scientists, educators, and food experts that I experienced that day, however.

DECOLONIZE YOUR DIET

A good example of the application of deep, traditional wisdom to our health issues today comes in the form of a sort of cookbook. Luz Calvo and Catriona Rueda Esquibel's story started in sorrow. Luz, who had been a vegetarian for fifteen years and considered herself very healthy, was diagnosed with breast cancer. As Luz endured surgery and follow-up treatment, Catriona struggled to find food that her partner would eat, and that would enhance healing. Their research showed that Latinas have an exceptionally low occurrence of breast cancer until they move to or are born in the United States. Both felt that good food could make a difference, and set out to grow and prepare a smarter diet. Their discoveries are shared in their lavishly illustrated book from Arsenal Pulp Press, *Decolonize Your Diet*.

Decolonize Your Diet is not exactly a cookbook—it's more of a manifesto, although a very gentle one. It offers both a thoughtful response and a generous offer to the community at large on how to improve our health. In other words, Calvo and Esquibel have brought their eating habits in line with their medical and cultural needs as only hands-on local farming allowed.

Many of their conclusions align with mine—principally that a local, indigenous, plant-based diet is more likely to afford a healthy life than taking pharmaceuticals based on research that has little to do with my genetics and background. These ideas are echoed by Bryant Terry, author of, most recently, *Afro-Vegan: Farm-Fresh African, Caribbean, and Southern Flavors Remixed.* In the forward to *Decolonize Your Diet*, Terry describes the book as "part of a larger movement utilizing ancestral knowledge to help communities of color respond to the public health crisis."

Calvo and Esquibel live in Oakland, and finding traditional Southwestern ingredients is probably not as hard there as in Washington State. I'm comfortable finding and growing foods that thrive in my maritime climate, but I understand what they are saying: my body, genetically, needs corn, squash, beans, and citrus. It doesn't need fried foods, it doesn't need much animal protein, and it definitely doesn't need deep-fried Snickers bars.

As these two academics got the hang of small-scale, urban farming (which in their case, seemed to involve a lot of tearing up of concrete), they began to keep chickens for eggs. They sought out and adapted family recipes for their primarily vegetarian diet, and got to know their neighbors, including a Sephardic Jew from Rhodes, along with *their* cultural preferences and genetic needs.

One of the recipes in their book is for tortilla soup. I learned my version some years ago by eating it three times in a row at a restaurant in San Antonio, until I could figure out all the ingredients. My version is a glorified chicken vegetable soup, but the *Decolonize Your Diet* version contains no chicken. This allows the ingredient in the name, toasted tortilla strips, to shine through, rather than be obscured by the chickeny flavor.

The book includes lists of indigenous ingredients at the back, along with mail-order sources. As my local Town & Country has restocked after their remodel, I see that they are carrying a wider variety of dry goods in bulk food, including more brown beans and grains like amaranth, and more alternatives to processed sweeteners. I look forward to exploring the thoughts and recipes in *Decolonize Your Diet* as I figure out where everything is now located at T&C. I'm planning on trying "*enmoladas*: tortillas smothered in pumpkin mole" and "red *pozole* with medicinal mushrooms." I have several freezer bags full of Hatch roasted green chiles that are way hotter than advertised, so I will need to make them into salsas and beans.

For my son's birthday, I made tortilla soup. While it still had chicken in it, I included fresh squash from my garden and used a vegetarian soup base instead of chicken broth.

Poco a poco, the old people used to say, little by little.

SCHOOLING

What do we know about our food in the Northwest, and on Bainbridge Island in particular? And how do we pass that knowledge on to others?

- Children need to know early on where their food comes from, and who grows, harvests, and prepares it.
- Environmental, food, and farm education are susceptible to the same pitfalls and bureaucracy as other formalized education.
- We need to check which interests have our interests in mind, usually by tracing where their funding comes from.
- A robust internship program can do a lot.
- We need to save locally successful seeds and their histories.
- It is important who has access to and ownership of the land.
- The health of the land depends on the health of the sea.
- Our health depends on the health of the land and sea.

Haleets

The young fish, once it has absorbed all of the yolk sac, is now called a fry. It must venture out of the gravel bed in search of food. The fry rises to the surface and fills its swim bladder with air. However, outside of its protective redd, it too becomes potential food, and spends a lot of time avoiding predators. The fry seek out dark pools under fallen logs, venturing out to grab a bite of smaller fish or organic matter. Insects that touch down on the surface of the water are fair game. Rotting branches grow colonies of insects and aquatic plants, providing both food and cover. When they are big enough to survive, the fry begin their journey downstream to the sea.

When I think about the carved faces of Haleets, when and how they were made, I realize that they are the product of the gift economy, from a culture that values the unseen as much as the seen. Over the years, young people went out into the woods and waters to pursue their vision quests, and carvings such as these were often the culmination of these quests. Perhaps these faces were their gift back to the community that had raised them. While they stood in the shallows and carved—trying not to fall in as the rising tide sucked against their legs each day—people were preparing for them, waiting for them to return and share their stories. Or perhaps they remained silent during this transition back to tribal time from spiritual time.

Nowadays, most vision quests take place in a sweat lodge. These are not always pleasant visions.

As Coll-Peter Thrush recounts in "The Lushootseed Peoples of Puget Sound Country," Gweqwultsah, or Aunt Susie Sampson Peter (Kikiallus of North Puget Sound), described how her father prepared her in the 1870s to be a traditional doctor or healer, in a long line of distinguished healers. Whatever he told her to do, she did. This involved surviving on very little food, running far and fast, and swimming in the cold waters of the Sound at night. "Nothing was allowed to scare me. So, that is how I found this particular power which always helps me, even as I grow older. Even now sustaining me is this doctoring power."

This was also the time in which some young women received labrettes, lip plugs, or tattoos on their lower lips. The labrettes have since gone out of style at Suquamish, but one of the figures of Haleets appears to be wearing one.

Aunt Susie Sampson Peter never mentions which of the spirits gave her power. They are not to be talked about, and it is rude to ask. Some novices see "career" spirits that will help them fish, trade, or gamble. Other see protective spirits, and some encounter the most powerful and dangerous spirits of all. One of these is associated with Agate Passage.

If there are local spirits watching the island, Akio Suyematsu has joined them. I don't know if there is a farming spirit. I can hear him complaining about how people are doing things, that he doesn't have time for this while fussing over a tractor he has babied along for fifty years. Haleets, also grumbling, must make room for him at Agate Passage.

Without going all polytheistic, I think we can agree there are spirits of place. Most of them were personified at some point, and as stories about them outlived their mortal form, they joined the mythology of an area.

There are people who will scoff (maybe Akio himself) and say, "There are no spirits." I think of these people the same way I think of the colorblind—perhaps they simply cannot see spirits, but they are missing a lot. It's not necessarily their fault, having grown up in a culture that trains you to ignore the obvious.

Me, I see spirits everywhere, from the ravenous slug in my garden to mother ocean. And those spirits are a part of my spirit.

Farmer Karen Selvar with corn
harvested at Day Road Farm.

– 4 –

Growing Our Own

WHEN A FRIEND OF WAYNE'S ANNOUNCED that he was starting a public radio station in Western Colorado, we decided to help him, whether he wanted help or not. We loaded up a moving truck with our few belongings and, with Wayne's brother Marty and his girlfriend, Libby, to drive the truck, headed out. We followed in Wayne's old Volvo wagon.

Libby worked in a food co-op. She was passionate about natural, unadulterated food. It was 1979, and the first time I had heard that packaged food was tainted with preservatives, and otherwise robbed of its goodness by having been processed. We ate in truckstops and juke joints along the way, so she did not eat that much. I remember she had Marty bring her a bowl of prunes once. I think she brought a few things to eat, maybe a bag of nuts and dried fruit, but I don't know how long they lasted. Libby carried a shaker of cayenne pepper to sprinkle on whatever she ate. Not a bad idea.

We knew we were close to our destination when people began to wave at our little caravan. Paonia turned out to be a town of twelve hundred people on the west side of the Continental Divide. It is set in a valley flanked by the West Elk Range, and by mesas quilted with farms and orchards. At night, the lights of a hard-rock coal mine pulsed above the town, causing people to call it the Mother Ship.

Our friend, Campbell, was a little stunned that we had offered to move here and help him start a radio station. He had volunteered at the station in Denver where Wayne had worked before moving to Washington, D.C. Campbell was using his own property on Garvin Mesa as the location for both the station and the tower. An FM station requires a direct line of sight to the tower, while AM sends a signal up in the air that then settles down upon its receivers. In either case, his farm was a good location for the tower.

We moved into Campbell's old farmhouse, set in the middle of an organic apple orchard. He was trying to make a living on this orchard when organic was still a small, specialized market. The orchard was filled with beautiful, obscure types of apple trees that have since been eliminated from the monocrops of most modern orchardists. A "natural" pesticide had to be applied to the apples and had to stay on long enough to deflect a particular moth from laying its eggs on the fruit. It might have had something to do with the stage of the moon. Deer had to be deterred by setting off M-80 firecrackers in the orchard. Eight-foot fences had to be mended, although the deer still seemed to get over or under them. The trees had to be irrigated. It wasn't too many acres, but it was a lot of work. Campbell would be out at odd hours, diverting water from one ditch to the other at dawn, or chasing off deer in the middle of the night.

Donning the long, canvas bags used by pickers, about half a dozen of us harvested the apples that year, including a couple of friends Campbell hired for that purpose. You picked an apple with your right hand (whether or not you were right-handed) and set it at your left shoulder to roll into the bag on your back—theoretically. Like most things, it got easier with practice.

Campbell was living in the packing shed, because he had recently broken up with a girlfriend, and could not bear to be in the house. She was a good cook and baker, and the kitchen was still stocked with her organic supplies—flour, sugar, meal, spices—and I began to make apple pies out of our bounty. I had baked before, but never made pies. I'm sure I did everything wrong, but apples, butter, flour, and spices are pretty forgiving. We had arrived in the fall, and everything in Paonia was ripe.

The fall also brought hunters from Texas to hunt elk. There was a whole set of stories about the hunters, including a showdown in the middle of the main street, Grand Avenue, in which two drunk hunters had shot at each other. There was also the highly illegal practice of shooting "slow elk" if a local family was especially desperate, that is, poaching a cow from a local herd. The space between my shoulder blades itched each time we went out to cut firewood. I was sure someone would mistake me for whatever was in season that week.

Everything in Paonia was just the opposite of Washington, D.C. It was like opposite day in elementary school, when you were supposed to wear your clothes backwards and walk backwards. Since we had arrived directly from the center of political power, we were viewed with suspicion. Maybe we were there to take over the radio station. Maybe we worked for the CIA, or some other nefarious agency.

Part of the paranoia was that growing marijuana in the nearby national forest was a big business, as it still is in many rural towns in the western United States. This was long before methamphetamines or OxyContin became the illegal drug of choice for remote communities. When we got the station on the air, it had an "eclectic" program schedule. I hosted a program of classical music, using Wayne's records. People complemented me for my vast knowledge of the subject, which consisted of reading the liner notes. Others slipped anonymous envelopes full of cash under the station door with "Play rock and roll!" scrawled on the outside. So we knew what programming the dope growers supported.

Others lived in this beautiful valley because they were convinced they could survive a nuclear attack this far from either coast, believing that weather patterns were such that the wind would blow any fallout away from the North Fork of the Gunnison River. It did have delicious water, the sweetest I had ever tasted. It made you feel invincible. All the children were blonde, no matter what their parents looked like. Women wore long dresses and went around barefoot much of the year. This was the late seventies and early eighties, but it was still the Age of Aquarius in Paonia. I made do with my corporate clothing and whatever remnants were left of my college wardrobe.

I added a pair of black rubber boots purchased at Farmer Frank's. I still use them.

Potlucks were common here. Every main course—lasagna, spaghetti, stew—had a choice of vegetarian or nonvegetarian options. What did I take to them? Maybe the pies I was baking. Maybe Spanish rice. I couldn't get the ingredients I thought I needed for more elaborate Mexican food.

The Fourth of July was celebrated in Paonia with a street fair. The high point of the street fair, as far as I was concerned, was the booth run by the Mormon ladies who brought their cherry pies. Those pies were to die for, and no one thought twice about going back to buy second or third slices. I asked one woman why her pies were so good, and she told me she substituted honey for the sugar in the cherries.

Food was part of the social conversation of everyday life in Paonia in a way that I had not experienced before. It was a way for neighbors who might not have anything else in common to engage with each other—at potlucks, the parade, across the fence. This was where I learned how to make small talk by asking what vegetables someone had decided to plant this year, and how they planned to eat what grew in their gardens. The conversation of food is the conversation of seasons, of cycles, of children growing up, of chickens thriving or meeting a bad end.

We tried to buy a home in the area, but were unable to get a loan for the one we really liked—a dilapidated ten-acre ranch at the foot of the West Elk Range, backed up against the forest, with beautiful views in every direction. It is possible that, had we purchased that home, we would still be there. Instead, we found a more conventional home on two and a half acres in a larger town, Montrose. It was an hour away from Paonia, and as we got paying jobs and spent more time there, we spent less time with our friends in the North Fork Valley.

Montrose, or more specifically, Spring Creek Mesa, was where I started keeping a big garden. It was a form of therapy, going outside and putting my hands in the soil. I saw this with my in-laws as well, who kept a big garden behind their home in Denver.

Spring Creek Mesa was a mix of houses and farmland west of downtown Montrose. The soil was sticky with red clay, and the sun was abundant. Best of all, our property came with water rights. Water rights are the most precious commodity in the West. Once every two weeks, we had the right to divert the water from a ditch that ran along the road, and fill the ditches and furrows on our own property. We used our water to grow a lackadaisical crop of hay that we gave to the neighbors for their horses, and to water our vegetable garden.

I planted a garden about ten feet by twenty feet. This felt huge to me, compared to the small raised beds my parents had cultivated. At the beginning of every season, the plants seemed small and unresponsive. By the end of the year, there was too much to store, eat, or harvest. I learned how to can relishes and tomatoes. This was something Wayne's mother had learned from her mother, and it seemed like second nature to her.

I had never even seen anything put into a canning jar. But all around me, food was unfolding according to the seasons. Fields were planted in crops of onions, alfalfa, and corn for fodder, cattle were driven onto the Uncompahgre Plateau in the spring to free-range all summer, and brought down in the fall. We could hear the pounding of a thousand hooves for hours before the cattle drive came past our house twice a year. Calving took place in the nearly fallow fields around us in March or April, and the cattle were taken to slaughter next fall. Men and women raised food and cooked and canned in an unending cycle that gave them great satisfaction, as long as there was enough to eat. This was the first time I had lived in a rural agricultural community, although like most of the west, it was about to be transformed.

Everyone in Montrose ate meat. The farmers who talked politics hung out at the Stockman's Café, and the farmers who wanted to get into trouble hung out at the Lariat Lounge. There was an invisible line that bisected the Uncompahgre Plateau south of which ranchers ran cattle, and north of which shepherds ran sheep. It might have been the outcome of a small range war at some point. While there might not have been any written agreements, both the Bureau of

Land Management and the National Forest Service were aware of and respected this divide.

Our "next-door" neighbor and his son went out one day with shotguns to hunt pheasant. They got a few yards out their back door before bringing one down. When they really wanted a challenge, they went out in the forest armed with hunting bows.

Losing a job in an area this remote took a toll on families. During the early eighties, the excitement about oil shale gave way to a bust, taking a lot of jobs with it, and people sold their homes at a loss or lost them outright. The bank officer who had given us our loan, a gentle, middle-aged farmer whose family had lived in the area for two or three generations, committed suicide. He might have felt responsible for the misfortunes of the families that did not make it.

By the time we left Colorado, Wayne and I had each cycled through a couple of jobs. Our big achievement was bringing public television to the small communities of Western Colorado via a series of broadcast translators. Before that, it was available only by subscribing to expensive cable channels, and then only if you lived in an area dense enough to have cable. All that technology is obsolete now.

I remember giving away bags of tomatoes and zucchini that last fall before we left. It had taken me four years to figure out how to grow good tomatoes before we moved to a new climate for new work and new opportunities.

LIVING AS A FARMER

It turned out that one of my early questions to Betsey Wittick, of Laughing Crow Farm, had been really important to her. I had asked her who her heroes were, and she had told me Judy Wicks, an entrepreneurial activist, and David Suzuki, an activist economist. She had in turn asked one of her potential business partners as she considered taking over management of the adjacent winery, but she wasn't thrilled with the results. "He said Joel Salatin [a farmer in Virginia whom Michael Pollan's work has made famous] and Ayn

Rand," she told me. "I realized he might not be the best person for me to work with. He never asked my heroes. I'm a collaborator."

On my second visit to Laughing Crow Farm, Betsey had just finished feeding breakfast to four interns in their twenties, all women: Becky Warner, Stacy Kinsell, Erin Jakubek, and Renee Ziemann. All were local except for Erin, who is from Portland. There was one male farming intern on the island that year, at Tanith Farm. All were college graduates—a farm internship is considered post-graduate education. They receive room and board, but no pay, in exchange for their labor.

Without leaving the dining room table, the interns began to sort heads of garlic to break into nine thousand cloves and plant as garlic starts. They set aside the smaller ones, because small starts grow small garlic bulbs. All the garlic heads had a rose-colored peel and were large, as garlic goes. The variety names were Rosewood and Chesnek Red. As they worked, I thumbed through a catalogue and some books. The Purple Stripe variety wins flavorful "best baked garlic" contests according to the Filaree Farm 2006 garlic catalog Betsey handed me along with a book called *Growing Great Garlic,* by Ron L. Engeland. On Betsey's farm as well, people were learning about farming from books.

The clove itself serves as nutrient for the young plant, while the basal plate sends out shoots. Garlic, it turns out, grows easily in our rocky soil, but it takes lots of fertilizer. This year, Betsey used her own manure pile from the three horses and the chickens she keeps. Now she wants her own manure spreader.

Betsey's farmhouse has stacks of publications about farming scattered around the living room and up the stairs as far as I could see. Some of the interns live in the main house, and a couple live in a trailer parked nearby. Very Paonia, as my husband would have said.

Betsey and I returned to our earlier conversation about her taking over the winery from the Bentryns. Although I knew about

Bainbridge Vineyards, I hadn't planned to write about wine growing on the island, because I did not think of wine as a food necessary for survival. But the more I thought about it, the more I realized that no food from off the island would also mean no medicine from off the island, and a significant percent of the medicines people take are for pain mitigation. When I researched my book about old Tucson, set in the late 1800s, drinking was a big issue, and the cause of many of the city's sorrows. But in a rough and tumble frontier town, alcohol was probably the only relief from toothache, arthritis, and other common ailments. If Bainbridge Island had to grow its own food, it would also have to grow its own medicine.

Originally from New Jersey, Gerard and Joanne Bentryn started the wine business on Bainbridge Island in 1977. Earlier farmers had planted grape vines in Grapeview, a community farther west, and near Mount Baker, in the Cascade Mountains north and east of Seattle.

Gerard had worked on satellite technology, and upon being drafted during the Vietnam War, was sent to Germany to work on missiles. There, the Bentryns became enamored of the local food system. "You can see everything you eat out of the window," Gerard had told Betsey. That view also included small vineyards. When they returned to the States, Gerard worked for the National Park Service, which he found "completely bureaucratic," but the two of them volunteered at wineries, and learned how to make wine.

When Bentryn was transferred to the West Coast, he bought property on Bainbridge for its similarity to the Mosul region in Germany, which he had grown to love. The wines grown there, he said, were more delicate, more fragrant, and had a lower alcohol content than wines from the sunnier south. The Bentryns started their vineyard and winery at a location just north of my house, in a natural bowl with an open, south facing slope. Since then, the Bentryns have moved their vineyard to the Day Road Farm and sold the original land to developers. It is now a collection of homes and condominiums called Vineyard Lane, connected to my Cave Avenue neighborhood by a footpath and a bridge.

The Bentryns have one of the earliest bonded numbers for winemakers in the state. They worked with Robert Norton at the Washington State University Experimental Station in Mt. Vernon to find grapes that would work on Bainbridge. At his suggestion, rather than using California grapes, they planted a different set of varieties from Europe: Siegerrebe, Müller-Thurgau, and Madeleine Angevine. They still grow these, along with varieties of Pinot Noir and Pinot Gris that can tolerate our wet climate. Betsey noted that most of the wine industry in Oregon is near the wetter coastline, not in the arid eastern half, as in Washington.

Betsey mapped out garlic-planting work for the rest of the day, and promised that each intern would get to drive the tractor that day. After watching her and Brian MacWhorter at work, I've realized that one of the traits of a successful farmer is the ability to estimate the amount of labor needed and to assign it in a way that feels equitable, but also assures that the work gets done. Betsey's interns were directed to rototill an area that had been planted with a cover crop. If she had time, Betsey said, she would use the horses. The rototiller will chop more, because the blades are circular, while the disk pulled by the horses just flips the soil.

"There is a method called no-till which we should probably do," she said. In this method, which is more challenging to do correctly, farmers use a heavy roller to crimp the cover crop, killing it without turning it under.

We walked by the two young draft horses, now in the paddock attached to the purple shed. They are Suffolks, shorter than her old draft horse, Samantha, but wide. Maybe we are all just used to Samantha, but the younger pair seemed to lack Samantha's charisma.

As we walked past the interns, who were now hunkered down in the field to plant garlic, Betsey said this had been the toughest year for grapes in the twenty years she has worked with them. Growing grapes is labor intensive, like all farming. "We want food, but we don't want to do the work."

I asked if strawberries could ever be grown on the island again. "Maybe we could grow strawberries," she said, "but there is a fungus that has built up in the soil. We've got to get really savvy about crop rotation, learn to grow organisms that will replace the fungus." That's true of most organic farming. Farmers used to use nicotine and copper to deter pests, but now both are considered toxic, and using copper is not considered organic. Back to the earth means back to seasons, back to Native and indigenous connections to what can be grown in each specific place.

We walked through a patch of clover to higher ground, where the vineyard begins. "Farming is getting to be more holistic, and the interest in small farming gives me hope. None of the interns are from agricultural backgrounds." Betsey herself is from Newark, New Jersey, where her father was a fireman. "We are beginning to get it, partly because restaurant chefs have brought the concept of farm-to-table to light, but we are not there yet. The fact that we are bringing animals back into agriculture is a good sign too." When the island was incorporated as a city, Betsey worked to merge city and county laws in order to protect agricultural zoning. As she became less politically active, she got more involved in farming. "This is my activism now."

We were now at a high point on Day Road Farm. A slight breeze rustled the leaves on the vines. We could look east to where Betsey's couple of acres snuggled into the landscape, or north to the Day Road Farms entrance. There, schoolchildren were disembarking from a bus to explore the farmlands.

The vines, with their broad leaves, grow on open fencing strung between sturdy posts to just above head height, about six feet. Because the Bentryns had both been ill, and the dark, wet summer was hard on the grapes, there had been no grape harvest that fall.

Birds had been allowed to eat the fruit off the vines. Though the harvest had been small, a few other vineyards and wineries on the island had participated in "grape crush," the annual grape picking and crushing. Most of the new wineries buy grapes grown in Eastern Washington, rather than growing their own grapes. Typically, Bainbridge Vineyards would have hired migrant pickers as well as a few Indipinos who still work the area. A few volunteers help as well, but as Betsey said, "volunteers don't transfer knowledge" to the next generation. I hadn't thought about that before. Even interns take what they know about the local landscape and spirit it away to new landscapes.

I asked Betsey how, really, growing and processing grapes on the island could be made to work economically. "Educating people about food is a long-term process," she answered. "There is a huge proliferation of wineries bringing grapes over from Eastern Washington. Right now, consumer taste is for heavy reds, but wineries want to offer the full range." The Pinot Noir grapes have been in since the late 1980s, and the first harvest was in 1992. In other words, Bainbridge Winery has tried to respond to the market, while continuing to grow its own grapes. Much of Betsey's job will be to position the business in a broader marketing landscape.

Gerard and Joanne Bentryn are in their seventies, and it has been a struggle to find the right transition for their business in order to retire. Most of the vineyard property, like the rest of the Day Road Farm complex, is now owned by the City of Bainbridge Island, to be kept in perpetuity as agricultural land as part of the community commons. The Bentryns talked to a couple of groups interested in taking over operation of Bainbridge Vineyards, but none connected with Betsey. She has since found a coalition of like-minded partners to manage the business. Betsey is committed to the *terroir* of this place. She looks young, but her hands and fingers are thickened from years of working the soil. Again, in talking with her I have the feeling that much more is at stake than the financial gains and losses of this work, this property. "In perpetuity" sounds like strong, secure language, but I worry that the beauty of the land will make it susceptible to market forces stronger than agriculture.

Jon Garfunkel of EduCulture plans to fold the vineyard and winery into its mission of reconnecting adults with the land and teaching the younger generations about the importance of knowing where food comes from, but possession is nine-tenths of the law, right? And a lot of people have wanted to own this land over the last one hundred years.

CHATEAU POULET

There are people on the island who could be described as survivalists. Not as many as in other parts of the county or state, since we live relatively close to Seattle and any survivalist worth his or her carefully stored salt opts to live farther out in the countryside. Say, Idaho, or Alaska.

But there is another group that even realtors are catering to. Let's call them preppers, since they like to think that they are prepared for anything, just in case. I don't think my friends Linda Meier and Stephen Hubbard will object if I describe them as preppers. They work hard at it, and have put a lot of thought into the idea.

Their farmhouse is filled with art, including Northwest Coast pieces by Native artists, with a mix of red kilims and Persian carpets on the floor. Next door, a new building was under construction during my visit, in a style—nouveau rustic?—that uses old shapes, but new materials such as corrugated steel.

Linda and Stephen moved to Bainbridge in 2001, shortly after 9/11, in part because they knew my next-door neighbors, Hilary Hilscher and Neil Johannsen. Before, they had lived in the fashionable Seattle neighborhood of Montlake, which Linda says was "noisier, crowded, less fun."

Stephen was in private practice as a cardiologist at the time. Diagnosed with idiopathic urticaria (hives of unknown cause), he needed to take antihistamines to control them. Stephen continued to perform minimally invasive surgeries such as implanting pacemakers, stents, and angioplasty balloons. One day, a pharmaceutical rep asked if he was still performing such procedures, and he realized he needed to stop, since antihistamines can make you groggy and impair judgment. That was 1998. Shortly after, he was hired by Harborview Medical Center in Seattle, which is affiliated with the University of Washington, as a teaching physician, which pays one-fourth the salary of a practicing physician. However, his insurance policy, which recognized that he was now disabled, made it possible for him to give up direct practice for teaching.

"We decided to look around Bainbridge and see what popped up," said Linda. "I had four years left on my mortgage in Montlake."

Stephen had grown up in Sacramento, where he was a 4-H kid. "I already think this is where I want to live," he told Linda, on first seeing the farmhouse on ten acres with the chicken coop in front. There was an offer pending, but they made a second offer and got it. That was in August 2001.

Their moved had been planned for soon after, September 11, 2001. Everything was delayed. They moved a week later, and all the ferries blew their horns for one minute in commemoration of the deaths. "I cried," said Linda, deeply affected by the tragedy, although she did not know anyone directly involved. "We haven't looked back since."

Did you intend to raise livestock? I asked.

"Not really," said Linda. "I had a little glimmer of someday living on a farm." Within a month they had chickens in the coop.

Linda and Stephen also grow all of their own vegetables, and keep bees. They started with three hives last year, and are down to one. The others were lost over the winter. They also had honey the first year, but not since. "Just dead bees," Linda said. They might have died of mites, or fungus—Linda and Stephen aren't sure.

I asked what they do when they travel, which is often. "Somebody has to stay here. It's not that big of a job, but it's daily. We live on a septic system and a well. Systems can go bad." The eggs need to be picked up daily, although the chickens have three or four days of feed set out, and their water is automatic.

The sheep also have an automatic water system, as well as grass and some supplemental feed. There are eight sheep right now, to be reduced to three or four when Linda and Stephen return from their next trip. I asked Linda if I could return when they slaughtered the sheep. This seemed to surprise her, but she agreed.

They also have a rescue goat, a Nubian named Annie. She is just a pet, Linda emphasizes, not expected to contribute milk or meat.

In with the nearly three dozen chickens are six all-white call ducks, a type of miniature mallard. They are used in England, Linda said, to "call in" wild ducks. They are very talkative, and also lay eggs from April to July that can be eaten.

Linda and Stephen first started selling eggs five years ago, when they realized they had too many. At first, they sold them out of a cooler at the end of the driveway on an honor system, then halfway up the long drive, and now from the porch of the house, figuring that it will take a lot of nerve to come right up to the house and take eggs without paying. "People love them," Linda said, "I've had people follow me up the drive just after I've changed the sign to 'available.' Often."

I asked how much feed costs for all the animals. It took Linda a while to estimate, but she finally came up with a figure of between $250 and $275 a month. The amount they receive for the eggs "might break even" for chicken feed alone. "We do it because we love it."

I asked if there is a philosophy behind this, or if they consider it a hobby. "Both," Linda said. "The philosophy part of it has grown, with the idea of getting food close at home, and knowing what your animals have been eating, what they have been nourished by."

Once they began raising chickens, their friends began sending them a gift subscription to *Backyard Poultry*. Linda recommends it. Someone else gave them a copy of *Minnie Rose Lovgreen's Recipe for Raising Chickens,* an island classic and a "great source." A young

English immigrant, Minnie Rose came to Bainbridge Island in 1912, where she married a Danish immigrant and kept a dairy farm for thirty years. She dictated the book to her friend Nancy Rekow during her last illness. "Keep the chickens happy," was her main advice.

Otherwise, "When chicken farmers get together, they talk about chickens. And sometimes you can't get them to shut up."

The two most common questions she is asked, Linda volunteers, are: Do you have to have a rooster (no); and how many chickens do you have? (about thirty).

"Chickens are in," Linda says. In 2011, the Bainbridge municipal code was updated to allow up to five chickens in the backyards of private homes, reflecting a general trend toward allowing small-scale food production throughout the region. My own neighborhood has covenants prohibiting livestock or permanent outbuildings, although people have sporadically tried to raise chickens.

This leads to one of my rules about food: birds always come to a bad end. Even if they aren't named (and people usually do name them), chickens are often the target of predatory animals, including pet dogs that run loose at night. Domesticated birds are also prone to various viruses and other illnesses.

A couple of years ago, Linda and Stephen received a call from BITV, our local cable channel, asking about salmonella. This was during the recent case of tainted eggs from a big Iowa supplier, in which thirteen hundred people were sickened nationwide. They did not return the call. If pressed, they had agreed with each other that they would say "people should consider all raw poultry and all raw eggs to have the potential of salmonella."

"After all, you have to remember where the eggs come from," Linda said, meaning, the rear end of a chicken. In the Iowa case, the feed itself was contaminated, so the chickens were sick internally.

The USDA has been trying to document all the chickens in the United States. They sent out a thirty-five-page survey, which Linda and Steve threw away. The USDA also called them about ten times, she said, and came by once.

"The reality is," Linda said, "you can't control all the chicken farmers in America. There are more and more. The survey was ridiculous."

We went outside. The original farmhouse is a kit-built loghouse erected by the first winners of the Washington State lottery in 1982. In front of the garage are three, three-thousand-gallon tanks resembling small silos that collect water from the roof. There is also an expansive deck with a view over the treetops, north across Eagle Harbor.

In front, sheep grazed on the fenced land. "They are Katahdin sheep, no personality. Just sheep." Annie the pet goat, who is very sociable, came right up to the fence to visit with us. The sheep ignored us.

Like many households on Bainbridge, Linda and Stephen keep guns to protect their livestock from predators, such as coyotes. It is legal to hunt deer on the island in season, as long as the hunting takes place on private property, with permission from the landowner, and well away from the road. Although the island is not overrun with deer, people regard them as a nuisance for getting into vegetable beds or eating the roses.

The chicken house has an enclosed mesh run outside it, so the chickens can go in and out as they please. There were previously two peacocks, which have since died. Most chickens only live four or five years. Then they are eaten. A huge fig tree shades the chicken house, related, probably, to a tree in my neighborhood. These trees, too, have a story.

I ask if they could live off the produce of their property if they had to.

"It's a possibility," Linda says. They have three freezers, but do not can. They are learning the best ways to freeze food. They grow more tomatoes than they can eat, and are using them in pastas and soups in the winter. "We go through a lot of Ziploc bags." I ask Linda what her response would be if there were a food shortage. "The good news is, if there were a food shortage, we have a lot stored away. The bad news is, all our friends and neighbors know it."

I asked if there was a way I could trade labor for food, if it came to that.

"Oh man. How do I answer that? If you were friends and family, we would share, on a short-term basis. On a long-term basis, I don't know.

"Right now it's a joy to share," she said.

SHEEP SLAUGHTER

The call came at 2:15 in the afternoon. The slaughtering crew was due at 2:00, Linda said, but were running late. She was sorry for the abrupt notice. Did I still want to come over?

I pulled on a jacket and jumped in the car. Linda and Stephen of Chateau Poulet were having their sheep slaughtered today. While I have eaten meat all of my life, I have never watched any animal bigger than a chicken prepared for consumption.

When I got there, a wooly sheep was tethered near the drive, struggling with the rope. A man named Kent and someone I knew, Gordon Black, were standing next to it. The sheep, named Confucius, turned and twisted, trying to free himself. Kent is Gordon's neighbor, and he had brought Confucius to meet his end along with four of Linda and Stephen's sheep. Gordon has a station wagon with one of those dog dividers in the back, so he transported Kent and Confucius.

"That's the first time I've had a sheep in my car," Gordon said in his thick Scottish brogue.

The day was damp and overcast, and after another phone call establishing that the slaughtering crew was still busy at the north end of the island, we all went inside for tea. As time passed, Kent and Gordon decided to leave Confucius to his fate and went home. There were no emotional goodbyes.

A little after 4, a plain white twenty-six-thousand-pound truck pulled into the muddy driveway and positioned itself by the pasture. I went out with Linda and Stephen, who began to collect and tether the four yearlings they had designated for slaughter: Cocoa,

Gaucho, Lambretta, and Caramelo. These sheep looked different than Confucius, who was half hair sheep, half wool sheep. Linda and Stephen's are Katahdin sheep from Maine, and they have a sparse hair covering. Confucius had been fathered by Linda and Stephen's ram, Obahhhh-ma. As we walked around the pasture, Annie, the pet Nubian goat, went from one human to the other demanding attention. Unlike the sheep, which avoided people, she was very social, staying close, making eye contact, and putting her head under your hand so that she could be petted.

Two middle-aged Mexican men and a young Anglo man got out of the truck and introduced themselves, then set to work. At that point, Linda excused herself and went back inside. Fred, one of the older men, appeared to be in charge. He carried a .22 rifle. While he began, the other two opened the back of the truck, which had two winches that folded neatly across the doors and swung out from either corner. All three wore bright yellow waterproof aprons and red rubber boots, but no gloves.

Fred asked which one was first. Stephen indicated Confucius, standing right in the drive by the truck. Fred calmly walked around the sheep until he got just the right angle, then delivered a single shot to the back of his head, pointing the rifle almost straight down. The sheep dropped immediately, and Fred pulled a knife from a stainless steel scabbard at his waist and severed the sheep's throat in one motion. In fact, I missed it. Within three minutes, Confucius had bled out and stopped moving altogether. The youngest worker, thin and blond and probably not more than nineteen or twenty, put slits behind the tendons of the back legs, fitted hooks from one of the winches in the slits, and hoisted the sheep up. He began to carefully cut the hide away from the legs and work it down the outside of the carcass. I noticed that he had a Band-Aid on one finger. The smell of lanolin rose from the sheep.

Fred went to the next sheep, tethered inside the pasture, and did the same. Although the second sheep had witnessed the death of the first, it did not seem aware of any danger, only struggling in annoyance against the rope on its leg. Fred seemed to admire the hair sheep, and I could see that for the purposes of slaughter they were neater and cleaner to work with. I noticed that the male sheep died harder than the one female lamb, going into cardiac arrest about halfway into the bleed, although the brain was long dead.

Annie the goat stayed close to me, curious, but also seemingly unaware that she might be in any danger.

Fred dragged the second sheep out of the pasture, and the third worker got busy. Each hide was pulled neatly down and off the heads of the sheep, the workers slipping their hands between the body and the skin to loosen the fat that held them together. They asked if Stephen wanted the skins, and he said no. They were put in a barrel brought along for this purpose. The slightly bluish carcasses were then carefully slit across the lower belly, and the workers reached in and removed the inner organs all in one sac about the size of a basketball. They asked if Stephen wanted the heads, and he said no. These went in the barrel along with the intestines. The sheep smell was stronger now, richer, but not repulsive.

Stephen asked them to leave the livers, hearts, and kidneys of each sheep. The rest of the whole carcasses would be taken to a small facility in Port Orchard that specializes in processing meat for hunters and small farmers. There, the meat would be hung for three days in a cooler, then divided into parts and each placed in a box and frozen. Stephen said that the parts of a processed sheep fit in a box about twice the size of a shoebox.

During all of this, Stephen was completely relaxed, moving among the men and sheep, talking and joking. The butchers were exceedingly polite.

I mentioned that my neighbor had told me Stephen sometimes ate roadkill. Stephen said that he had eaten roadkill about three times: once when Linda found a deer that had just been hit on the road near their house, once when he picked up a raccoon, and another time when he and his father found a deer near his parents' place in Stanwood, north of Seattle. His advice was to cook raccoon "a really, really long time" because it is tough.

When they finished, the three workers hung the carcasses in the truck and placed the barrel full of offal inside. They hosed off their aprons, their boots, and the metal holsters holding their knives before closing the doors and folding the winches back up. There was no way to tell what the truck was used for from the outside. The entire process was done by a little after 4:30.

They told Stephen he could pick up his meat in about three days.

As I prepared to leave, Stephen asked if I wanted some liver or kidney. I said I didn't know how to cook kidney (they grill it), but that I liked liver, so I followed him up to the house. There, he and Linda began to divide and freeze the organ meat. He placed about half a liver in a plastic Ziploc bag for me, and I took it home. I was aware that it was still warm as it sat on the car seat next to me.

At home, I prepared the liver in a covered skillet. Stephen said that they throw almost everything on the grill, but we only fire ours up for salmon. I sautéed a leek and some carrots from the farmers market in olive oil before adding a little Malbec wine and the liver, which I cooked for ten minutes. We ate it with French lentils, salad with Greek olives and crumbled feta, and olive bread. It was good. I had stopped buying calf's liver at the grocery store some years back, in part because it is not carried as often as when I was a child, but also because I was concerned about the way commercial beef is raised. But I had seen the pasture where this sheep were raised, and as I cut into it, the liver had no abscesses.

I sent an email to Linda the next day, thanking her. She said they had put their liver on the grill and eaten it with potatoes, chanterelles, and leeks with half and half, and a spinach salad with gorgonzola, avocado, and sunflower seeds.

"So there," she said. "Enjoy."

PERSEPHONE

Persephone Farm lies about twenty miles from Bainbridge, north of Suquamish in Indianola. It must have been grandfathered into the Bainbridge farmers market, since it is about the same distance away from Bainbridge as Holt Ranch, which was never allowed at the Bainbridge farmers market because it is out of the North Kitsap area. For ten years, Persephone was located on Bainbridge Island, and when it moved to rolling hills near the Port Madison Reservation of the Suquamish, Rebecca Slattery took on Louisa Brown as a partner in the endeavor. North and east of Persephone are tribally owned forest lands. Beyond that is the town of Kingston.

It had been a long time since I had driven to Indianola, on a road that leads only to the little settlement. It is either on or awfully close to what had once been Suquamish land. From what passes for a downtown—a general store and a public pier—one can gaze southeast to Agate Pass Bridge and the pricy homes on the Port Madison area of Bainbridge. That is also where you will see Haleets gazing back at you.

Of the farm's thirteen acres, only two to three of them are under high-intensity cultivation. I had met Rebecca at our neighborhood Fourth of July party, and she had insisted that I come out to her farm and see her method of farming. Beyond the cultivated fields is pastureland that supports chickens and heritage turkeys. As part of her CSA, Rebecca supplies flowers to her customers, which she says are "easier on the soil" as she rotates them through with kitchen vegetables, using field peas and buckwheat as cover crops. Because of the patches of sunflowers and zinnias, Persephone was the most scenic farm I visited. Rebecca keeps an elaborate map of what is planted where, which is constantly updated as crops are harvested, plowed under, and replaced. Rebecca's farm was strong support for Brian's assertion that farmers could support our current population. Although not on the island, Rebecca's intense farming methods support forty to sixty subscriptions (averaging four people each) on just two or three acres.

Before coming out to the farm, I was researching indigenous diets. Native people in our area ate a lot of seafood and meat when they could get it, and many different types of berries, roots, and even the fresh growth on fir trees and ferns in the spring. With that in mind, I asked Rebecca how much grain we really needed in our diets.

Don't get me wrong. Stranded at an airport at eight A.M., I will be one of the first in line for a scone and a latte. But the scone, while it might be delicious, leaves me feeling full and still hungry. That's another reason I carry nuts and dried fruit when I travel.

I know that the baked goods we eat depend on eggs and oil, as well as wheat. When I looked up what bannock was made out of, thinking that it was an indigenous bread, it turns out to be a Scottish word applied to frybread, which is now eaten all over North America. Most indigenous food was traditionally steamed or boiled, but frybread is deep-fried. The frying adds more animal fat, since fat and oil are difficult to extract from the plants in this region.

I'm perfectly happy with corn tortillas, although I like flour tortillas because they hold up under extreme conditions like heavy sauces.

Rebecca looked perturbed at my question. "Most people want grains and fats in their diet," she said. "I know I do." Rebecca was raised on the *Diet for a Small Planet* approach, a book published in 1971 that emphasized the combination of various grains and vegetables in order to maximize protein. Grain is "pretty sustainable," and easier to produce than meat. "For animals, you either need a lot of space, or grain," Rebecca said. "Livestock need a lot of land." Grain can also be stored. I noted that it is hard to grow in our climate. "Not on Whidbey," she answered. "It grows pretty good in the rain shadow." Ebey Prairie on Whidbey, the island just north of Bainbridge, was, according to Rebecca, the most productive grain area in the state before water from the Columbia River was diverted for crops in Eastern Washington.

All the farmers I talked to seemed to regard this historic water diversion as a great tragedy, as though they would have personally received the water if it had not been sent east. Perhaps they are lamenting the disruption of the salmon cycle caused by damming and diverting the Columbia and her tributaries, but it doesn't feel that way. Western Washington could not sustain the population it does without the food produced in Eastern Washington, with its far greater amount of sun. That's just a fact: we receive the food and the income generated by industry and high-tech jobs; they receive unnatural amounts of water and subsidized highways. The people on each side feel superior, but this many of us could not live in the Northwest without each other.

Rebecca and I talked about the lack of water on Bainbridge. Even though it rains all the time, most rainwater runs off into the Sound. The more pavement, the more roofs, roads, and driveways, the more runoff. And in our short summer, it can go without raining for six weeks during the most crucial time for fall crops. The Association of Bainbridge Communities, a local group focused on conservation, issued a report a few years ago on the water situation that was quickly buried by developers. Real estate on Bainbridge Island is expensive and sought after, and the idea that there might be a finite amount of water available to islanders is not a selling point. New research at the county level confirms that the water table is dropping. "Development is seen as the highest and best use of the land. The [Washington State] Growth Management Plan mandates it," Rebecca said. Since then, local governments have revised regulations for development, and increased penalties for violating those regulations, while trying to conform to the state's Growth Management Plan.

If Rebecca were in charge of feeding the inhabitants of Bainbridge, how would she go about it? "I don't think there would be the water. No one is permitted to use county water for commercial use—otherwise the limit is five thousand gallons a day."

But if there were enough, "the only way to have this conversation," Rebecca said, "is to start with 'What would people eat?' Even to make vegetables palatable, we need seasonings and oil. I want grains and fat in my diet. Even lambs in the summer need more than pasture," she says. The farm tried raising lambs one year just for their own consumption, but the young animals did not thrive on pasture alone.

"Poultry are high on the food chain," she said, to my surprise. "Eggs are the first thing you would miss" because chickens also need grain, minerals, and organic supplements. "They are not very sustainable. We would need to exist on the wild birds that are here, such as quail." I saw quail in my yard last year. We also have naturalized Chinese pheasants, but no grouse. Before that, I had not seen quail for at least ten years. Given the number of dogs and cats and wild predators, I don't know how any still live on the island at all. But maybe, after we had eaten all the domesticated animals on the island, the ground-dwelling bird population, the quails and pheasants, would rebound.

Shellfish farming, on the other hand, is sustainable. "If it was a priority to have fish and shellfish, it could be done." Shellfish are relatively easy to seed and manage, and my neighbors went out this spring to start oysters they will harvest next year. The oyster starts are planted in nets that hang in the water, then hauled up and harvested a year or so later. Because they are in open water, they are not treated or supplemented in any way. Their health depends on the health of the surrounding water.

There is a commercial salmon farm on the west side of Bainbridge Island, which generates some controversy. Only Atlantic salmon are used in fish farms, for some reason, and they are not supposed to mingle with wild salmon. They are dosed with antibiotics, but still harbor diseases that can affect the wild fish. The state and Indian tribal attempts to bring back native runs, or transplant fish from one run to another, have also met with mixed results. Hatchery salmon lack the vigor of wild salmon, maybe because they don't necessarily originate at that site, and so lack the homing instinct to return. A dam in place since the early 1900s was recently taken down on the Elwha River near Port Angeles, about two hours drive west of Bainbridge, to great fanfare, and salmon will soon be able to leap upstream again. Tentatively, the tribe chose to bring in non-Native salmon in hopes of increasing numbers at a more rapid pace. This plan is now on hold as the land and native salmon bounce back.

I asked Rebecca what area of Bainbridge she thought was the most fertile, if we were to devote more land to agriculture.

"One place I gardened was the old Bucklin Hill Farm. It had been gardened continuously for one hundred years. But now Hyla Middle School is located there. The school has done a lot of water diversion, so it is no longer good farmland. They created an athletic field, and there are contaminants from runoff, clear-cutting, and erosion. There are just too many stakeholders with different agendas on Bainbridge."

Looking out over the patchwork of cultivated plots on Persephone, where half a dozen people were harvesting, I asked what good farming practices were in a restricted area like ours?

She thought about this for a moment. "Give back to the soil," she said. "Build soil, which is a big challenge as vegetable growers. Make all your own compost. Use cover crops, and turn the crops in. Use mineral adjustments for the plants. Bring in horse manure, use spent salmon from the hatchery, use leaves and wood chips."

This conversation, like so many others, made me realize that the decisions we make now will determine whether or not the island could ever sustain itself agriculturally. I asked what some of the negative practices going on right now were. "Development, taking down trees, putting down more pavement. If each of our pockets (of land) is part of climate change, we can't think of Bainbridge as an island. There is the little picture and the big picture—we all need to be planting trees." I could see Rebecca's wheels turning now, as she tried to hold the whole picture in her head, the various systems involved.

"The county is doing a lot of good—controlling storm water runoff, creating catchments to reduce pollution but also to recharge the aquifer. This is a change for the county. On Midway Road from

Indianola to the farm [a steep, uphill gravel road] the county will now require new developers to capture water."

What other positive practices were in effect? "Farmers on Bainbridge are trying to make the soil better. This is less true of home gardeners. The farmers take a pretty holistic approach, not just mining resources. They are starting a food policy council, conducting food education in the schools, and participating in commercial composting. Even the people with restaurants are getting involved. The owners of Blackbird Bakery are worm-farming.

"We raise and sell heritage turkeys. If there was more demand, we would raise more." One of the things I have been hearing from Marilyn and Cliff of Holt Ranch is that restrictions on how poultry and livestock can be slaughtered are a big issue. For small slaughters, there is one mobile poultry butcher in the area operated by the Kitsap Poultry Growers Association. Customers must sign up and pay ahead of time, and be willing to pick up the meat on a specific day. This offers none of the convenience of a supermarket, and requires individual consumers to own full-size freezers, since the butchering does not reduce the meat to cooking-size portions. When Cliff and Marilyn took the leap and built their own slaughter facility, however, it seems to have made the difference in the success of their farming operation.

"People who make it a priority will spend the money on local, organic food. Almost everyone in the United States could buy local, organic food if they wanted to."

Here, I had to beg to differ. Food at the farmers market is extremely expensive, maybe four or five times as much, compared to even Town & Country, and the true working class goes to Safeway and Wal-Mart for their food. "I know artists with almost no income who buy their food at the farmers market," Rebecca said hotly.

I wondered if she had ever lived in a big city. It's true that some poor people can choose a lifestyle that supports local, sustainable food. But if you work for the phone company and pay rent and commute and have a family to feed, Safeway looks mighty good in terms of convenience and price, and Wal-Mart looks even better. I have the leisure time to spend washing and trimming organic vegetables, and the income to buy them, but there are plenty of people around who do not.

People worked dawn to dusk—perhaps an office job followed by small-scale farming at home—before World War II. The chemicals and chemical companies left over after the war put their resources, with a great deal of financial support from the government, into developing products that would enhance the short-term growth of food plants, preserve food, and present it in an easily consumable manner. This was also part of the campaign to get women out of the job market and back into the kitchens, by showing them how clean, lovely, and efficient the modern kitchen and home were. In all fairness, the United States also provided thirteen million dollars in money, food, and supplies to a starving Europe at that time, under the Marshall Plan. But the country never returned to sustainable, locally sourced food. Commercial production and distribution of food is still highly subsidized by government rules and regulations, from the Department of Transportation to the USDA. Local, small-scale organic farmers do not have any of this support system, and presumably, living and eating strictly on an island, we would not have that system in place, either.

Are people just lazy now? Working only one job, then kicking back in front of the television in the evening? We also live longer now, and suffer the sorts of maladies that come from lack of exercise and a sugar- and fat-laden diet. But plenty of people work hard and raise their kids without access to the best food. Michelle Obama might be working on these things, but she is up against Big Biz, Big Ag, and Big Pharma.

What would we miss? I asked Rebecca, if we had to live on what we grew on the island? "Coffee," she said, "although maybe we can substitute chicory. They are growing tea in Snohomish. We would miss olive oil." Rebecca had zeroed in on the same foods as the other farmers and chefs.

Naming a farm after the Greek goddess of spring, Persephone, evokes lush images of trees and fields in bloom, but also implies a seasonal restriction, a time of cessation when the earth sleeps, and Persephone must return to her husband, Hades, in the underworld. During that time her mother, Demeter, stalks the earth gloomily, missing her daughter. Persephone is not entirely free of Hades because she consumed four pomegranate seeds while in his company. This can also mean that winter is the time of latent fertility, and if we are patient, the earth will awake and bear fruit for us. The local Salish tell similar stories.

If there is not water, the fruit will not thrive. Rebecca reminded me that, even if Bainbridge is an island, it is situated over one end of an aquifer that extends under the saltwater and continues on under the Kitsap Peninsula to the northwest, so that practices on the peninsula affect conditions on the island, and visa versa. All our salt waterways are shared, and a healthy Puget Sound would be a big part of making life on the island independently sustainable.

PLOWING BY MOONLIGHT

On Friday night, there was a full moon. It was the second moon of September, a harvest moon, and many of the farmers on the island stayed up all night celebrating. There was a bonfire and food at the Day Road farms. Photographer Joel Sackett was there, eager to capture black-and-white photos by moonlight. In particular, he wanted to get one of Betsey Wittick with her horse Samantha in harness, plowing by the light of the moon.

Saturday was the usual farmers market, albeit with sleepy farmers. There was a particular urgency on this, one of the waning days of the market. People bought scads of ripe tomatoes, bags of lettuce, buckets of potatoes. Whatever price the farmers named, we pulled it out of our pockets and purses without question; no one bargains at the Bainbridge farmers market, although one day when I came up short of cash, the farmer gave me my carrots anyway.

The next day, a Sunday, was the harvest fair at the Johnson Farm, another traditional farm preserved by the city from further development. It was drizzly and overcast, as usual, but this did not dampen the spirits of the young families attending the fair. There was live music, and hay bales to sit on while listening. The smell of good food carried from a motley assortment of booths, while raffles and demonstrations were under way. Tom the Turkey was there in a cage so that prospective ticket buyers could inspect him before a raffle, the details posted on the cage; good thing he couldn't read. There were sheep to pet and apples to press. In one paddock, a woman was shearing sheep in front of a crowd of parents and children. The sheep put up with being held awkwardly on their backs and did not seem offended by the process.

This was definitely a different crowd than the one I usually saw at the weekly farmers market. These were the children the farmers hope to educate, to win over by showing them how to start tomatoes and where potatoes come from. Their parents were about evenly split between the "we are growing most of this ourselves anyway" crowd and more affluent commuters who need something to do with their children on the weekend.

I had hoped to see Joel here and find out how the shoot had gone on Friday night. I knew it was before noon, but I figured he might have recovered after a full twenty-four hours. Betsey Wittick, whom I had expected to see, maybe with Samantha, was also not present. Another family was giving rides in a wagon hitched to a pair of docile ponies.

I had a piece of blackberry pie and a great cup of coffee from the Treehouse Bakery. I visited with a friend, Roger Lauer, who was starting an artisanal co-op modeled on one in Green Valley, Arizona, where he and his wife had a second home. He was staffing a booth at the harvest fair where interested parties could sign up. The co-op is a workspace with tools where people can take classes or bring projects for crafting.

Finally, around one o'clock, just as I was about to leave, Joel showed up, desperate for a cup of coffee. It turned out that Betsey had decided that conditions were not right for Samantha on Friday, and that the newer pair of horses was not yet ready to plow in the dark with lots of strangers, fires, and general carryings-on around them. But Joel had some good shots, he said, of Betsey and Samantha from earlier times.

What neither of us knew at the time was that Betsey had been up all of Saturday night with Samantha. On Saturday morning, Betsey had not noticed anything unusual before leaving for the market. When she returned, Samantha was lying down. She was foaming at the mouth and appeared to be having an allergic reaction, possibly to something she had eaten in the fields on Friday night. Her gums were white. Betsey called the vet, who was home with the flu, and gave her milk of magnesia, and shots of a muscle relaxer, according to his directions.

Samantha did not get better, and continued ill into the evening. Finally, Betsey had to call the vet and ask how to tell if she was dead. The vet told her to touch the sclera on her eye and see if she reacted. She did not. It was 8:45 P.M.

Samantha, was buried "like an Egyptian queen," Betsey told me later. They worked all night by moonlight and flashlight. The horse was so heavy, at eight hundred pounds, that they didn't know how to move her. The vet, still by telephone, told her to truss Samantha like a turkey before rigor mortis set in. This would make her the most compact shape possible for burial. Betsey, her interns, and some other farmers then put a chain around the horse's neck and dragged her with a tractor to the edge of the field. "We buried her near a white oak tree that I had planted a few years back," Betsey wrote in her blog, "my favorite tree species because of the grace and strength they develop with age."

Samantha, a handsome chestnut Belgian, was probably the most photographed horse on the island, Betsey said. She appears with Betsey in one of Joel's books. I asked how old Samantha was, and she said twenty-six. I remarked that twenty-six seemed pretty old for a horse, but Betsey said that wasn't old at all. On her blog, Betsey listed the horse as twenty-seven, so perhaps older than Betsey had realized. She talked calmly about the death. If I had been discussing a working companion of twenty years, I would have been weepy about it. Maybe it was the practical farmer in her, or maybe it was shock.

In her blog, Betsey admitted that Samantha was in fact reaching the end of her expected life span, and had suffered from a choke, an esophageal obstruction that is fairly common in horses, a week or two earlier. Betsey had already purchased the younger horses, anticipating a time when Samantha would be gone.

Samantha was originally purchased by Bainbridge Vineyards to cultivate between the rows with a minimum impact on the soil. It turned out she had a taste for grape leaves, however, and ran away with the plow a couple of times before they decided not to use her in that capacity. "The kids could drive her," however, because she was steady and slow and sensible enough, and Samantha became an integral part of the farm education program. She didn't seem to mind being around children, although she was not especially social on a one-to-one basis. She often turned her nose up at a proffered carrot or apple if it was not up to her standards.

"I feel fortunate to have been with her during her passage with the moon once again shining," Betsey wrote. "I will miss her."

In death, it turned out, Samantha completed the metaphor for which I had been grasping, our direct relationship to the land, both joyful and sorrowful. Rather than the gauzy idyll of a horse in the moonlight, Betsey was left with the hard grief of dragging a companion across the cold ground to her grave. Samantha lived out the full cycle of her life in tune with the agricultural calendar, dying under the harvest moon, in the same way that the moon dies and is reborn each month as a promise of continuation. Samantha was an aloof, hard-working animal much appreciated by the people around her. She embodied the simple reality of the farmers on Bainbridge, working every day, day in and day out, and sometimes into the night, to produce food while most of the population of Bainbridge Island slept.

JOEL SALATIN

A chilly June day brought those of us on Bainbridge an unexpected visit from farming guru Joel Salatin. Marilyn Holt, co-owner of the Abundantly Green CSA, sent me an invitation to hear Salatin at the Day Road Farm, just up the road from my house. The talk seemed to be only for farmers, but I signed up anyway. Maybe I know the secret handshake by now. All that the young farmers asked when I showed up was my name, and that I follow the directions for parking. There had been an event earlier in the day geared to a general audience.

Salatin first became nationally known when he proved to be a feisty advocate for small, local farming and food consumption in the documentary *Food, Inc.* He was later visited and quoted extensively in Michael Pollan's book *The Omnivore's Dilemma*. He has since become a rock star in the food business, using his platform to skewer Big Agro and promote the agenda of the individual farmer.

First they fed us. The Harbor Public House, a local business, prepared food for a hundred or so attendees, served at tables under a tent. Dogs had been welcomed, but not children, although both were in abundant attendance. I saw at least two pregnant women with large families in tow. The people at this event were bursting with fertility. Only a few of them were the farmers I knew. The Harbor Pub is one of the local restaurants that buys directly from local farmers. It even features local beer. It was one of the Harbor Pub owners who had the connections needed to bring Salatin out to the island on short notice.

"Who are my heroes?" asked Salatin once he had been introduced a few times. "Those who touch the earth's womb hole and leave it essentially, aromatically, romantically, improved."

This was followed by whoops at his daring language, and there was a long, dramatic pause.

Salatin went on to describe how his parents had purchased and lost a farm in Venezuela before returning to the United States and buying Polyface, a "completely worn out" farm in Virginia that he now owns and runs. They could buy it because it was cheap. "Every person who has made a name in sustainable agriculture," he said, "started on a rock pile.

"What we offer is landscape healing—to the land, the food, and the landscape culture. We are increasingly damaged by separation from the earth."

He described one of his interns, who left an office job to work for him. "Today," he quoted the intern, "I was with real people that I could touch. We made something with our hands that will make chickens happy. At the end of the day, we could touch each other and touch what we had made."

"As our culture moves more and more into the virtual world," said Salatin, "there is this deep yearning in our soul to have this visceral relationship with something in our lives.

"We are the new Native Americans," he said. It might have occurred to him that there was at least one Native family in the audience, but if he did, Salatin simply plunged ahead. "We are the repository of that knowledge."

Salatin clearly enjoys playing to a crowd. "I've got a real PhD—it's called post hole digger."

He went on to describe a science experiment in which students buried processed food they had brought to class, and the teachers buried fruits and vegetables. A few weeks later, the food buried by the students looked the same, while the fruits and vegetables were gone.

"Why would you want to eat something that worms won't eat? If it won't rot, it won't digest. What we do is 'a ministry and a mission.'"

"Farmers markets need to be year-round," he continued, "and have a common cash register. When a farmer and customer talk, we need to be free to tell our story."

This is what I wanted to hear, Salatin's take on the farmer's story and how it fit into this larger system I had come across. But each thing he said seemed to be the beginning of a conversation, not a whole conversation with a beginning, middle, and end. The talk was more of a political stump speech than an assessment of the farmer's place in the food pecking order, or a call for action, or a reassurance that farmers had made the right choice in pursuing this occupation.

No matter, the farmers ate it up. And I think they also loved being around each other. It isn't that often that so many farmers are gathered in one place at one time.

CONVERSATION WITH MY SISTER

I visited my sister and brother-in-law's farm recently, and learned more about what they grow. After twenty-five years of living in a small town close to their acreage, my sister and her husband moved into Fargo, so Scott now commutes an hour north each day to work the land. Not everything they grow is from GMO seed. Generally speaking, grains such as wheat and rye, are GMO, while pinto, black beans, and soy are not.

My earlier conversation with Aida about conventional farming practices had lingered with her, and not surprisingly, she had discussed it with her husband. Scott's grandmother had homesteaded in a sod hut in eastern North Dakota, a place about as bleak and unwelcoming as one can imagine. Against his parents' advice, my nephew, David, is also in the business. Aida wrote to me:

> I thought I should say something about Monsanto since we are farmers and like most farmers in the United States and the world, for that matter, we use GMO seed. I asked Scott what he thought about Monsanto and he said, "We all hate Monsanto." Why? Because it is a multinational conglomerate which eats up all the competition and manages to suck everyone dry. If farmers happen to have a good year, you can be sure that Monsanto will immediately jack up the prices for seed.
>
> As far as GMO seeds, Scott says that the seeds that are not modified actually require the farmer to use more toxic chemicals to kill weeds, etc. Also, he says there have been

a couple of French studies that have shown GMO seeds to have negative effects on people. However, those who ran these studies refuse to turn over the data so that the studies can be evaluated and replicated to see if they are even scientific. Scott says until he sees that data, he has to rely on the studies by the USDA that have shown GMO seeds to be just as safe and healthy as organic seed.

A few years ago I saw a documentary on PBS about Norman Borlaug, the so-called father of the green revolution. His aim was to do something about world hunger. He began his research on seeds first in Mexico where he was able to increase crop yields dramatically so that Mexico is now an exporter of food. He also worked in India and Africa to help revolutionize farming practices. He is credited with saving billions of lives in third world countries by helping the people to produce harvests that could actually feed the people. He received the Nobel Peace Prize and the Congressional Medal. He believed that increased food production for the world could only come through GMO seeds and that criticism would come mainly from people who do not know what it means to be hungry.

Aida and her husband believe that there is no other choice than GMOs if we want to grow enough for everyone, but much of the food in the first world is thrown away. I asked her if she thought there might be methods of distribution that would make a difference even bigger than that of GMOs.

Well, I haven't really researched this and maybe I should. But I have heard several well-respected farm experts speak about this. In our part of the country farming is a big gamble. We rely on the weather and so many other variables are out of our control. For instance, last week we got five inches of rain. We only have half the crop in the ground and now planting will be delayed even more. David

has some land that he will not be able to farm because
it is too wet and there won't be enough time for it to dry
out before we hit the deadline for getting the seed in the
ground. GMO seeds help control some of the variables
of farming by out-yielding conventional seed and making
it easier to eradicate weeds and control some diseases.
Each year in farming brings surprises, but that is the
tension and risk of farming.

There seem to be several issues going on with Monsanto and
GMOs, I wrote back. One is a patent issue. Monsanto won a court
ruling that it could protect its patents, but like Amazon, it has done
everything to wipe out any competition. It has aggressively pursued
even small farmers who want to save seed for the next crop, and
made only its own seed available overseas, so that farmers have to
buy new seed from them each year. The company has spent millions
to reach this point.

That GMO seeds grow well with only RoundUp is one thing, I
wrote, but what happens if people cannot afford the seed, or Monsanto can't supply it because of a transportation issue or a natural
disaster?

Of course, people have been modifying and experimenting with
genes since before Friar Gregor Mendel noticed he could track the
features of pea plants in the 1800s. Mostly, people just want to be able
to choose for themselves. If a GMO apple, labeled as such, were offered in a grocery store for fifty cents, and it was next to a non-GMO
apple offered for one dollar, most people would buy the modified
apple. But everyone would rather make that choice for themselves.
Right now, the big companies are fighting to keep GMO food un-
labeled.

I didn't include it in my letter, but I was thinking how here on
Bainbridge Island, farmers recently staged a demonstration, picket
signs and all, against GMO products. They hoped to make the public
aware that, to make enough income, they really have to grow organi-

cally (which means they cannot use GMO seeds) and charge a premium, or they cannot compete with fruits and vegetables trucked in from California that were grown on a much vaster scale with minimally paid labor.

I also didn't mention the dead zone in the Gulf of Mexico. Scientists seem to agree that it is due to the discharge from the Mississippi River of pesticides and fertilizers from the farm areas. It is killing off big tracts of ocean. The negative effects of agricultural chemicals are felt all over the world. We have to look, I wrote to her, at short-term versus long term effects. Yes, Norman Borlaug showed us that people could use "modern" farming methods to increase production, but at what global cost in the long run? Might we slowly go back to more local, organic methods? Or do we just tell our children and grandchildren that it is their problem?

This is my third year of keeping a very small garden, I continued in my letter to my sister. It just provides a few sprouts a week right now, and will have peas and carrots later. I don't always buy organic or local. But I sure like being able to choose, and have confidence that if there is a big disaster, we will have food locally for at least awhile. I don't claim to have all the answers, or to tell farmers how to do their work. But I would like people to take a longer view of consequences. I think of how people on Bainbridge treat waterfront properties: some are restoring fish runs, while others are pouring concrete to try and keep the edges of their properties from washing away. These things work against each other. And I really don't like business monopolies, which is what is going on with Monsanto. They hurt all but a very few people.

During my last visit to North Dakota, the recent energy boom was evident everywhere. As we drove by, Scott pointed out the tenth-largest ethanol plant in the world. Locals can take tours of the Bakken oil fields, and Scott warns Aida to stay well back from railroad crossings when an oil train, which can consist of up to 110 cars, goes by. They are both thankful that regulations for tanker trains have been tightened, after several fiery wrecks in other towns.

Fargo has seen an increase in crime, as thousands of itinerant workers flock to the state in search of high-paying jobs, only to find housing shortages and outrageous prices. Scott, used to small-town living, still leaves his keys in the ignition when he parks his truck at home, but I think he no longer does so in town. As the boom has cooled, thousands of unemployed men have been left in its wake.

With Bakken oil and ethanol replacing domestic coal, the market for that coal—long criticized for how it is mined and how it burns—has shifted to the rapidly expanding Chinese market. That means shipping coal through West Coast ports like Seattle. This has generated protests, as the railroad tracks run right through downtown Seattle and along the waterfront. Any problems, such as derailed or exploding trains, miles and miles of uninterrupted cars, and toxic spills would affect Bainbridge Island, too, because that is where the ferry that connects us to the mainland docks. At some point, the United States will have to figure out that shipping our problematic energy sources to others does not solve the energy problem. It will blow back in our faces sooner or later.

Even if Scott, Aida, and David were to suddenly decide to grow produce for the organic market, it would take three years before their fields could be certified as clear of pesticide. During that time, the fields would need to be left fallow or the produce sold under conventional, nonorganic status, but without the growing advantage of chemical applications. Extension agents would be able to provide them with some information and education about organic approaches to farming, but organic food sales still account for only about 4 percent of the market.

Their son David, who now has a wife and two small children, completed a degree in mechanical engineering and worked in that field for a couple of years before returning to his first love, farming. He uses software that helps him track the grain markets and decide when to sell. As Scott and Aida prepare for retirement, Scott has slowly shifted the business onto David's shoulders, allowing him to choose when and what to plant, but also allowing him to assume the annual loans needed in order to acquire grain and seed for planting. While I was there, an order of organic hops that they were to grow on contract got mixed with other grains at the distributor, and had to be shipped from the supplier again. They needed to get the grain quickly in order to plant in time, and had to get the distributor to pay for the mistake.

I sense a shift in my sister and her husband's attitude toward organic farming and fossil fuels as they are directly exposed to both its profit and problems. With grandchildren in the picture, they are more sensitive to the environmental issues that surround exposure to so many toxic chemicals, and would have preferred that their son not continue in the farming business. I think they would love to see alternatives to fossil fuels and chemicals that offer practical solutions to farming. But as they enter retirement, they don't see themselves as active participants in the issues. David is wrapped up in the daily demands of farming and having a young family, and like all of us, would like someone else to get busy and come up with solutions.

CHOOSING WHAT WE GROW

As I continue to write about our relationship with food on Bainbridge Island, the climate continues to change. Not just the literal climate, with global warming, but also the climates of the market and of what people think they need.

In the last few years, regulations were changed concerning where grapes can be grown and local wineries. This has resulted in a number of new wineries on Bainbridge Island. Unlike the Bentryn's Bainbridge Vineyards, which grows its own grapes, these wineries process grapes brought over from Eastern Washington, where higher temperatures and Columbia River water allow for a greater variety and abundance of grapes. Their wines are merely bottled here. The advantage is access to a ready market of visitors from Seattle who ride the ferry over and can visit tasting rooms for the day.

After State Initiative 502 passed in 2012, a new commodity entered the legal market: marijuana. Washington State was the second state, after Colorado, to legalize recreational marijuana, and although Bainbridge has greatly restricted its growth and sale on the island, it will eventually be grown here.

I've never used marijuana—though there were evenings when the hallways in college were pretty hazy—but I have no problem with its legalization. I figure it's better to have it regulated than not. I also think it is a more benign drug than alcohol. I don't think it is going to ruin the children or scare the horses.

What concerns me in both cases is the possibility that the high prices commanded by wine and marijuana will divert resources from growing real food. Marijuana in this country is usually grown in greenhouses with artificial lights, fans, and lots of water. Especially if it is grown on the island, it will use a lot of our resources. Is this a product to which we would like to give priority? I think we should at least talk about it as a community. Marijuana is easy enough to grow in other parts of Kitsap County and bring to a retailer on Bainbridge. Right now, its sale is restricted to the one industrial park on the island that meets the distance requirements from schools and public parks.

In both cases—wine and marijuana—I'm most interested in having a discussion about how we use our water. Where do we want it to go? Is there an optimum balance of tree cover, development, and farming? Do we have enough water for all of it?

Food fads have hit other parts of the country. There was a time when wine growers in California took out long-established vines to replace them with olive trees in order to grow and sell artisanal olives and oils. Just as many growers got into the business, hoping to ride the front edge of the popularity of a domestic product, California began to suffer drought conditions, and growers went back to concentrating on products that command higher prices, such as almonds, pecans, and oranges. But the drought is affecting all of the farmers in the Central Valley, which is where much of the food for the entire country is raised. As resources become scarce, we might want to distribute them more carefully.

Because we love our addictions—the lottery, alcohol, marijuana, shoes—and can afford them in this country, I have no doubt that those interests will be served. I just hope that we reserve space for a few carrots.

As I contemplated these systems that seemed beyond my ability to grasp, I remembered a book that a writer friend, Francis McCue, had tried to get me to read a few years earlier. I had picked it up and attempted to read it several times, but could not fathom what it had to do with my concerns as a writer and citizen. Maybe it was something only poets could understand. But there had been something in there about potlatches, I recalled. This time I picked up the book and it began to make sense. In *The Gift: Creativity and the Artist in the Modern World,* Lewis Hyde describes the ways in which the world of art and the world of commerce interact with each other. The artist must find a way to monetize her work in order to survive in the world, without compromising the intrinsic value of the art in the process.

But what I saw, as I read, were the parallel economic systems that exist between the natural world and the world of commerce. While I don't think this was the author's primary intent, he would likely embrace my interpretation as compatible with his own. Humans have been participating in the first system, the natural one, for tens of thousands of years. The indigenous people of the Northwest modeled their rituals on the gift of natural abundance—they understood that the world provided what people needed to survive, as long as they honored the delicate balance between need and want, between short-term greed and long-term maintenance. This is what all their stories were about—plants, animals, and spirits talking in ways that people understood, but only to remind us of what we have always known.

European settlers, who had grown up in systems that emphasized scarcity, Hyde says, stepped into a system that emphasizes the value of the gift as reflected in the potlatch, in which those who have a lot share with those who have less. In fact, Hyde uses the potlatch as the first example of this concept in his book. The more that is given away, the more status accrues to the giver. The abundance of gifts attests to the giver's affluence and alignment with both natural and supernatural forces.

As part of the potlatch, Hyde continues, specific objects of art are given away. After that, the art objects—a clay pipe, a special medallion—are meant to be given away again and again, challenging the European concept of individual ownership. The "owner" is merely a custodian of the object, which is not valued for its commercial worth, but for the esteem it imparts to the person who is temporarily taking care of it. In times of scarce resources, everyone benefitted from the conservation and sharing of those resources, either in status for the wealthier, or sustenance for the poor. What white men saw, when they came upon the elegant canoes, elaborately decorated longhouses, fish drying on racks, and meticulously made baskets and blankets, was loot.

Haleets

Salmon are much more complicated than people. While we go from infants to children to teenagers to adults, salmon go through at least five stages of development. Salmon that survive the fry stage progress to becoming smolts. Smolts are the young adults that must not only leave the protective shallows of streams and riverbeds, but venture out into the open, salty sea. To me, this is the most amazing transformation of all—from freshwater to saltwater fish. The changes that come over their bodies—becoming longer, stronger, with a protective coat of scales and gills that can process oxygen out of saltwater—must feel much like pregnancy does for women. Aches and pains, a ravenous appetite, a body that seemed familiar transformed into one remade for a specific purpose.

This is where the many species of salmonid begin to distinguish themselves from one another. Some take a year or two for this transition, while others change more quickly and dramatically. Some will stay out at sea for a long time, while others return to spawn more than once during their lives. I think this diversity means that the fish are more likely to find a steady supply of food when they come upstream. Likewise, the salmon provide an evenly spaced source of protein to the forests, animals, and people waiting for their return. A catastrophic weather or geological event is less likely to wipe out all the salmonid species if their various moments of return are staggered over time.

I remember walking the beach up to the lighthouse in Port Townsend, Washington, northwest of here. A salmon swam up to the shore and stayed, sampling the waters with her gills. There must have been a stream there once, dropping down from the steep, sandstone cliff behind, before the road, before the campground, before the signs and cement and asphalt. There must have been a stream, and the fish could taste it, the waters that led back to the very spot her ancestors came from.

At the Our Food Is Our Medicine conference, I heard that the fish can taste the oils from the cedar trees—and that each area, each stream, has a distinct flavor. The cedars and the salmon, the elders said, cannot exist without each other.

I wanted to help the salmon I saw on the beach, to pick her up and carry her to an existing stream, the right estuary so she could lay her eggs and lay her weary head down to die. But I could not. Her stream was gone. I failed that salmon, as I fail thousands of them every day, all year long. I eat them, but I do not nourish them. This is what is wrong, what Haleets bears witness to, the times in our lives when the system is out of balance, out of the harmony that is such an important concept in Lushootseed culture.

Is it up to the spirits? Or up to us to bring harmony back to the rivers, lands, and waters of Puget Sound? There are no portrayals of salmon on Haleets.

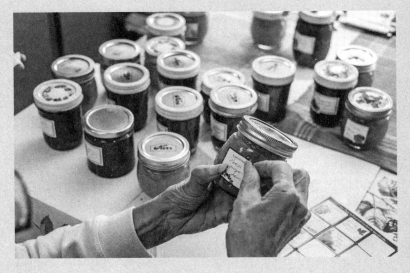

Kay Nakao making preserves.

– 5 –

Feast or Famine?

OR MANY YEARS, I grew no food at all. Our property on Bainbridge has tall, second-growth Douglas firs along its south and west boundaries, and they block most direct light. A bigleaf maple grows strategically southwest of the house, casting shade on it during the summer months. These trees absorb much of the noise we would otherwise receive from the highway and street west of us, as well as much of the runoff when it rains. An arborist described the majestic Douglas fir at our northwest corner as a sentinel tree, a sort of anchor for the other trees in the neighborhood. These trees determine our neighborhood weather.

A little sage lurks under the decorative plants in front of the house, and oh yes, a big clump of lavender grows by the mailbox. Our mailperson does not like the bees it attracts. She does not like the tiny spiders that frequent our mailbox, either. There is also catmint in a pot near the back door, which practically grows itself. In the deep shade on the west side of our house, presided over by that bigleaf maple, perennials grow around a couple of ash trees, understory to the evergreens, in the fallen needles and decomposing leaves. Our yard, all in all, is comfortably messy, my favorite kind of garden.

Instead, during our first years on the island, I concentrated on growing a little boy, which was a delight, and on writing books and teaching creative writing. I suppose those activities could be considered a form of "growing" something, but they are just part of life. People who really need to grow plants would not take any of these as a substitute. My husband, for his part, remembers to water the outdoor plants when we have a dry summer, and grows a variety of houseplants, from a Christmas cactus to a sea onion.

About ten years after we moved to Bainbridge, Neil Johannsen and Hilary Hilscher moved in next door. They built raised beds in order to grow vegetables in their sunnier yard, and soon after that, offered me one of them.

It had been so long since I had grown food that I needed to learn all over again. Reading directions. Planting seeds or starts, weeding, checking for insects. Remembering to water. I grew a little kale and mesclun, a greens mix. I grew peas and a few stunted carrots. There is nothing else in the world like growing something, pulling it from the ground or vine, and putting it directly into your mouth.

The writer Jamaica Kincaid, an obsessive gardener, once said that as her hands turn over the soil, her mind turns over the words, so that when she puts pen to paper, her work requires very little revision. To me, writing is very different from gardening, in that the words stay put when you place them on the page. They do not dry out, or blow away, or get eaten by birds. Squirrels do not dig them up, although sometimes I wish that were the case. Starting to grow food again made me go outside and consider the weather.

I remembered that, in Colorado, even if I had nothing else in common with someone, we could talk about our gardens.

In 2007, my doctor called to say that my cholesterol level was out of control. And suddenly I was forced to think about food in a new way, as a part of the puzzle of keeping healthy while not dedicating all of my time and energy to nutrition and diet.

In addition to my mother's death by stroke, her father, my grandfather, had died of "hardening of the arteries," arteriosclerosis, which we now know is caused by a buildup of fat. His wife, my grandmother, was half Opata Indian, a group closely related to the Tohono O'odam, who are said to suffer from the highest occurrence of diabetes in the world, along with heart disease and high cholesterol. Diabetes also occurs in my family. Since I eat well, exercise, and don't suffer from obesity, my doctor said that my high cholesterol was most likely genetic. Nevertheless, she agreed to let me try to bring it under control through diet. I cut out all butter, almost all cheese, and most eggs. I also baked less, since good baking involves sugar, butter, and eggs.

Several years passed, and I was unable to bring my cholesterol down below around 235. I finally agreed to try medication.

The first eight months on statins resulted in discomfort so acute, I considered giving up eating all together. I kept thinking that my body would adjust to the daily regimen of lovastatin. After a fall, winter, and spring on the medication, I had my cholesterol tested in June. It was 210, almost normal, as far as I was concerned. In addition to the medication, my husband and I had been buying produce from a farmer friend, and washing, cutting, cooking, and eating vast quantities of vegetables, some of which we had never even heard of before. Potatoes and garlic? Northwest favorites. Beets? Yes, those too, although neither of us is wild about them. Root vegetables thrive in our low-light climate, requiring little more than water, well-drained soil, and thinning.

I discontinued the statins over the summer, smug in my conclusion that the healthy diet had brought down my cholesterol levels: end of story, happy ending to this book.

In the fall, my doctor tested my cholesterol again. It was back up to 214, which I still thought was pretty good. Not so good was that my triglycerides were also 214. My cholesterol is supposed to be under 200, and my triglycerides are supposed to stay below 150.

After my protests that the statins made me feel as though I was trying to digest ground glass, she put me on a form of niacin called Niaspan. I took this while away at a nearby town trying to teach and write. Not good. My bowels and bladder were so irritated that I wondered every day if I would make it back to my cabin after class without having an embarrassing accident. I gave up on the Niaspan after two weeks. I never did develop the skin flushing for which niacin is famous, which causes many users to turn a deep red as the medication is dispersed through the body.

When I returned home, I tried an over-the-counter supplement called CholestOff. The reasoning behind this concoction is that if the system is flooded with plant statins, called sterols, the body will not absorb as much cholesterol from food. This also irritated my intestines, if not as much, and I took a small dose of it every day until I saw an endocrinologist in February. I went to this appointment reluctantly, loath to try any more medications. As it is, I am allergic to opioids and sulfa drugs, and I seemed to be building up a repertoire of Things That Make Me Feel Really Bad if I swallow them. Who exactly are these medications tested on? None of my relatives, clearly.

Dr. Subramanian looked at me suspiciously, unsure what to do with this normal-looking woman whose own physician had given up on her. I'm sure she is used to seeing diabetics with metabolic syndrome, since I was asked at least twice as I was checking in at the front desk if I had my insulin pump with me. Finally, she focused in on the triglycerides.

"I can treat these separately," she said, "and doing that would give you different side effects." That did not sound terribly promising, but she didn't prescribe anything that minute, so I was happy.

For years, I had taken a low dose of estrogen to control monthly cramps and heavy bleeding. "Go off your hormone," she said, "and come back in July. Taking a hormone can affect your lipid and triglyceride levels." I was in my fifties now, so it was possible I didn't even have a period anymore without the artificially elevated estrogen level. I had stopped it one time around the age of fifty, and all my symptoms had come roaring back while I was—yes!—traveling. So I agreed with some trepidation.

Meanwhile, the doctor planned to deliver her baby and read my books while on maternity leave.

On the sheet I took with me upon departure, with the doctor's diagnosis and instructions printed out, was the word "hypertriglyceridemia." A couple of days later, I looked it up. Like diabetes, it can be either an inherited or developed condition. Judging from the photos online, it was not inherited in my case. Those who inherit it seem to have knobby growths on the hands, elbows, knees, and feet. Or maybe these were just extreme cases. That explained why Dr. Subramanian had looked at my hands and feet so carefully. She also said she was checking the pulse in my feet, which I have been unable to find myself.

I also saw online that alcohol can affect triglyceride levels, so I stopped drinking wine altogether unless I was out at a social event. As it is, I am a moderate drinker. But it couldn't hurt.

Finally, the online literature (the boon of all hypochondriacs) indicated that hypertriglyceridemia is more common in Hispanic women than in other populations, especially those with certain physical traits linked to metabolic syndrome. Metabolic syndrome is a condition that combines excess weight, type II diabetes, and the "apple-shaped" body that stores fat in the abdomen. One article suggested that women with a waist circumference of more than 85 centimeters (33.5 inches) are more likely to suffer from any or all of these symptoms, all of which are tied to heart disease. My guilty secret is that my waist is 36 inches around, only two inches less than my hips. In addition to going off the low-dose hormone I had been taking for decades, I now planned to lose those extra ten pounds I have been carrying around my waist since the birth of my son.

Clearly, all these were signs that something was off-kilter about my body. The normal checks and balances seemed to be missing.

This seems to be true of land use on the island as well.

LAND DEVELOPMENT IN THE AGE
OF SUSTAINABILITY (A RANT)

My thirty-year-old neighborhood had been valiantly battling further development. The developer had purchased the property—forested land on the edge of a ravine, between Highway 305 and Cave Avenue—some years ago. It is shaped like a long triangle, and runs behind the properties across Cave from our house. Mysteriously, it received R-8 zoning adjacent to our R-4.3 zoning, meaning that it could have eight housing units per acre versus four. When we moved in, we were told that it was possible, but unlikely, that the property would be developed in our lifetime, since it presented so many practical as well as environmental problems. Nevertheless, in 2010, the owners, longtime island residents and developers, submitted plans to develop the site into urban-style, multifamily housing.

When papers were filed in 2010 to develop the property, the neighbors began to fight the plan on the basis of the property's unstable slope, inappropriate zoning, traffic patterns, and the lack of a sidewalk to accommodate pedestrians on our narrow, dead-end street. We fought it on the basis of the number of trees that would be cut down, adding to the slope instability and surface runoff. And we lost. Ground was broken in 2014. What it boiled down to is, yes, the subdivision is legal, if wrong. A small forest of evergreens was cut that included over eighty "significant" trees, which meant at that time, trees with a "diameter at breast height" of ten inches or more. Oddly, regulations at the time called for the careful documentation of every significant tree, but also allowed them to all be cut down. As a result, I have a map from the city that documents what is now a ghost forest.

This area had served as both a buffer from the highway for our neighborhood, and as a place where wildlife such as deer, raccoons, pheasants, quail, and many other birds could rest and forage. North of it is a steep ravine that provides a natural wildlife corridor. South of it are five wild acres that will soon be developed by another company. However, that parcel is mostly blackberries and scotch broom—both invasive plants. Its development will be a further blow to the wildlife, but will not impact our neighborhood the way the first development has.

Destruction and construction have been ongoing ever since. The owner prefers to do much of the work himself, with his own backhoe, so weekends often find him puttering around the former forest. Three duplexes and one single unit now stand, surrounded by bare earth, with an asking price of almost a million dollars for each double unit. As of this spring, none of them have sold. If they do, more dwellings will follow. It doesn't really matter now—the trees are gone. Some of the neighbors have said that those eventual duplexes will act as our buffer from the highway—absorbing the noise on our behalf, but not putting the water back into the ground once supplied by the Douglas firs.

What responsibility does an individual developer have to the future of the community?

And what responsibility does a local government have to make development profitable at the expense of the community? This part gets tricky, because the city has to look at development in terms of resources and tax bases. As the population grows, the city must continue to provide services, either by expanding existing resources or using them more efficiently. Most would say the developers should pay for upgrading infrastructure such as sewer pipes and roads, but developers can just as easily say, "We are enhancing your tax base," that is, that tax revenues from the new residents will pay for it, along with those from the existing residents whose taxes go up.

But resources are not unlimited, even if somebody is able to pay for them. The island taps into a number of aquifers, and as Rebecca Slattery of Persephone Farm reminded me, Bainbridge shares this underground body of freshwater with the Kitsap Peninsula, our kissing cousin across narrow Agate Passage. Once, the two bodies of land were joined even more closely, but time and geology have driven us apart. On the peninsula, the Suquamish reservation holds just over four thousand people, while the next town over, Poulsbo, has just under ten thousand. This makes Bainbridge island the more densely populated at twenty-three thousand people. In addition, the Suquamish have forest and fisheries staff to manage their natural resources. We do not. Our farmlands and patches of forest are at the mercy of a bewildering quilt of city, county, state, and national regulations that do not always work to the common good, whatever that might be. The fish and sea life in surrounding waters have their own set of regulations.

If I have earned the label "tree-hugger," I am not alone. When another, larger property came up for development on a highly visible corner a mile north of downtown Winslow, the Visconsi development, more island residents protested quite vociferously, and formed an organization called Islanders for Responsible Development. A nineteen-year-old college student, Chiara D'Angelo, even sat in a tree on the property, just like Julia Butterfly Hill, who tried to save a stand of redwoods in California. Chiara's sit-in worked for a few days, drawing attention to our collective ire, but as soon as the developers threatened legal action, she came down, and the acres were clear-cut the next day. They are now covered in concrete. There is a pharmacy and perhaps there will be medical offices, and in a few more years, most people will not remember the tall firs and hemlock, small mammals, and many birds who lived there. For years, there was a pheasant so tame that we routinely slowed on the highway to allow him to cross.

I THINK THAT I SHALL NEVER SEE . . .

This picture grows more and more complicated. I had thought that the question, "Could we feed ourselves with food grown on the island?" would have a simple yes or no answer, but it is really about a set of interlocking systems that need to sustain each other: agricultural land, forests, water systems, and of course, mutual support as neighbors and storytellers in order to cultivate and harvest food, and pass on information about the land. I decided to seek out Olaf Ribeiro, a famous tree pathologist who lives on the island. If we had to feed ourselves from food grown on the island, farmer Betsey Wittick had said, the first thing we would miss would be the trees. We would have to cut many of them down in order to clear the land and take advantage of what little sunlight we have.

Olaf agreed to meet me at the Bainbridge Historical Society, which is walking distance from my house and has three heritage trees in front, thanks to Olaf. Even in an Indiana Jones hat and a heavy leather coat, Dr. Ribeiro resembles Mahatma Gandhi, with his compact stature and round, wire-framed glasses. The son of immigrants from Goa, India, Olaf was born and raised in Kenya before immigrating to the United States.

It's easy to imagine him chaining himself to a tree to protest its removal. He has threatened to do so on a number of occasions, but as far as I know, his adversaries have always blinked first. There are a lot of trees on Bainbridge. In the 1890s, the Port Blakely Lumber Mill, at the southeast corner of the island, was the largest in the world, turning trees into lumber as fast as they could be felled. Most of the lumber went to build ships at the Hall Brothers Shipyard in Eagle Harbor, just downhill from my house, where the ferry now lands. Every single tree on the island was cut down—those that we see today are second or third growth, although a few look older. The trees on my property are second-growth Douglas firs, and over one hundred feet tall. That is about four or five times as tall as most houses. Much of the undergrowth on the island has been taken over by invasive species, such as ivy and blackberries, but the trees are mostly native to the Northwest.

Second-growth trees are also a big deal because they fall down. Having grown up quickly without the natural diversity of a forest, they lack deeper roots. They depend on each other to break and filter the wind, and to provide shade and sustenance for new trees, as well as a few plants. When people remove some of the trees in a grove, or a big wind comes, or especially, both of those occur in succession, the trees fall down and take the power lines with them, or smash cars and houses. This leads people to regard all trees as nuisances, and they often move to cut down the trees on their property without waiting for an accident.

But all of the freshwater on Bainbridge Island comes from underground aquifers. No one ever talks about it, but aquifers must be recharged by surface water. Every time we cut down trees to build new houses or streets, more rainwater runs off the surface and returns to the ocean without stopping to visit the aquifer. This may seem an odd concern in the Pacific Northwest, with all our rain, but on an island, freshwater makes a difference. San Juan Island, north of us, regularly runs low on freshwater. Desalinization plants are in use there and on Whidbey Island, but they dump extra-salty water back into the Sound, causing its own problems.

Bainbridge Island's aquifer was designated as a single-source aquifer in 2013, meaning that it is replenished only by rainwater. If the water table falls too low, not only does freshwater become scarce, but also the water table becomes more vulnerable to saltwater intrusion from the surrounding Puget Sound. Pressure from the freshwater in the aquifer and the wells that tap into it keep out the saltwater.

I asked Olaf about this. Each mature tree, he said, absorbs three to five hundred gallons of water a day. When you take out these trees, there is no place for the water to go, and it causes surface flooding. "A good example is Halls Hill," he said, an area at the south end of the island that recently experienced flooding after some new development. "The rule of thumb for replacing these trees is that it takes twelve large trees to replace one huge tree, and then it takes twenty years for those trees to grow."

In Seattle, Olaf has found that developers can be persuaded to change their plans to accommodate trees. "They say [Bainbridge Island residents] are tree-huggers," he says, but the city does not effectively protect its trees. Bainbridge only recently passed an ordinance meant to protect mature trees. In contrast, Hunts Point, Mercer Island, and many other upscale communities have had tree ordinances in place for some time that require permission from the city to remove a tree. Part of this is the culture. Hunts Point and Mercer Island are in King County, the same as Seattle, and are largely urban in nature. The property owners are wealthier, and do not make their living from the land.

In contrast, Kitsap County, which includes Bainbridge, is mostly rural in nature. Until recently, many of the residents made their living from industries related to the harvest of trees—lumber mills, construction, land development. It also has a high military presence, with an accompanying high regard for individual property rights. Like many people in Washington, Oregon, and Northern California, the residents of Kitsap County have had to find new occupations as the lumber industry slowed. Often, those new occupations are related to tourism. Bainbridge, too, depends on tourists on an outing from Seattle to ride the ferries.

On occasion, Olaf is called in to mediate disputes between property owners. Often, it is just a question of a waterfront view. When people want to cut down all the trees that block their view of the water, Olaf advocates a "filtered view," suggesting that owners take down just two or three trees. He convinced some property owners to retain the trees on their property, and they later thanked him. They find themselves, he said, watching the eagles and other birds that perch in the trees as much as viewing the water beyond.

Years ago, I posed my husband and son by a cluster of huge trees before they were cut down to widen and "improve" the east end of Winslow Way. In the photos, the trees dwarf the little figures below them. I had to stand across the street and about a block away to get the spreading bigleaf maples and hemlocks in the frame. When I looked at the photos recently, I realized that I had already forgotten what the street looked like with those towering canopies and textured trunks at street level. Others have moved here since, and have no idea there used to be big trees just north of the ferry terminal. I had duplicate copies, so I gave a set to Olaf.

He looked at them sadly. The Winslow Way development had

saved a couple of big trees behind buildings where most of us cannot see them, but Olaf is not satisfied. "They did a terrible job," he said, "and have done nothing to keep those trees alive."

Olaf and I went outside to look at and talk about the trees in front of the Historical Society: a sycamore, an American elm, and a red oak. We both remember when the same spot held a pet store with parking under those trees. The city purchased the lot in order to create a work yard for its utility trucks, and planned to cut down the trees. Olaf testified to the city council about the value of the trees, which had been planted in 1880, and included the story that the cuttings had originated at Kew Gardens and been transported around Cape Horn. In the nick of time, just like in a movie, a woman came forward with the original notes her father had kept as he nurtured the little trees in his cabin during the rough voyage around the Horn.

"These trees were brought across the ocean from Britain," Olaf said. "They're the last of their size remaining in downtown."

The city was convinced to save the trees, and even came up with the money to dig up the broken asphalt and compacted gravel surrounding the roots, to improve their health. The soil was so rocky that they had to keep sharpening the blades on the excavating equipment. Olaf put down a mulch that a company in Olympia donated, containing a "mix of biologicals"—beneficial organisms—to help keep the trees alive. How do they look now? I asked.

"They look good, but need another shot [of biologicals]."

Olaf now has a financial resource for his tree activism, the Save Bainbridge Island Trees Fund. "People send me money," he said, "but I save it as a contingency in case I need to sue the city." In the past, a local attorney gave his time pro bono. It costs $550 even to file against the city.

"The biggest stumbling block is money. I'm always amazed when people are passionate enough to give money."

Olaf recounted other instances where he was able to intervene and save trees targeted for destruction by construction, street widening, or the power company. Several times, he threatened to chain himself to the tree until the issue was resolved. Olaf points out that trees are good for the local economy: "The city doesn't realize that tree tours are getting bigger. People will pay to look at trees." People often come over to the island by ferry from downtown Seattle, without their cars, and are looking for things to do in Winslow. Olaf occasionally leads tree tours himself, and has prepared a walking guide to the "Historic and Champion Trees of Bainbridge Island," describing notable trees in the downtown area.

I asked about the fruit trees that have been brought to the island over the years. I knew that I had walked past a huge fruit tree in a yard on Cave Avenue for three years before realizing it was a fig. Since my father grew figs at our home in the high desert, I didn't think they grew in this climate. The tree, it turns out, had been planted by a member of the Loveritch family, the same Croatian American family that helped to start Town & Country. At that time, the house it stands next to, built in 1906, faced east across a field of lentils as far as Ferncliff Avenue, and as far north as High School Road. There are several fig trees scattered across the island, all related to this tree, all descended from a tree somewhere in Croatia.

"All of downtown was [once] an orchard," Olaf said, imagining the past. "Twenty acres. Most of what you see here was once apple trees."

He began to tell me stories about some of the trees he had saved. Olaf threatened to chain himself to an English walnut at a onetime bed-and-breakfast called the Captain's House, and managed to save it. "Oh my god, I hope he lives forever," said Meg Hagemann, standing near the one-hundred-year-old walnut tree outside her Parfitt Way home. "He is an island treasure."

When a developer announced he had permission to take the walnut out to make way for a utility pipeline, Meg didn't know what to do. But Olaf came to the rescue, with documents showing the tree had been planted by Winslow pioneer Ambrose Grow, and negotiated a compromise that routed the pipes beneath the tree's roots.

"I've had visitors come, holding hands, and ask me to take their picture under it," Meg said. "It's what we all long for. It's an oasis of peace."

In another case, "the biggest maple on the island was cut down," said Olaf. No one saw a reason to save it. "Today I would have better luck," he said, "because of email," which allows him to rally his supporters quickly. "The climate has changed enough so that people get incensed to act," said Olaf. "Time is a friend."

Getting back to my quest for local food, I asked him if there were any native nut trees. "Filberts are native to this area," he said. I had heard of filberts, but did not know what they were until we went out and looked at some. Filberts, it turns out, are native hazelnut trees, and in fact the squirrels were busily burying them around the lanky trees that flank the Bainbridge Performing Arts building. These trees, too, were saved when the city built the plaza next to City Hall, where the farmers market convenes—it had planned on cutting them down. A volunteer, Sandy Shoupe, now does most of the maintenance on them. Before, Olaf told me, "you couldn't see the trees for the ivy."

I asked about the relationship between trees and fungus, his specialty. The relationship is both good and bad, he said. Fungi are good, part of the tree, and it is a symbiotic relationship. "Without mushrooms, trees would not survive."

I described the various mushrooms growing under my trees that year, an unusually large and varied number. "Douglas firs can host many types of fungi," he said. "If not, they need nutrients, including fungi." A study in Britain, he told me, showed that one tree can support 170 different life-forms. Olaf himself found forty on one local tree, including microorganisms. However, in the British study, he said, fungi reduced the height of certain trees through stress, limiting height and causing them to put out more branches from the trunk.

Olaf insists that with proper care, trees can live forever. He visits Britain on a regular basis to give talks on how to bring back the health of ancient trees, and has received attention in the *Wall Street*

Journal and on NBC's *Today Show* for his work with the Doomsday Oak and the Tortworth Chestnut, in Gloucestershire. Trees brought back from near death are dubbed "phoenix trees." "People are in awe of these trees," he said. "There is dead silence when they see them, the trees have so much power."

Once on a weekend vacation with friends, I visited a giant spruce near Lake Quinalt in the Olympic National Park. The tree is so large, at 191 feet in height and with a trunk of almost 59 feet in circumference, that the mind cannot entirely encompass it. You can look at the base, and you can look up toward the crown, but it is too large in total to really apprehend. My friends and I posed, reclined on the knuckles of the huge roots, so that we could take photos of each other, as much for perspective as anything else. I try to imagine such trees on Bainbridge. The Suquamish once harvested planks from such giants without felling the trees. Anthropologists call these culturally modified trees. They were carefully maintained in order to provide materials for canoes and longhouses, as well as just about everything else that once made up the material culture of the Suquamish. None exists on the island anymore. Now we struggle to maintain even the twenty-year-old trees that shield houses from traffic noise and pollution.

"There are people who are really passionate about trees," said Olaf. "People saved the trees on Kahlgren Road," he tells me, at the north end of the island. When a bulldozer operator came out to take down the trees in order to widen the road, "a woman came out and put her chair in front of the bulldozer and read her newspaper." Someone came out from the planning department to see what was going on, and "was very difficult."

"Why not widen the road on the other side?" Olaf asked the planner. A second person came out who was familiar with Olaf and his work, and the trees were saved.

"On Bainbridge," said Olaf, "all that is required by the planning department is that the drainage around the proposed houses in a development be clear. The developers are not accountable for the surrounding area. But when the trees are removed, there is flooding. There is no regulation on where water goes from the development."

Since 2010, city code has been revised to strengthen sanctions against the illegal removal of trees. Trees of a smaller diameter are now protected, and developers must pay a much higher amount for any trees illegally removed. Appropriate trees for urban sidewalks have been defined, with Olaf's help, and regulations adopted that will require developers to fund a "tree bank" if they remove trees illegally and the trees cannot be replaced in the same location. The penalty for illegal removal has been substantially increased to discourage a tendency to cut trees and apologize afterwards. This set of regulations, part of an update to the city's Comprehensive Plan, took hours and hours of committee meetings to define, meetings that included city staff and council people, as well as citizens like Olaf. While all this shows a change in attitude from what Olaf had become accustomed too, he worries that it might be too late.

NASA satellite photos, says Olaf, show an increasingly diminished tree canopy on Bainbridge. I have since wondered if there is a minimum amount of tree cover the city should maintain, to make sure that the island never exceeds its water capabilities. The north end of the island might be protected, in that it maintains its own water system and a private watershed of about one hundred acres of forest.

I asked if it was possible to strike a balance between the needs of people—housing, transportation, and food—and trees. "Balance?" he asked. "Yes, we can't do without trees. It is part of our psychological and sociological makeup. We've got to have them in every neighborhood. Not just in parks." Is there an optimum ratio of trees to people? "Well, more trees, as far as I am concerned." I told Olaf about Betsey Wittick's remarks, that the need to grow food would mean cutting down most of our trees. "One of the staples we need are fruits," he said. "We need apples, cherries, and apricots to complement vegetable gardens. It's true, you can grow more vegetables in a small space. But if we grow just vegetables, we would spend a lot just importing fruits." At some point, he told me, a physician on Euclid, a secluded street at the north end of the island, was growing every variety of apple to see which would grow best. "He kept books and books of records," but Olaf failed to get them, or copies of them, when the doctor retired and moved away.

He thought about it some more. "We could have a complete balanced diet if we grew fruit trees. In fact, I'm surprised Akio [Suyematsu] never planted fruit trees. If not fruit trees, at least some trees." I checked later, and Akio did grow a few Christmas trees. There are a couple of Christmas tree farms on the island—they are seen as an easy way to bring in cash from agricultural land that is not under cultivation.

Olaf gave me a copy of an article he had been preparing to send to the local paper. It is full of the peppery indignation I found in him in person. He quotes First Nations documentarian Alanis Obomsawin: "Only when the last tree has been cut down, only when the last river has been poisoned, only when the last fish has been caught, only then will you find that money cannot be eaten."

NOTES FROM A FISHERIES EXPERT

Washington is the only state on the West Coast to allow private ownership of shoreline, and Bainbridge has fifty-three miles of shoreline, 60 to 70 percent of it privately owned by 20 percent of the residents. Shorelines reinforced with concrete or stone to resist tidal change— that is, much of the privately owned shoreline on Bainbridge—limit fish survival. When shorelines are reinforced, not only are the swampy plants and small organisms that the fry need to eat and hide in deprived of habitat, but in many cases the creek mouths that give access to upstream spawning grounds are blocked or completely eliminated. At first consideration, reinforcing the shoreline makes a sort of sense, in that it fixes shifting rocks and sand in place and allows owners to build piers and anchor their boats closer to shore. But over time, these bulwarks inevitably fail, and in the meantime they often cause more damaging erosion to other parts of the shoreline. That lonely salmon I saw in Port Townsend lingers in my mind, looking for a stream that is no longer there.

Shorelines are a huge political issue on Bainbridge Island and all over Puget Sound, because shoreline owners see any efforts to restore shoreline habitat as an infringement on their property rights. Often, their properties were already equipped with bulwark and docks when they purchased them, and they want to keep it that way, come hell or high water. They worry that without artificial strengthening of the banks—which can involve cement, rebar, and in the past, creosote-soaked logs—they will lose waterfront to erosion. After all, what will they leave their children? The effects of recent king tides, however, which easily overcame many of the waterfront barriers, might convince waterfront owners to take a second look.

Haleets listened in when Jay Zischke, the non-Native manager of the Suquamish fisheries for the last twenty years, talked to a Bainbridge audience about his work just across Agate Passage. A tall man with a mustache, a Suquamish potlatch vest, and khaki pants, he resembled the early twentieth-century image of an outdoorsman—except for the PowerPoint presentation. His talk took place in the auditorium of the new art museum on the island. A Bainbridge audience can be deceptive. They may be dressed in old clothes, with grubby shoes and self-administered haircuts, but any gathering, for any reason, can have more economists, scientists, and PhDs than a typical mainland gathering.

Zischke started by providing context for current tribal practices.

Puget Sound is an inland sea, surrounded on three sides by land, but open to the San Juan Islands, Canada, and the greater Pacific Ocean to the north. There are three main basins suitable for fish rearing in Kitsap County, all in East Kitsap: Liberty Bay Basin, Dyes Inlet, and Sinclair Inlet. Each has freshwater streams that flow into either freshwater lakes or protected bays before entering the larger and less protected environment of Puget Sound. According to Zischke, the Washington Department of Fish and Wildlife conducted a count in early 2012 that found no viable Chinook population in our area. And there should not be, Zischke said. They are a large fish and require deep waters and significant habitat in order to survive. In other words, this is not an appropriate or natural environment for Chinook salmon. Yet that is what is raised at the Suquamish hatchery, a facility where fish eggs are expelled from the females and fertilized with spawn cut from the males in a definitely unromantic procedure. The eggs are protected until the finger-length hatchlings are deemed big enough to release downstream, where they mingle with wild fish and everything else in the Sound waiting to eat them.

Of the five species of Pacific salmon, Coho, said Zischke, spend about two years in freshwater, then one in saltwater. Chinook and chum stay out in the ocean for three, four, or even five years. Spreading out their return is a good survival strategy. Pink or humpback salmon are a two-year fish, returning every odd year. The fifth salmon in the Pacific group is the sockeye, though sometimes steelhead are included as a salmonid cousin.

The questions start right away. I don't even have to turn around to recognize some of the speakers. And I'm happy to hear them here, asking the questions I don't feel qualified to ask.

So why are the Suquamish rearing Chinook fry, rather than chum salmon, also called keta or dog salmon, which is the most common in Puget Sound? "Tribal fisheries concentrate on Chinook because they provide more commercial value" to restaurants and consumers, said Zischke. Consumers have been trained to look for the deep-orange flesh of local and Alaska Chinook, and ignore salmon of many other species. Puget Sound Chinook salmon and the Hood Canal summer-run chum are listed as endangered species—but so are tribal fishermen.

"The tribes are trying to create opportunities for their fisherman. They would not be in the fisheries business if they did not have to be," Zischke said. The tribal elders are afraid that, if there are not commercially viable fish to be caught fresh and sold every year, people will stop fishing and lose the knowledge, and the markets, that go with it.

Zischke listed some of the dangers faced by hatchery fish. Everything can go awry. Some of the hazards presented to and by fish reared in and released from hatcheries, according to Zischke, include overharvesting due to the mix of hatchery and wild fish, in which the wild fish get overfished; disease; genetic interaction between the hatchery and wild fish; and competition and predation, which cloud the true status of the wild population.

Hatchery managers must also test to make sure that commercially farmed salmon in the area (including those from the fish farm on Bainbridge, located just south of Fort Ward State Park off the western shore of the island) are not infecting the wild salmon. Farmed salmon—which are almost always Atlantic stock, since Pacific salmon do not thrive in fish farms—carry a number of maladies, such as sea lice, that are not carried by the wild or hatchery-raised population. Farmed fish never leave their pens, if all goes well, until they are harvested, but they share the same waters as the hatchery and wild fish that run through Rich Passage between Bainbridge Island and the West Sound region. Farmed fish also add waste to the commonly owned waters of Puget Sound. Escaped Norwegian salmon (and escape happens regularly) eat the same larvae as the wild salmon, providing further competition. An outbreak of an influenza-like virus called infectious hematopoietic necrosis, or IHN virus, caused the owners of the fish farm to destroy their entire stock in 2012. Zischke compared the farmed fish to children in a preschool, who are potentially exposed to more diseases. The hatchery fish raised by the tribe must swim past the pens of the farmed fish in order to reach the open ocean.

The Suquamish tribe is not supportive of the farmed fish facility, but it is legal. The Atlantic salmon facility on Bainbridge is controversial to its neighbors on the island as well. The fish pens are just offshore, and machinery keeps the water moving around them. The generators that run this machinery provide a constant background noise along the shore of this high-end neighborhood. The fish farm also attracts sea lions, seals, and cormorants to the area. The farmed fish are fed and tended by workers. All the water that goes through the pens goes back out into the open waters that the wild salmon must traverse. Zischke is careful as he delivers this information. He is paid to be a scientist and fisheries manager, and to convey the official line of the Suquamish elders.

The fish farm, PanFish USA, was started by a subsidiary of the Campbell Soup Company in 1972, but is now part of a much larger corporation that owns several fish farms in the area. It is one of the few industrial businesses on the island. In Puget Sound as a whole, Zischke told us, over ten million pounds of salmon are produced annually by commercial fish farms. Recently, the Wild Fish Conservancy—a coalition of scientists, conservationists, and sports fishermen—filed a lawsuit against federal environmental and fisheries managers for allowing commercial salmon farms in Puget Sound. Environmentalists argue that the fish from these farms should not be labeled organic, since they are fed fishmeal that cannot be certified as organic. "The Agriculture Department says it will propose standards for the farmed organic fish this year," Zischke tells us. "That means the seafood could be available in as few as two years— but only if USDA moves quickly to complete the rules and seafood companies decide to embrace them." The USDA was set to propose rules for organic fish in 2015, but nothing has come of it so far.

With oversight by a state fisheries biologist, the Agate Passage facility run by the Suquamish is trying to replenish the fish that thrive in small, close-in fishing areas, like the chum in Chico Bay. In 1997, an estimated nineteen thousand chum salmon were consumed in Dyes Inlet by the resident orca population, themselves a protected species under the Environmental Protection Agency—that was almost the entire annual run. Zischke gives this information with a slight shrug. He almost smiles. This is what happens when you rear fish in an artificial environment and turn them loose in the Sound.

There were huge runs in 1998 and 2007. The chum catch—what the orcas don't eat—is mostly exported to Asia, along with the roe.

A few hatchery Chinook also manage to escape and spawn naturally each year in September. Sea lions eat them, chum spawn on top of them, and low water levels mean there is less than a 1 percent chance that juveniles will survive. This is part of the natural process of fish production: lots of tiny fish hatch, a few find shelter and get bigger, and even fewer survive the hazards of the wide open sea to return to their creeks of origin. Very little, after all this intense scrutiny, is known about the life of the salmon while out at sea.

As for catching nonfarmed salmon, most tribal fishing rights are defined by a 1974 ruling by U.S. District Judge George Hugo Boldt, *United States v. Washington*. This was a landmark decision defining tribal fishing rights as well as territories, and it decrees that tribal fishermen are entitled to half of all harvests each year. Originally, the ruling seemed to pit nontribal fishermen against tribal interests, as well as to set up conflicts between commercial and recreational fishing, both tribal and nontribal.

Under the *United States v. Washington* decision, the salmon population is co-managed by the state and the tribes. They try to agree on a plan each year for the number of days of fishing, and the numbers of each species that are allowed to be caught. A subsequent ruling, the 1976 Magnuson law, has been very useful in preserving fish runs by extending fisheries to two hundred miles offshore. This means they can be more strictly monitored and controlled. In 1985 and 1999, treaties were signed with Canada to protect stock that crosses the border. Fish don't carry passports.

We are figuring out that, from the creeks running across the lower ends of our properties on Bainbridge Island to the crashing breakers of Neah Bay, our area is one continuous habitat for the salmon, these creatures that provide sustenance for just about everyone and everything carbon-based in the Northwest.

Now, what was once an inherited series of negotiated agreements between tribes has moved into the modern legal system, with tribes suing each other about where they can fish. The definition in the ruling is "usual and accustomed places," but in many cases, these areas overlap. Suquamish in particular, as Dan Rapada told me earlier, has one of the largest "usual and accustomed" fishing areas, and use of these has been challenged by the Skokomish and Tulalip tribes. In Hood Canal, the tribes are now pitted against the U.S. Navy, which seeks to limit their ability to fish around its proposed wharf at Bangor. On the other hand, the Suquamish tribe is cooperating with the Muckleshoot tribe on a fish hatchery in Snohomish County. Income from commercial fishing remains a major source of hard cash for many tribal families in the state of Washington, and brought them 260 million dollars in 2011.

The records of these "usual and accustomed places" are maintained in part by the staff of the Suquamish Museum, which keeps documents about which areas have been fished by the tribe. In other words, there is a continuous link between the past and the present, verified through stories, artifacts, written records, and common history as understood by the Puget Sound tribes.

Working with the Bainbridge Island Watershed Council and the City of Bainbridge, the Suquamish are also helping to restart salmon runs on Bainbridge. So far, two salmon streams have been restored, Springridge Creek and Cooper Creek, and Murden Creek is being monitored. Fish also run in Issei Creek, and up the ravine near my house, although I have never seen them. Zischke tells us that the number of salmon that are spawning naturally is determined by foot surveys—walking the streams during a run—and estimating.

I spent a few days one fall hanging around the weirs on Springridge Creek, trying to spot a returning salmon after the heavy rains. Miracle of miracles, I spotted one dark-gray fish in the dark-gray stream, splashing its way up the edges of the weirs, which are wide, shallow basins with an opening down the center lip to admit returning salmon.

Are we talking thousands of fish returning to Bainbridge? Hardly. At most, fifty to seventy-five adult salmon have been returning yearly to our streams, where they are monitored by the Watershed Council.

What struck me throughout Zischke's presentation is that low tech and high tech are constantly bumping up against each other. In order to participate in salmon fishing, one of the fundamental activities of the tribe—what might be their defining group activity—the Suquamish must resort to the most high-tech tools available. Nature's cycle is much too complex for people to second-guess, especially now that we have put it out of balance.

Zischke ended by assuring us that salmon are extremely resilient. They are managed according to three Hs: harvest, hatchery, and habitat. Maintaining the shoreline buffer is crucial, he said, and we need to maximize the vegetative buffer between houses and the shore.

But Zischke might be speaking too soon. Salmon survival in Puget Sound itself, according to Phil Rockefeller, island dweller, former state senator, and recent chair of the Northwest Power and Conservation Council, is threatened. He views temperature increases due to climate change as potentially lethal to salmon. Acidification, also linked to climate change, is "another potential threat to the food web of the salmon." Add to that the spring runoffs, which are now occurring several weeks earlier, and the question becomes, "What is the limit of the salmon's adaptability?"

After spending hours poring over dozens of studies, guidelines, newspaper articles, and websites hosted by dozens of organizations, the only thing that is clear to me is that the salmon probably need their own lawyers. As of April 2016, according to the Washington State Department of Fish and Wildlife, there will be a drastically reduced fishing season for salmon in the waters of Washington and Oregon State, due to low numbers of returning salmon. Although the tribes raise and release hatchery fish for all—commercial, tribal, and sports fishermen—the sportsmen greatly resent restrictions to their access.

LOVE AND STEWARDSHIP

Some people inherit or buy land, then consider it a burden. Others buy land because it has a house on it, and in the house they will place a dining room table, beds, a kitchen, and a bath. They will live there, and call it home. There are people who see the land around their house as a good place to park cars and maybe boats. Some people keep elaborate gardens that require hours of tilling, planting, fertilizing, and pruning. Finally, there are people who buy or inherit land and find themselves the loving stewards of its natural landscape.

Frank Stowell is one of the latter. He and his wife, Mary, raised two daughters in what passes for a conventional house on Bainbridge Island—not too large, but beautifully finished in knotty pine paneling that sets off the Craftsman-style tables and chairs he inherited from his parents. A river-rock fireplace automatically makes the living room charming. Outside, sheep and chickens do their thing on lumpy, but mostly level pasture. An exuberant dog completes the scene.

But Frank's charge lies beyond this, across a small access road, in an area called Bucklin Hill Woods. The land there is sectioned off into plots of eight to ten acres, and each owner is permitted to build a house, but not much more. Frank and Mary have, so far, chosen not to build on their property, but the two of them walk the land every single day.

A compact man in his mid-sixties, Frank leads people to the property the way a boy would show his cousins a secret fort. He is pleased and proud of it, but mindful that little of it is his own doing.

Bucklin Hill Woods is protected by a conservation easement, which means that most of the property can never be built on. Like the Fortner's property, the taxes are reduced as long as the land stays vacant and undeveloped. If the owners were to develop the land, not only would they begin to pay taxes on it, but they would owe all the back taxes as well.

This is one way that municipalities have found to protect wild lands—which in Bainbridge, includes wetlands and a few of the seeps and danks that once fed the streams providing refuge for salmon, as well as other woodland creatures.

The fifty-acre subdivision that Frank and Mary's land is on was split off from the old Bucklin Hill Farm, where Rebecca Slattery once had Persephone Farm. The developer, John Green, decided to offer conservation easements and divided the land into five properties of varying sizes, each of which could hold just one home. As the lots were sold off one by one, the property closest to the Stowells', 17.5 acres, remained. The other owners invited Frank, as a member of the Bainbridge Island Land Trust, to all of their meetings. He helped plan how the properties would be developed. The developer took the 17.5-acre parcel off the market in 2002 when it still had not sold. The Stowells realized how attached they had gotten to the land, a place where their children had held magic tea parties. They finally bought the parcel in 2005.

Walking on the property with Frank, I realize that these are the places that salmon yearn to rest after their long sojourn at sea—always shaded by tall woods, mosses coating almost every surface. I could feel my moisture-sensitive hair curling up tight around my face. I breathed deeply, because I could tell this was some of the cleanest air on the planet. It was being generated right here, right out of these tree trunks and springy ferns.

Unlike on my property, the bare earth here is never visible under these second-growth spruce and cedars. Layers and layers of fallen leaves and needles combine with the moss and undergrowth to provide beds for the deer and other small mammals that make their way here.

When we paused for a moment near a grouping of cedar, a small hiss filled the air. "Did you hear that?" asked Frank. "That's an owl letting us know it sees us."

Frank spends much of his time in the woods communing with the owls that call the property home. The owls raise their chicks there, and engage in the kind of owly conversation we sometimes hear outside my house around four in the morning. I've never heard birds that gossip so much. But that day, a single hiss was the only evidence that they were watching.

As we made our way along the loosely diamond-shaped track that Frank and Mary have worn into the woods, we had to stop every few yards to exclaim over yet another grouping of mushrooms. Frank would dutifully take out a worn book of identifying photos, de rigueur for the true woodsman in these parts, and pick out their names. But I could tell that he did not really care what they were called. Frank reveled in their beauty, their singular insistence on reappearing every year that conditions permitted, a single eruption in a beam of light, or a swirl of shelf-fungi that suddenly turned a dark, wild space into a Victorian cupboard.

Foraging mushrooms on Bainbridge is a popular pastime. Nowadays, one can hardly move on the island without stepping on a professional forager, happy to lead you out into the woods to pick the ferns, spruce tips, mushrooms, and nettles that would make a true, Northwest dinner.

No salmon return to this property. Closer to the water is a conduit under a road that stops them, and Frank once applied for a grant to correct it, but was denied. He hasn't said if he will try again. Enough water runs in the small streams crisscrossing the land that I'm sure a healthy population of salamanders and frogs call the mossy hollows home. Still, these woodlands are essentially dead without the return of the salmon, the sacrifice of their bodies after spawning and the nutrients that would have been returned to the soil. This is the condition of most of the once-fertile land on the island.

On the way back to their home, we paused at the one-third acre site that is designated for a house. Frank and Mary seem happy to live just across the way, where sunlight can enter their windows in the morning, and the sheep and chickens can graze to their hearts' content. While we see plenty of houses surrounded by trees on the island, people and trees don't really need the same habitat. People need light, and trees need other trees. My own property seems like a good compromise, with trees on two sides, but open to the east and north. Unlike the live oaks of California, which stand apart from each other at quite a distance, the trees on this conservation easement seem to grow in family groups, with a tangle of undergrowth weaving them together. When one of them falls, it acts as a "nurse tree" for smaller trees, offering up its crumbling body to the roots of new growth.

This small open space sparks the imagination. It is the kind of place where one can imagine Alice dozing over her lessons before a rabbit with a pocket watch runs by.

Every election year on Bainbridge brings out a wide array of statements and accusations that only the voter patient enough to look up the regulations for herself has a chance to understand. Conservation groups line up on one side, and developers on the other. Voters, whether resistant shoreline owners or tree-huggers, must look over the candidates and decide which are most likely to represent their interests. Even when candidates try to remain somewhere between the two camps, someone is bound to give them a shove in one direction or the other.

Right now, Bainbridge is not a significant spawning ground for salmon, although at least three kinds—Chinook, Coho, and cutthroat—have been spotted in our streams. But its intricate shoreline, full of pint-sized bays and inlets, continues to offer a great deal of cover for fry where it has not been damaged or blocked off by shoreline development. Without the cooperation of its human citizens, however, the native fish population faces increasingly long odds against survival.

A recent study by the Puget Sound Partnership, a state entity, shows tiny improvements in specific measurements, but overall, the health of the Sound has continued to deteriorate. Is it important that salmon be able to return to their ancestral creeks? Besides the Suquamish inheritance, the health of the air and waters of the Sound directly affect the health of everyone who lives here. Salmon are not only the basic food and sustenance of the area, but the main indicator of the health of the rest of the system. We could continue to cut down trees and pave over wetlands, but if an island as progressive as Bainbridge cannot reverse this trend, no one else will be able to, either.

THE WORST CASE AND THE GIFT

As climate change continues to advance, more and more former skeptics are convinced of its reality. I might be overly romantic in hoping it is not too late to reverse course, that if enough of us pick up our shovels to remove the levees and farm the edges between the forests and the beaches, modify our eating and driving habits, we can bring this downhill trajectory to a standstill.

Others are not so optimistic. The earth is heating up, and only someone with her head in the sand is not prepared for the Worst Case Scenario. Climate change aside, there are so many other disasters for which to prepare: forest fires, earthquakes, tsunamis. Where I grew up, in earthquake country, our household always kept a little food and water someplace. Even if it's just the power going out now and then, nobody likes to go hungry or thirsty, even for a little while. Since beginning this book, I have become more serious about this, filling a backpack with a few things I would like to have with me if we need to leave the house suddenly, things like a headlamp, a ground cloth, water bottles, and sneakers in which to run away from the dinosaurs unleashed from their long sleep in the bowels of the Marianas Trench. I mean, things meant to help my husband and me survive for a night or two. I'm not too concerned about official documents. Maybe I should be.

Some people have made a lifestyle out of this approach. These are the preppers, also known as survivalists, although some prefer the first term. Let's just say that they are people who realize that the imbalance we have created in our society, between the rich and the poor, the haves and have nots, and those who have access to the bounty of the land as opposed to those who do not, is likely to come to a head in the near future.

In *The Gift,* Louis Hyde refers to the quantity in each transaction that cannot be assigned monetary value.

Why are these opposing points of view? Preppers assume that there might be a time and circumstance when they will need to be able to live "off the grid" because the existing system of food and water delivery will break down. This includes growing and storing food and water for themselves, and being equipped to physically defend themselves from others if a shortage occurs. The more serious have spent thousands of dollars building bunkers in more remote parts of the West, such as western Idaho. Like our friends in Paonia, they expect to survive the Big One—war, earthquake, famine—and continue with life as I prefer not to know it. Except they have more guns.

The Gift, by contrast, describes the role of art in the exchanges that make up our interactions with each other, that mark culture and civilization. It details how some objects not only have no monetary value, but lose what value they have (prestige for the "owner") if not passed on to others. In modern commerce, objects of art are made that deliberately have a value that cannot be measured in money, but pass into the monetary realm when they go on the market.

The worst case scenario happened to Native Americans when the first European explorers showed up. Devastated by smallpox, pushed off their hunting and farming grounds and relocated to reservations, or sent off to boarding schools, tribes would seem to have lost the entire concept of the gift in the transition to a mercantile economy. And yet an account of labor practices in the late 1800s, including those of Squamish women in particular, shows that they adapted immediately to the new concept, selling berries and other foraged foods for money in a "doorstep economy" that in turn was used to purchase goods for *sgwigwi* activities, "that foolish custom of giving away property to the other tribes for the sake of praise such extravagance obtains." The trouble with money is that it was too easily converted back to the mercantile system, and so tended to fall out of the gift system much more easily than an object of beauty.

Where does our food fall in all this? The current food system relies on the extraction of time and labor from people who are underpaid to work in our fields. This leads to an artificial pricing for the food in our supermarkets, and explains why we pay so much more for the food we purchase in farmers markets: we are paying the true value of the food, including the labor it took to produce it and make it available in the market.

While considering these topics, I read *The Black Count* by Tom Reiss, a biography of Alex Dumas, father to the novelist Alexandre Dumas and grandfather to the playwright Alexandre Dumas. The elder Dumas was born in what is now Haiti, his father a white French aristocrat, and his mother a black slave "stolen" from her master. They had three children together, but only Alex was taken back to France by his father, where he became a successful professional soldier under the monarchy. Alex Dumas embraced the ideals of the French Revolution, and became a high-ranking general in the Revolutionary army. He eventually came under the command of Napoleon Bonaparte, who disliked this charming, accomplished black man. Bonaparte also tried to roll back the human rights instated by the Revolution when he saw how much income France accrued from slavery.

In reading about the history of slavery in the Caribbean, I realized with a shock that we depend on a similar system: as long as we demand cheap food and encourage farmers to underpay their workers, there will be a slave class that labors under poor conditions. People do not "choose" to live like this.

Underpaid farm work is not a gift, but a forced extraction of labor.

My own family story is caught up in this history. My father was fortunate in that he was plucked out of this system by a sympathetic classmate and his father. This single event changed all of our lives. One of my cousins married an undocumented worker when it was possible for him to gain citizenship by marriage, but otherwise, I don't think any of my close relatives had to cross without papers or work in the fields. The relationship between Mexico and the United States has been an ebb and flow of workers allowed into the United States when labor was needed, and expelled when not needed. When borders were less defined, and papers less easily traced, that relationship was more fluid. The Mexican Revolution occurred at a time when the United States needed labor to build the railroads, bringing my parents and grandparents north. My father's uncle was able to purchase land in the Central Valley during the Depression and to establish a small truck farm. I remember visiting cousins there when I was about twelve—they owned the ranch where they lived. More recently, I spoke with men who had worked in the United States at some time or other before returning to their home cities in Mexico. Before the drug wars got so intense, it was a common practice for the laboring class to spend three or four years here as older teens, then go back to start a family. One told me he had worked as a truck driver, and another said he had spent three years maintaining golf courses in the South. It was their equivalent of a year abroad offered by many colleges in the United States. After their experiences here, and after having earned enough money to marry, they were usually happy to return to their hometowns of Guanajuato, Aguascalientes, or San Miguel de Allende.

As Mexico's economy improves, there will be less incentive to brave an illegal crossing. That will leave the most desperate, and most exploitable, at the mercy of coyotes and employers who hire people to work in many trades in the United States: from farm work to construction, restaurant work to hotel maintenance. With refugees from the Middle East, Central America, and North Africa sending international migration to an all-time high since World War II, I expect this third economy, the exploitation of desperate workers, to encompass some of these new refugees.

If the crutch of underpaid labor were removed, food suppliers would have to charge more for the food we consume. Cheap labor subsidizes the extra cost of transporting food for long distances—if we had to begin to pay the full cost of that long-distance food, local food grown in smaller quantities by people paid a living wage would become more competitive.

Families that could not afford the higher prices might pay less in exchange for harvesting the food themselves. This, in turn, would encourage a return to keeping individual garden plots for easier-to-grow foods, and to purchasing local foods from dairies, butchers, canners, and beekeepers, as we once did. This would not eliminate the need to grow large quantities of basics such as rice and wheat, but might save our overall system a lot of time and money by encouraging people to buy seasonally and grow locally.

If we kept this in mind, we would be in much better shape if a real emergency struck.

WHO GROWS MOST OF OUR FOOD?

This, as they used to say in San Bernardino, is where the rubber meets the road. I can rhapsodize about the beauty of Bainbridge, the farmers who by grit and determination wrest a living from the land, and the wonders of our locally owned grocery store. But this accounts for very little of what most people eat on the island. Even if I grew more vegetables, eschewed all meat and gave up coffee, I would buy most of my groceries from Town & Country. And T&C must operate within the reality of the food retail business. Not all of their suppliers are going to be perfect employers; not all of their sources are going to pay a living wage.

An especially painful dilemma is posed by the Sakuma Brothers Berry Farms. One of the families sent from Bainbridge to the camps during World War II, the Sakumas did not return to the island. Rather, they settled in California and in Burlington, Washington, where they continue to grow berries for a commercial market.

Today, the workers at Sakuma Brothers are in a continuing strike that started in 2013, with workers now pushing for a union contract. Mostly members of the Mixteca ethnic group from Oaxaca, they have formed their own organization, Familias unidas por la justicia—

Families United for Justice—in order to fight what they see as the violation of workers' rights at the farm. These are traditional family groups who have organized along the model used by Cesar Chavez.

I learned about their struggle in a dim room at Kiana Lodge, where Rosalinda Guillen, a short, sturdy woman exuding confidence, stood before a mixed crowd of healers, farmworkers, writers, and educators from the United States, Mexico, and Peru. She spoke in both English and Spanish. I know Rosalinda's brother from the years he spent as an arts activist in Seattle, but this was the first time I had met Rosalinda.

Rosalinda introduced herself to the crowd. She was born in Mexico, and moved with her family to Washington State when she was ten years old, in 1960. A migrant farmworker until her twenties, Rosalinda then took a job with a Skagit Valley bank and worked there for the next sixteen years. Four years short of retirement, she quit her corporate job to advocate for farmworkers through the United Farm Workers, the union founded by Cesar Chavez. She also worked for the Rainbow Coalition during Reverend Jesse Jackson's 1988 presidential campaign before returning to the fields to organize workers. One of her great successes is the Chateau Ste. Michelle Winery, which now uses union workers. "We believe another world is possible," she told her audience at the Kiana Lodge.

Besides wage and labor issues, the Sakuma workers' complaints include the use of chemicals that aggravate eye injuries, including a commonly used mix of Captan (a fungicide), Malathion (an insecticide), and Carbaryl (another insecticide) in a spray guaranteed to "eliminate insects and diseases at the same time." Captan can cause dermatitis and conjunctivitis, as well as acute toxicity. Malathion and Carbaryl are known to cause nerve injury to workers exposed to them—exposure symptoms include diarrhea, headache, nausea, and vomiting. The combination spray is marketed to the general public by Rescue and Bonide for use on fruit trees.

"We all have to work together," Guillen said. "The harm done to some of us by pesticides will come around to all of us."

Sakuma Brothers recently hired, for the first time, an experienced CEO from outside the family in an attempt to maintain profits and accommodate worker demands. Sakuma Brothers is listed as a partner business on the Town & Country website, but Rick Nakata tells me that the produce department is not placing orders with them until the labor issues are settled. The question of how workers are treated is another reason to be knowledgeable about where our food comes from.

"We are allies with small family farmer organizations. Why not a land trust for food production? Why not aim for 15 percent organic? Only 3 percent of crop land in Whatcom County [north of Seattle] is organic," says Guillen. "Why not a twenty dollar minimum wage, and the production of a domestic fair-trade product? The term *organic* originally implied that food was grown in a socially just manner."

Later, I looked for evidence of this last statement. The concept of organic food started in the 1800s in Europe and Britain. It was as much a philosophical approach as a practical one, treating the land and its workers as integral parts of the living system that results in food. One could argue that it started with the Jains in India, who refuse to harm any living creature, but I don't know if they had any influence on the Europeans. Farmers in France, in particular, embraced organic farming from the beginning. By the 1900s, scientists in the United States were writing books on the subject, but I didn't find any particular concern for farmworkers who did not own their own land and its produce until 1985 when the Rural Development Center (RDC) was founded in California. The RDC pioneered the idea of a "Farmworker to Farmer" program, in which agricultural workers gain broader skills leading to their advancement into farm management or possibly farm ownership.

Guillen's vision is that farmworkers can earn enough to own their own land, grow their own food, and produce enough extra to sell for cash. Like the Fortners on Bainbridge Island, these farmworkers want to live self-sufficiently on the land, and produce value-added foods and handicrafts that can be sold in the marketplace, be that in the United States or their country of origin.

WHEN EVERYTHING WAS SCARCE

In 1993, Nancy Turner and Alison Davis, two Canadian anthropologists, published a paper called "'When Everything Was Scarce': The Role of Plants as Famine Foods in Northwestern North America." They applied modern methods to older data collected by a range of anthropologists, especially interviews with Native elders. Based on these interviews, Turner and Davis created maps and tables that showed the seasons and availability of indigenous plants used for food. The interviews encompassed a territorial arc that that stretched from British Columbia to Newfoundland. They also preserved a few of the stories that describe the roles of these plants, and the cultural responses to times of famine. Here is one of them, a Kathlamet text collected by Franz Boas in Oregon in 1901:

> The people of mythical times were dying of hunger. They had only sagittaria-roots to eat. They had only small sagittaria-roots and skunk-cabbage and . . . rush roots to eat. In the spring of the year the Salmon went up the river. They had first arrived with many companions. . . . Then the Skunk-cabbage said: "At last my brother's son has arrived. If it had not been for me, your people would have been dead long ago." Then the Salmon said, "Who is that who is talking there?" "Oh, that is the Skunk-cabbage who is talking." "Let us go ashore." They gave him five elk skins and put war clubs under his blanket, one on each side. . . . Then they carried him inland and placed him among willows.

These stories are noteworthy because they represent thousands of years of practical knowledge of what grows here, when and where it is available, and how humans have endured harsh and extreme circumstances by relying on these foods.

Turner and Davis's research notes the use of over one hundred species of plants, from those considered delicacies to those used only in times of absolute emergency.

As ethnobotanist Gary Paul Nabhan pointed out in the talk I attended at the University of Washington, northwestern North America, especially the Northwest coast, is rich in naturally occurring food resources. Turner and Davis quote other anthropologists saying that on the Northwest coast, "both land and marine fauna are exceptionally rich. . . . Coastal waters teem with fish," and "the potential food supply is consistent and dependable."

But food still needed to be harvested and stored on a seasonal basis, and crises could occur. Those caught short would suffer and sometimes starve. Reasons for these times of scarcity, or even famine, varied—from a late salmon run to an attack by a rival group in which food stores were stolen or the residents were separated from them. The most common time for a food shortage was late winter or early spring, when food stores from the previous year had run out, and the spring salmon run was late.

Turner and Davis report one instance, from the work of Kennedy and Bouchard (1983) on the Slianunon (Comox), when "the berries did not ripen, the salmon did not come and the animals seemed to have left the country," resulting in famine, but note that such occurrences were rare. For the Kwakwaka'wakw (Kwakiutl) of British Columbia, starvation was also rare: stories of famine occur more often among families living at the heads of inlets, rather than close to the open sea, where marine mammals such as seals and sea lions, and fish such as salmon and halibut remained plentiful.

Farther north, conditions of scarcity increased in frequency and severity, making the Tsimshian on the north coast of British Columbia and far Southeastern Alaska even more vulnerable to famine. People living in the north had a slimmer margin for human error or the unexpected.

Food scarcity could also be due to natural catastrophes. Turner and David report that another anthropological team, Hayden and Ryder (1991) concluded that a major prehistoric cultural collapse among the Lillooet was probably due to catastrophic landslides that dammed the Frazier River of British Columbia, disrupting salmon supplies upstream.

Some of the stories Turner and Davis collected about food shortages describe families or individuals running out of food while traveling or hunting. For example, a hunter might prefer to go hungry rather than return empty-handed, especially if on the track of game. As thirst or hunger pangs set in, the hunter might resort to emergency foods or hunger suppressants in order to continue. Or a traveler might get lost, or simply run out of food before reaching her destination. Finally, a family might lose a provider, and be unable to accumulate enough food to survive the winter. In these cases, emergency or famine foods would come into use.

Turner and Davis divided these plant foods into four categories, with some overlap: regular foods that became more important under certain circumstances, largely due to extended availability; alternative, less preferred foods, used as a minor part of the diet except in times of scarcity; starvation foods or products never used under normal circumstances; and hunger suppressants and thirst quenchers, last resorts during short periods of food and water deprivation.

I would like to think that there is a divine order to this, in that less desirable foods were held in reserve for times when more desirable food was missing. They might also have taken longer to renew themselves, and so could not take the intense harvesting to which more commonly consumed foods were subjected. An exception to this seems to be clams, which thrive in carefully constructed clam beds that serve three purposes: protecting clams from predators, making them easy to find and harvest, and building up shoreline for the small and microscopic plants and animals that need these shallow waters. These include the most desirable food of the area—and one of the most desirable foods in the world—salmon.

Also, what was considered a famine food, used only in emergencies, and what might be considered a delicacy, eaten on special occasions or when available, varied quite a bit between indigenous groups, regions, and preparations. For example, black tree lichen was considered a delicacy by the Flathead of Montana, especially when mixed with dried, powdered camas root. It was described, when cooked together with alternate layers of wild onion, as "one of the best liked of all vegetable preparations." But in other areas it was not highly regarded.

Normally, the preparation for black tree lichen was complex—harvesting large amounts from a pre-tasted source, soaking in freshwater overnight, pounding, and shaping into loaves before pit-cooking. The cooked loaves were then dried. In the research reported by Turner and Davis, most people who knew about this lichen agreed that cooking was essential to make it edible. Cooking broke down the complex lichen carbohydrates, which are mostly indigestible for humans. The cooked, dried loaves could then be stored without deterioration for three or more years, and travelers could carry them on long journeys. Black tree lichen could also be eaten raw and unprocessed in times of extreme need. Why eat uncooked black tree lichen when people knew it was easier to digest after it had been processed and cooked? Because they lacked the energy or means to do so.

Even in the best of times, black tree lichen was not as highly regarded as salmon. In a Lillooet story, "The Abandoned Boy," Raven got salmon from the boy during a food shortage, after the boy had obtained special powers from the Sun. Raven, not wanting to reveal his good fortune to the other villagers, told them that the food he had was black tree lichen bread, with the implication that this was not a particularly desirable food.

Many of the old-time ideas about less-preferred foods line up with what we would consider less-preferred foods today: fish heads, storm-killed small fish or birds, certain shellfish, and small predatory mammals, including dogs, martins, and wolverines. But those are North American preferences. In parts of Europe, small, migrating songbirds have almost been hunted out of existence because they are considered a delicacy.

Alternative plant foods included rose hips, gathered and dried in quantity when other foods were missing, black hawthorn berries, considered "dry and mealy and . . . eaten only if nothing else was available," and soapberry, which was eaten "only in lean times" in southern Canada, but was considered a delicacy farther north and west when whipped into a confection or used as a beverage base.

True famine foods were eaten only in times of extreme hunger. These included raw black tree lichen and raw Nootka lupine roots. Some of these foods contain enzyme inhibitors and other toxins, and cause symptoms ranging from headaches to nausea and dizziness. Yet, in desperation, people turned to such foods.

Hunger suppressants and thirst-quenching strategies included foods or alternatives used in ways familiar to those of us from the Southwest. They might include holding a root in the mouth to stave off hunger and thirst, or finding potable water in the hollow stems of the giant horsetail. Gum from certain trees was sometimes chewed for pleasure or as a hunger suppressant, and teas may have been used to alleviate hunger or provide nutrients.

The importance of these foods should not be taken lightly. In some cases, the nutritional value supplied by alternative foods meant the survival of a group of people for the days or weeks until more food was available.

This is illustrated by the following story from Nlaka'pamux (Thompson) elder Annie York, recollecting stories of famine told to her by her great-aunt, Josephine George of the Nicola Valley in southern interior British Columbia:

> But one time, that year was the famine. They had nothing, no fish, everything was scarce. . . . So they went up Broadback Mountain . . . to try to get up to where this avalanche lily may be . . . they went up there in the spring. And the people that eats cow-parsnip was the ones that survived. . . . They're very valuable food, when Indians had that spring beauty, what they could dig out, they survived. But the ones that didn't eat them, they're just trying to get a deer or something, then they died.

The prickly-pear cactus, they always eat it all right
enough, but they had to eat it during a famine; my grand-
aunt told me, "We eat that three times a day!" she says.
There was no fish, nothing. And that cactus was all the
children, even to the babies, had to eat . . . after they steam
it. That was in springtime.

Turner and Davis also calculated the nutritional value of the
foods used during times of scarcity. After a winter spent eating dried
foods, people were in serious need of vitamin C and other nutrients
available only in fresh foods. vitamin A, vitamin C, and B vitamins
(thiamine, niacin, and riboflavin) were necessary, along with the
pure calories needed to go out and gather food.

Turner and Davis also speculate on how cultural practices or
even food processing might have affected the availability or scarcity
of certain indigenous foods. For example, the Lillooeet, after their
regular food supply was disrupted by the landslides that blocked
the Frazier River, dug, cooked, and ate more root vegetables. This
in turn caused overharvesting and eventually a population decline
around their major villages, as continued famine conditions caused
people to move away.

Many cultural practices are closely related to limitations in food
supply, Turner and Davis point out. Within the last century, controlled landscape burning, once used to encourage plant food production in landscapes such as camas prairies, has been suppressed
by U.S. Forest Service policies, causing the depletion in quantity and
quality of some indigenous plant foods. In fact, I don't think I have
seen an active camas prairie since moving to the Northwest over
thirty years ago. According to "Reading the Washington Landscape,"
a blog kept by Dan McShane, certain tribes once specialized in growing camas for trade with other tribes, as part of an elaborate system
of trading and giving. "The southwest Washington prairies provided
a key source of carbohydrates for thousands of local people as well
as thousands more via active trading," according to McShane. This

system had already begun to fall apart in the early 1800s due to the high mortality rate caused by exposure to new diseases.

More recent problems include overgrazing by livestock, use of pesticides, and the introduction of invasive species, all of which have caused a deterioration in traditional plant foods. On Bainbridge, there are no prohibitions against the use of legal pesticides or herbicides, except in wetlands or shoreline buffers, so many of the plants that might have once grown in abundance and served as food in times of scarcity may no longer grow here. And runoff from private land, as well as failing septic systems, has compromised the quality of the waters surrounding the island.

Another cultural aspect of food scarcity is that food preferences, like fashion, shift over time. Now that we can import food from not only all over the country, but all over the world, we have developed exotic tastes, enhanced by health claims and food fads. I'm not immune to this. While I love cacao and tomatoes, both indigenous to the Americas, I also drink coffee (indigenous to Africa) and eat oranges (indigenous to Asia). And none of these foods grows near where I live. I have eaten *nopalitos*, cactus, and it is okay, especially when mixed with scrambled eggs and hot sauce, but if I had to eat it for every meal, as Josephine George did, I would be tired of it after, oh, a day. If Bainbridge were cut off from outside food supplies, would there be anything left of the foods that naturally grow here? I'm pretty sure I've found some black lichen in a nearby neighborhood, but it is high in a tree, and I'm not motivated enough to knock it down and sample it.

Nowadays, much indigenous food would be treated as famine food—we might only eat it if nothing were available from the grocery store. Many who once had knowledge about these foods have probably forgotten it, and many others never received it. Still, every family, no matter their origins, has versions of "preferred" foods that are rare, expensive, or take a great deal of preparation, and so are treated as special delicacies, as well as versions of "peasant" foods, or common foods, that are easy to grow or buy and fix in quantity to stretch further. This might be something as simple as beans and squash, which together with corn, form the "three sisters" of Southwest Native American food, or something more complex like a stew made from animal parts that are discarded or fed to other animals during times of plenty.

As Gary Paul Nabhan points out in his book *Why Some Like It Hot,* people of different genetic makeups need different foods. Those of us who live far from our genetic places of origin need to find local equivalents in order to stay healthy. Of Lebanese ancestry, Nabhan, who lives in Arizona, says that he substitutes tepary beans for the fava beans of the Mediterranean. When you think of it that way, many of us may be suffering famine conditions without knowing it—symptoms of obesity may be a sign that our bodies are searching for what we truly need to eat, rather than what we crave.

We have been taught to want certain foods through advertising, often for foods like sugar, corn, and milk that receive government subsidies. Some of these subsidies were put in place during the Depression, when they enabled families to have access to foods that might otherwise have been out of reach. Other foods, such as corn and soybeans, are subsidized because of lobbying efforts on behalf of the meat and processed food industries. None of these subsidies has anything to do with the regions in which they are grown or produced, much less local production or seasonal availability. The only fruit or vegetable that provides a notable subsidy to growers is the apple. Although many subsidized foods contain dairy, many indigenous people, as well as African Americans and Asian Americans, are lactose intolerant.

The major difference between how people in this region ate in 1850 and how they eat now is that most indigenous people participated in a "seasonal round" that enabled them to travel from place to place and take advantage of the foods and resources available in a variety of localities and habitats. Unlike agrarian societies, said Turner and Davis, where people live in one place and are dependent on just a few crops for their sustenance, hunter-fisher-gatherers like the Native peoples of the Northwest use a wider diversity of foods from a great range of environments. In addition, they trade with others they come in contact with for food that originates much farther away. This was once a way to mitigate food scarcities, because they were less reliant on any one crop. If a particular food was late or didn't show up at all, the families moved to another location.

Until 1854, when George Meigs built a lumber mill at the north end of the island at Port Madison, people did not live year-round on Bainbridge Island. The Suquamish came to Bainbridge to harvest trees and their accompanying products, such as bark, roots and fresh, edible shoots, to pick berries, and especially, to gather clams. They camped on the beaches for weeks at a time, feasting and harvesting, smoking clams to preserve them for trade and supplies, then loaded up their canoes and moved on.

Having tied ourselves to the land year-round, we are now dependent on most of our food being trucked in. It is possible that we could survive, at least for awhile, on food obtained solely from the island, but it would turn ugly fast. Blackberries, which we love and curse at the same time, would quickly become desirable and then scarce. Deer, now equally cursed for the damage they cause to flower and vegetable gardens, would briefly be a source of meat. Raccoons would be seen in a whole new light, but as Stephen told me, we would have to be sure to cook them for a really, really long time.

CLIMATE CHANGE

Another factor, of course, is climate change. A United Nations panel, the Intergovernmental Panel on Climate Change, released a report in 2014 that includes a great deal of information about the effects of climate change on food production.

The good news, according to the report, is that many areas that were once too cold to grow food before may now be able to do so. The bad news is that, overall, climate change may reduce food production by 2 percent each decade for the foreseeable future. Meanwhile, population growth and the increase in wealth among some of the population will call for a 14 percent increase in demand for food. And yup, the oceans are rising. There is no reversal of these trends in sight. Most of the carbon dioxide released into the atmosphere will stay there for thousands of years, while the oceans continue to heat up. This will change tide and weather patterns. Hot, dry seasons will get hotter and dryer, while cold, wet seasons will get colder and wetter.

The only way to offset the need for more food will be to put more land into production, which means chopping down forests, thus accelerating climate change. The increased demand for food, says the report, will place its greatest burden on the poor.

This is not an abstract "poor." One day, a Native American friend who uses social media as a sort of open diary of her musings, posted a cry that cut me to the quick. It asked for prayers for relatives in her extended family. They have suffered age-related falls, accidents, bad health. They suffer the stresses of worry, asthma, diabetes, and heart disease. They fear change, because change is "powerful and demanding." She asked for kind thoughts, positive images. She realizes, she said, that many of us do not understand the stress of being poor. She thanked the Creator for everything she has. She did not mention that she, herself, suffers from most of these conditions.

Even before looking at the climate report, I realized that these changes will fall mostly on the poor of the world, and that I, at least for now, am not one of them. But those who have been active for food justice have known this all along. Like Gandhi before them, these activists have used fasting as a way to draw attention to their causes. Perhaps because it is specifically about our relationship with food, fasting has become a tool by which to attempt change in the behavior of others. It not only calls out the fact that we can choose to abstain from eating while others cannot, it puts the activist's own health and life on the line in terms that everyone can understand.

I never met Gustavo Gutiérrez, the Opata peace and justice activist. He passed away in 2012 while taking part in a Peace and Dignity march. At the age of eighty, he was on horseback in the Grand Canyon when he fell, later dying of his injuries. I have seen him in videos, and he was a large man. I am pretty sure that he suffered from metabolic syndrome. Upon reflection, I should have gone out of my way to try to meet him. I am part of a chat group that seems to be made of the last remaining members of the Opata tribe in the United States. We post stories and photos, but only recently met as a group in person. Two other members live in Washington State, and I have met both of them.

Gutiérrez understood that we must take a holistic approach to the health of the land and the health of the people. Long before Aldo Leopold articulated this understanding of our health, the Opata and many other indigenous groups understood that the food we put in our bodies, and our nearness or farness from its sources, probably has a more significant effect on our physical well-being than anything else we do.

Cesar Chavez, Rosalie Guillen's inspiration, fasted on behalf of farmworkers, as did Billy Frank Jr., the Yakama fishing rights activist who fought and won back a few rights for Native American fishermen. These fasts were long, drawn-out affairs, with men risking their lives in order to effect social change.

Recently, Gary Paul Nabhan fasted on behalf of monarch butterflies, whose natural habitat has been reduced through the use of RoundUp and other chemicals used in growing Monsanto crops. It is difficult to separate these issues: poor stewardship of the land leads to physical and social ills. The indiscriminate use of chemicals and the burning of fossil fuels have finally put us over the top, unless the human race can pull a miracle out of the air to stop climate change. Everyone was heartened by the Paris Climate Accord of 2015, but the targets that were agreed to will still not stop climate change. We can snuggle up on our little island, but it is coming for us, sure enough.

Haleets

Adult salmon live lives we can merely imagine. That's how little we know about them. They go out into the open ocean and swim away from their home rivers. They grow strong in the currents, see that there are thousands of other salmon of every hue and origin, a universe of things to eat and be eaten by. Then the same salmon that left their rivers and streams as smolts—newly formed and enlarged bodies, ignorant of the dangers possible in the open ocean—return as adults with full, sleek bodies.

Some of them stay in the open ocean longer than others. They hear the whale's song, the soundtrack of the world, and when they return to freshwater, they no longer fear death. They know the end is coming, but only after the ecstasy of reproduction. Even if their ancestors have not made it back to the spawning grounds in generations, thwarted by dams and human-made blockages, the fish persevere, seeking that golden moment when they can perform their own part in the great ballet of life.

Warm Springs (Wishxam) artist Lillian Pitt tells a story about She Who Watches, Tsagaglalal, a petroglyph of a large, feminine face that overlooks the Columbia River Gorge. Back when people were "not quite people" and could still talk to animals, Coyote came one day and asked Tsagaglalal if she was a good leader. "My people live well," she answered. "We have lots of salmon, venison, berries, roots, good houses. Why do you ask?" Coyote asked who would look after her people after she was gone. When she said she didn't know, Coyote turned her to stone, so that she would continue to watch her people, whatever good or bad fell upon them. The Army Corps of Engineers came and destroyed the Wishxam village at Celilo Falls—and still Tsagaglalal must watch.

Boarding schools took the people's language away, engineers blocked the mighty rivers that supplied the salmon, and farmers turned under their traditional crops of camas and salal. Shipbuilders came and in one generation cut down the mighty trees that had provided planks for longhouses and canoes, bark for baskets and cloth, wood for fires, needles for food and medicine. A creosote plant filled the harbor with poison; it was declared a Superfund site by the Environmental Protection Agency in 1987.

Two figures at the left edge of Haleets provide a puzzle within a puzzle. One figure looms over another that appears to be upside down. One of the most powerful spirits known to the Suquamish is A'yahos, portrayed as either a two-headed snake or an antlered figure. One of the stories told about Agate Passage is that A'yahos once lived at the bottom of the pass. There was a great rumbling and shaking. The people screamed and yelled in fright. They looked out to see a two-headed eagle fighting with A'yahos. When it was all over, the eagle had won, and carried A'yahos away. But Agate Passage was much larger than it had been before, widening the waters that lie between Old Man House and Bainbridge Island.

A seismic event, estimated to have taken place around 800 CE, caused major changes in Puget Sound. Seismologists calculate it was an 8 on the Richter Scale at Agate Passage.

A'yahos, the shaking spirit, is associated with a number of sites around Puget Sound. In recent times, geologists have been able to match these stories up with known earthquakes and slides. Lidar technology can show earthquake activity under areas that are too built up to test. The stories are so accurate that scientists are pretty sure A'yahos lurks in these places as well, in the form of fault lines and unstable slide areas.

The figures on Haleets were probably carved by different people over a long span of time. In a video made in October 2012 by the Bainbridge Island Historical Museum, Dennis Lewarch, the tribal historic preservation officer for the Suquamish Tribe, suggests that some believe that before the seismic event of 800 CE, the boulder, still uncarved at the time, was much closer to the water. If the two figures at the left edge of the petroglyphs represent A'yahos and Thunderbird, then this is a recording of the struggle that took place between them. Haleets in that case would attest to a time in traditional memory when the north end of Bainbridge tipped up and the south end tipped down, drowning Wing Point, a long, narrow spine of rock, and submerging several camping and fishing sites of the Suquamish along the east and south sides. Did famine follow? Did trade strategy change? The people of Suquamish would have needed to regroup and rethink their relationship with other people, the natural world, and the spirit world.

These stories, like that of Tsagaglalal, remind us that there are consequences for taking the gift for granted, misunderstanding, or squandering it. The gift can be in the form of knowledge, or of songs that are sung during certain seasons. They remind us that we must be prepared, that life is constant struggle. If we ignore the lessons inherent in the stories, or forget the knowledge of plants and animals that is carried in the songs, humans suffer. We throw the system out of balance.

Haleets turns it back on us, facing away from the island. Maybe Haleets has given up on us, thinking that we are not worthy of the secrets it embodies. The designs are increasingly difficult to see, and those who once maintained the petroglyphs did not pass instructions on to their children or grandchildren. We are all unwell for lack of the knowledge and practice that were once our legacy. We watch the rising tides, and take stock of what we have left.

Brian MacWhorter and Akio Suyematsu at
Day Road Farms with vintage tractor.

– 6 –

What We Can Do Together

VEGETAL DREAMING

A S THE SEASON PROGRESSES, the community garden bursts with life. A neighbor kept my plants watered while we traveled for two weeks, and I returned to kale, mixed greens, and more kale! We have enjoyed it many ways—stir fried, as salads, as a soup with white beans, and in a frittata. We are almost caught up now.

The carrots are well established, and my yellow tomato plant survived its baptism of copper sulfate and sideways planting—*la jefa* of the garden, Anita Rockefeller, had me lay the gangly plant on its side and bury it, only allowing about eighteen inches at the top to curve out into the air. It seems to be working.

It rained intensely over the weekend, so there is no need to water. As I harvest and weed, two ravens greet each other overhead, elaborately and formally. I get the impression they have known each other a long time, but are not exactly friends.

Otherwise, it is quiet today. I was thinking how noisy it would be if plants made as much noise as the rest of us. Instead, they occupy the realms of sight and smell, attracting and repelling as it serves them. I remembered times I have crossed open fields in the hot sun and heard the crackle of wild oats and the popping of seed pods as they scatter their cargo. That's about as noisy as it gets. When I chop the discarded leaves and weeds for composting, the smell of arugula rises up to my nostrils, causing me to breathe more deeply. It makes me wonder if my sense of smell is coming back, or if it is just the intensity of the aroma.

The plant life here is palpable. Knowing this season of both full sun and rain is short and fleeting, the plants are growing as quickly as they can. They are concentrating. I feel as though, if I could just lean in close enough, I could hear the vegetables dreaming.

BALANCING

As in Paonia, small differences on Bainbridge Island can seem large. The single issue that generated the most letters to the editor one year was whether to put a roundabout or stop signs at a problem intersection near the high school. The roundabout won.

But there are more serious balancing acts as well. Property rights advocates end up pitted against environmentalists, who want more restrictions on how waterfront properties are developed. Property owners fear that if bulkheads or other "improvements" are banned, their properties will lose value. Advocates for the restoration of Puget Sound point out that Bainbridge Island has miles of shoreline that once provided shelter for salmon fry and the many plants and animals that accompany them. It's pointless to restore salmon runs if the newly hatched fish have no habitat in which to mature. Meanwhile, the number of returning fish drops almost every year.

Land developers fight any changes to zoning that would limit the number of houses they can place on lots, or that require adequate parking to serve their subdivisions. As long as I have lived on Bainbridge, developers and businesses have cut down tree buffers with little or no consequence. The fights seem to be about aesthetics, walkability, and impact on adjacent properties. Until recently, no one ever questioned how the removal of so many trees must affect the aquifer, our only source of freshwater. In one recent development controversy, the same one that saw Chiara D'Angelo sitting in a tree to block its removal, the developers, like one of the tenant businesses, were from Ohio. Their children don't go to school with our children. They will not walk or drive by this property every day, remembering the towering trees that once flanked the highway and provided a buffer for already existing high-density housing. They never saw the eagles and blue herons that flew overhead and made their homes nearby. Like previous commercial buildings on the island, lush landscaping, traffic calming, and walkability were promised, but the result is a clump of generic buildings that could be dropped anywhere—even Ohio.

This is the sort of place that investment brokers package and sell to people looking for ways to make money on their money—a deal backed by an investment company or two that probably doesn't show up even as a separate line-item on investors' quarterly statements. How can investors know what sort of good or harm they are doing? Because I have been self-employed most of my life, my small, slowly accumulated retirement fund is with a company that caters to educators. I don't invest in their real estate fund, but if I did, I would probably be helping to build developments just like this one across the country.

These conflicts put the city government in a bind. Everything the developers have done so far conforms to our rules and regulations. Everyone on the island wants to keep Bainbridge beautiful and livable. The town wants to be seen as a safe, welcoming place for businesses to invest—not only for the direct benefits from the development, like jobs, taxes, and cash flow, but also because development gives the city a higher investment rating, enabling it to borrow funds with which to build the things citizens really want, like parks, a new police station, and safer, smoother roads. If the city is perceived as hostile to outside financial interests, its financial viability suffers.

These are also the sorts of issues that pit neighbor against neighbor. Consequently, most people remain silent, amiable, until their own properties are directly threatened. After all, it's an island. We shop in each other's stores, our children attend school together, and we are members of the same churches, synagogues, and service organizations. By the time most people become civically engaged, it is too late to change specific zoning laws or tighten requirements, both actions that must be taken before a property owner or developer files plans with the city. The current City of Bainbridge Island comprehensive plan is great—high-minded, forward thinking, a document for the future as well as the present. But the plan is merely a set of guidelines required by the state—it is not legally enforceable except through local rules and regulations. The hard part—and it is really tedious—is making sure that city code conforms with the comprehensive plan, before there is little left to protect.

All over the state, municipalities are doing the same thing, with variations on the same cast of characters—homeowners, landholders, renters, commuters, elected officials and hired staff, consultants, and planners. How do you put all these great ideas into practice?

THE ROCK FARM

In 2013, Phil and Anita Rockefeller invited me (okay, I begged) to see the Rock Farm, a portion of their property that they have turned into a community garden.

When I arrived Sunday at 10:30 A.M., Phil and Anita were hanging what looked like prayer flags along the eight-foot-high deer fence. Up close, I could see that each flag had been designed by a community member, all of the flags stitched together by Anita. Maybe this is another way to exhibit community—or maybe it is so the deer can see the fence better.

The Rock Farm is a tidy one-third of an acre on the west side of the island, just the size of my own lot, but it is a very productive one-third acre. In the fall of 2008, Phil, a former state senator and now a member of the Northwest Power and Conservation Council, and Anita, a retired director of the Washington State branch of the EPA, were walking by the empty field to their mailbox, and realized that with the recession, people would go hungry. The idea to open the property for the public to grow food was born.

"In three minutes, it went from 'Should we do this?' to 'You should do this,'" said Phil, meaning Anita. "And you will probably need some help."

The farm is based on three precepts: that all the community gardeners are committed to growing food for Helpline House, which provides resources to those in need on the island; that working the farm will help people understand where their food comes from; and that farming in adjacent communal plots will give people a chance to tell each other their stories. Of course, they had me at "story."

Kathy Moore, a master gardener, acted as Anita's first mentor in the garden. Now, Becky Peddy, a volunteer with Helpline House, fills that role. She meets with the Rock Farm gardeners on a one-to-one basis to discuss productivity and suggest ways to improve it. Productivity, says Anita, does indeed go up after these meetings. Everywhere I looked, lush beds of kale, carrots, spinach, and the occasional patch of flowers spilled over the borders. Birdsong filled the surrounding forest of Douglas firs, and the sun was just beginning to break through the cloud cover.

When Anita cannot find an answer to a gardening question, she keeps asking people—not only Becky but also the staff at Bainbridge Gardens and other community members—until a solution is found. When tomato plants began to be infected with blight, she contacted tree specialist Olaf Ribeiro, who suggested that new tomato plants be treated with copper sulfate before bringing them into the garden. Anita now announces a day that she will spray tomato plants, and people bring them to the parking area for their baptism before taking them through the funky, wrought iron gate for planting.

When I first visited in 2013, twenty-six gardeners were participating in the project, working sixteen one-hundred-square-foot plots. In addition, there were five plots devoted just to produce for Helpline House. Now there are more plots devoted to Helpline House. People who want to join the garden tell Anita, and if there is room, each pays a small fee for the year that covers the cost of water and general soil amendments. There are small fees for additional compost or lime to "sweeten" the soil. The garden also employs some professional help. Almost all of the landscape and gardening business on the island is conducted by Mexican nationals, and Anita uses a landscaping service to help her with the heavier work of clearing and spreading compost in the garden. I had a long conversation with a gardener from Durango, Mexico, my mother's place of birth, who has been in the area for many years. He often works for Anita, and claims he can fix any motor.

On my first visit, Phil recounted the history of the field, which they have owned for over thirty years. He remembered clearing it of Scotch broom, an aggressive, invasive species in the Northwest. The property then served as a pumpkin patch for the Boy Scouts for a few years before it was left to go fallow. Today, the garden now sends thirty to fifty pounds of produce a week to Helpline House in the growing season, for a total of around twelve hundred pounds a year.

As we spoke, Phil began piling ripe raspberries on my notebook. "Feel free to visit anytime," said Anita, "even just to read or drink a cup of tea" at the plastic table and chairs centered in the garden.

The following season, I took the plunge. I paid my fifty dollars for a ten-by-ten plot at the Rock Farm. I don't keep a regular schedule, but I do try to time my visits to coincide with my use of the car for other reasons. It bothers me to get in my car to drive five miles in order to grow food. Why am I doing this? To decrease my carbon footprint? Bring down my cholesterol? It's better than trucking food from California, but I had gotten used to popping next door to water or gather a few tomatoes. I was still doing that, too, with a couple of tomato plants in pots on Hilary and Neil's back porch.

At the Rock Farm, lush forests of dinosaur kale and towering sunflowers flourish all around me. My plot looks hard-bitten in comparison, but only because I keep the kale well-plucked. There are only two of us at home, and if I let it get out of hand, we will waste food. I cultivate a productive row of broccoli for Helpline House, but they don't want our extra kale. Toward the end of the season, I froze bags of it straight from the garden, and later added it to pinto or navy bean soup. I grew a row of luscious carrots, and a crop of spinach early on. Who tends these giant vegetables all around me? Sometimes I see other community gardeners, but mostly I am there by myself. What are their stories? Some appear never to harvest their bounty.

Gardening at this slightly ramped-up scale is a lot more work than backyard gardening. Driving to the garden, tending the Helpline row, weeding, and watering—it all takes a lot of time. When I harvest, I need to trim and wash the vegetables, and package them so they stay fresh until I use them. Things rot quickly in this climate, even in the refrigerator. Of course, our weekly city disposal service collects and recycles green waste, so it goes back into the soil some-where. Although I already understood it intellectually, tending a plot at the Rock Farm has finally made me understand on a physical level the amount of labor that goes into our food. People paid by the bag or box, as are most workers in the produce industry, keep this up all day every day in order to make a living.

HELP

Helpline, and its sister organization, Fishline, provides fresh food for the hungry on Bainbridge and in Poulsbo. Their services offer a great way to feed people with produce that would otherwise go to waste. Both of the grocery stores on the island send them produce that is just past its peak, as well as other goods that can be used locally.

I had been handing off my broccoli to the next person headed for Helpline House rather than taking time to go over there myself. Again, I try to avoid unnecessary driving, but maybe I had been avoiding something deeper. It was August before I took in greens myself and discovered that each contribution is weighed, and the amount noted on a card kept for each individual who brings in food.

This came as a surprise to me, since I thought the Rock Farm contributed to Helpline communally.

Helpline receives city support, funds from the federal Supplemental Nutritional Assistance Program, and individual contributions. Even Bainbridge has people in need, and the recent recession made it worse. According to their website,

- The food bank serves about three hundred households (40 percent with children) each week.
- While the majority of food bank users are employed, they have a hard time making ends meet on their income.
- Close to one thousand people on Bainbridge Island are below poverty level. Of the cities in Kitsap County, Bainbridge represents 8.3 percent of the county's poor.
- The community-supported milk fund distributes over eight hundred cartons of milk on a monthly basis.

When I showed up, Becky Peddy was there in her other volunteer capacity. She showed me how to weigh and note my contribution on the card. Later, I asked her if she had attended the potluck held earlier that summer at the Rock Farm, when I was out of town.

"I never attend potlucks," she said emphatically, end of discussion. Too much waste? I wondered. Certainly a story there.

According to my card, I had made two other contributions that added up to about five pounds of broccoli. Not very much, really, in the scheme of things, and Helpline House is always bustling with activity. It's a good thing Anita has us all working part of the Rock Farm just to send food to Helpline House. She recently extended the area under cultivation.

Even though I had probably been avoiding the reality of it, I knew before my visit to Helpline House that there were hungry people on Bainbridge. Marriages go bad, jobs go south, and people want to keep their kids in school with as little disruption as possible. Rents on Bainbridge, while higher than in the rest of Kitsap County, are much more affordable than in Seattle. With other members of Kol Shalom, I volunteer once a month to make and serve a dinner, called "Super Supper," at the end of each month. Dinner is served each night that week at one of the local churches. We serve on Tuesdays at the Eagle Harbor Congregational Church, which is centrally located and has a commercial kitchen. The last week of the month is when food stamps run out for many people, and about thirty people show up pretty consistently to have a filling meal. Of those, about five people take food away to share with others, or to eat at a later time.

One evening we served chicken tacos, and I had to figure out how to make guacamole for thirty-five people. I used about five avocados and the food processor. It turned out pretty well, but I think it is hard to wreck guacamole. I admire people who can shop for groceries and cook at that volume without panic.

One of the guests that night was an American who had lived in Mexico City years before, and was delighted to eat some Mexican food. I think the fact that the meal reminded her of better days provided as much comfort as the food itself.

Sometimes I recognize people who I thought had retired from good jobs with pensions. We do not ask for any qualifying documentation before serving the diners, so some might come for the companionship, which is just as important for good health as a balanced meal. I make a point of talking to everyone a little bit as they pass through the buffet line, just being kind. I remember times when I was young and alone and even a kind word would have made me feel so much better.

Right now, the existence of a place like Helpline House, which receives funding from both federal agencies and the local community, is based on the idea that some people have a lot, and some have very little. If we find ourselves in the position of having only what we can grow or make, our bank balances will mean a lot less, and our physical abilities will mean a lot more.

Always, with food, we return to the problem of labor.

If the island were to achieve local sustainability, it would be the result not of nostalgia—as it might appear right now, with our attractive farmers and their picture-perfect animals—but of more practical problems like the costs of fuel and human labor. Ideally, people go into the food business because they love it, and honor the skill and craft that go into this sort of intense, local production. Local food will not take hold with the consumer, however, until it is economically comparable to buying mass-produced food in a supermarket. Remember the qualities the Nakata cousins looked for: quality, quantity, consistency, and availability. But even that is changing.

SUQUAMISH GARDENS

At the 2014 Our Food Is Our Medicine conference, I heard the Samish story of the Maiden of Deception Pass, and it struck me for its similarity to the story of Persephone (the namesake of Rebecca Slattery and Louisa Brown's farm in nearby Indianola). The Maiden story, as told to us at the conference, goes like this:

> Once there was a girl who fell in love with a man from the sea. He asked her father if she could be his wife, but the father refused. The girl began to fade away. The fishermen caught fewer and fewer fish, and the people began to starve. The girl got sicker and sicker. Finally, the father told the man from the sea that he could marry her and take her away if she was allowed to visit once a year, so that the family could check on her well-being. He agreed.
>
> The fish became abundant again. Each year, the girl returned to visit her family. She was very happy. Sometimes she came back with a new child. But as time passed, she was covered in more and more barnacles and seaweed, and it became more difficult for her to breathe, to spend time on land.
>
> Finally, the father released the girl and her husband from their promise. Now, if you look down into the roiling

waters of Deception Pass, you can see her long, green hair waving in the water.

The story makes clear that we are kin to the ocean dwellers—as Celtic storytellers have celebrated for generations in their stories of selkies—and also that we are bound to the same seasonal rhythms as the land and the sea. Seasonal stories told throughout the Northwest celebrate this connection. Stories explain our connection to the land, and a process was needed, the elders realized, by which these stories could be recovered and placed back in their cultural context.

Native American stories also serve to emphasize that our health is tied directly to the health of the land and sea. In 2005, at least ten Northwest tribes came together in the Traditional Foods of Puget Sound Project and asked the USDA Extension Service to help them bring back a nutritious, indigenous diet for the health of both the land and the people. Years ago, when tribes were assigned to reservations across the country, indigenous people were provided with so-called commodity foods for two reasons: to supplement their diets when they were confined to lands unable to sustain them, and to distance them from food that tied them directly to the land.

According to Rudolph Ryser (Cowlitz), chair of the Center for World Indigenous Studies, "the strategy was to wean people away from reliance on the land. Then they would not need access to deer, fish, and other traditional foods. They could become 'civilized.'"

These commodity foods included low-quality pig fat, beans, flour, and refined sugar. This explained the creation of frybread, which had never been part of the indigenous diet: it is made from the low-quality ingredients Indians were given to replace food they could no longer harvest from the land. During the Great Depression, the government began to support farmers by buying surplus foods and distributing them to Indians through the Commodity Supplemental Food Program. These commodity foods changed depending on what was available. Often milk- or wheat-based, they were sometimes entirely unsuitable for consumption by indigenous people. Many Indian people experienced growing up with commodity foods, including powdered milk that would not dissolve, poor quality meat, and processed cheese, according to Ryser. In this relatively recent history, the ills that we associate with the indigenous body began to take hold: diabetes, high blood pressure, high cholesterol, and heart disease.

One of the fundamental misunderstandings of first contact was about attitudes to land: Native people wanted to *access* the land, while white settlers wanted to *possess* it. While Indian treaties over the years supposedly allowed access to the land for the purposes of gathering food, these provisions are almost never honored, certainly not in a state like Washington, with its private ownership of the shoreline.

Many tribes still depend on commodity foods, but in the Northwest, the Native Food Systems Resource Center, from its home at the Northwest Indian College in Bellingham, is working to change that. Since 2005, it has facilitated tribes working together to improve the food available to their people, and to re-remember how to grow, gather, and prepare indigenous foods. A series of ongoing conferences, hosted by a different tribe each year, including the one I attended at Suquamish, bring together cooks, gatherers, storytellers, and tribal staff to exchange and explore ideas related to food sovereignty. A wonderful book, *Feeding the People, Feeding the Spirit: Revitalizing Northwest Coastal Indian Food Culture,* by Elise Krohn and Valerie Segrest with help from many others, has come out of these conferences. It is not a screed or a manifesto, but a simple-to-use guide to finding, growing, harvesting, and preparing indigenous food. For example, I learned that bull whip kelp can be peeled, cut into rounds, and pickled. Without passing judgment on how people eat now, the book clearly explains the health and social benefits of natural foods. *Feeding the People* includes equivalent foods for those that are scarce, and the nutritional value of each. It even provides a healthier version of frybread, using whole wheat flour.

Across Agate Passage, I was pleased to read that Suquamish has three gardens featuring culturally significant plants and nutritious foods. Hot lunches are provided for the elders, using food from these gardens. Individuals are also encouraged to start their own kitchen gardens and, this is my favorite part, the tribe will provide a whole kit—boards for building raised beds, soil, and seeds—for those who would like to do so. These are provided within a context that offers respect as well as advice.

As the Suquamish tribal newsletter says, "Our hands are up to the tribal council for their love and goodness they give to their tribal elders."

I wondered why there was not a similar program on Bainbridge that afforded gardening opportunities to the elderly.

Modern American life tends to segregate people not only by economics and education, but also by age. Since there is no undergraduate college on Bainbridge, most of our young people leave after completing high school. According to the Chamber of Commerce, only 3.6 percent of the island's population is between the ages of eighteen and twenty-four, while 12.8 percent is sixty-five or older.

Some of our kids return, if they can figure out a way to make a living, but most do not. At the same time, Bainbridge has become a haven for the elderly who can afford to live here, often those who move to the Northwest when their children or grandchildren relocate to Seattle. Our slower pace of life and self-contained community offer a nice counterpoint to the big city. Junior law partners can bring their kids to visit Grandma in her condo in the country, and if they time it right, visit the harvest fair and pet a goat.

But Grandma would be a lot healthier if she got out and pulled a few weeds. She might even be able to drop some of her medications if she was growing and eating fresh food. Most of the farmers, grocers, food activists, gardeners, and others I have talked to so far are the children or grandchildren of people who worked hard all their lives, mostly growing, catching, or cultivating food. Spending their last years in a sealed, air-conditioned condo would not have been their idea of a good time.

In 2009, Sue Cooley purchased a valuable corner lot downtown and had it turned into a community garden with raised beds, now called Red Pine Park. The lot had once been the site of Junko Harui's house—Junko was the force behind the Bainbridge Gardens nursery. The property, when it went up for sale, came with a map of the beautiful plants and trees already on the land, including a small orchard. The neighbors tried and failed to raise enough money to purchase the property, which was otherwise slated to become another set of condos and a small hotel. Cooley finally stepped up and bought it herself. Although she is now in her nineties and too frail to garden actively, the park is located where she can watch the activities from her window.

Red Pine Park now belongs to and is managed by the Bainbridge Island Parks and Recreation District. I've got my name on a waiting list, along with about ten other people, for when a plot opens up. It is just a few blocks from my house, and I could walk there to garden. It is also located where the population is denser, and probably offers more opportunities to work in conjunction with others than does the Rock Farm.

WALKING THE FOOD FOREST

When I first heard about it, I thought something called a "food forest" might also be a way to integrate these two parts of our system—the elderly, and the all-ages need for food and physical activity. But nothing is ever simple.

What is a food forest? It is land on which edible plants will grow in an environment using the fewest artificial resources, while attracting and supporting the insects, animals, and people that enhance its well-being.

I first heard of the food forest idea from a Canadian friend who posted a story about Todmorden, England, a town that landscaped its public space in edible plants. Seattle, our big sister across the Sound, has also broken ground on a food forest on Beacon Hill.

At a workshop offered by Chuck Estin and Demi Rasmussen, I learned that Bainbridge might get its own food forest, on the 13.5

acres that was once the M&E Tree Farm. The property had been donated to the city in 2002, with the restrictions that the land could not be used for commercial purposes, nor could new buildings be erected (two small shacks already stand on the land). Turning the land into a food forest, to be managed by Friends of the Farms, would meet all of the stipulations. In addition, the property is adjacent to the publicly owned Day Road Farm complex of vineyards and farms, so food forest volunteers could take advantage of the farm implements and help already available at that site.

After the workshop, I visited the proposed site. The terrain slopes south and west, and is bisected by a stream originating at ponds created by the Suyematsu family to serve their properties, all now part of Day Road Farm. The stream is joined by several natural seeps and enters a beautiful ravine, lush and cool with ferns. There are several points at which water could be diverted to irrigate fields.

Generally speaking, an acre of land takes thirty-five thousand gallons of water to cultivate, according to Estin. There are a variety of methods for getting that water to plants, including *hugelkultur*, as practiced and taught by Austrian Sepp Holzer. This consists of shaping small terraces and ponds to collect and distribute water evenly. It sounds a lot like the *trincheras* used by Pueblo cultures all over the Southwest, many of which can still be seen today.

The plants in a food forest, according to Estes, are grouped by guild—meaning, their specialties: Do they attract bees? Fix nitrogen? Inhibit grass? Each grouping of plants, whether in a keystone planting that faces south to accumulate sunlight in its center, or a raised bed that can compost at its foot, needs to include plants from the various guilds, just like a small community of people. Tall fruit- and nut-bearing trees need to be on the north side, so as not to shade out smaller berry bushes and vegetables.

Plantings also need to attract humans to weed and harvest them, and insects to pollinate them. In other words, humans are just another organism to a food forest, one that needs to be integrated into the needs of the forest. This is an entirely different approach to growing food than endless rows planted by machine, doused with chemicals, harvested, and processed. It is also different than using even a small tractor or plow on fields of monocultural plants.

What good is a food forest to people? It is a public space where those from all walks of life can see where their food comes from, and take an active part in it if they choose. The food is available to all whether they help grow it or not. The philosophy behind it is that of abundance, rather than scarcity. I can see the deer now, trying to figure out the quickest route to the food forest. But maybe they, too, are part of the attraction.

Indian Country News did a piece about the Seattle food forest, which is in the Beacon Hill neighborhood, and emphasized that the food forest could be a congregating area for ethnic communities. It quoted Glen Herlihy, a member of the Friends of the Beacon Food Forest committee, saying that in addition to Native people, "there's Vietnamese, Chinese, Filipinos, and Africans in the area. The Beacon Food Forest is a place where all ages and ethnicities can meet."

While this seemed like an intriguing idea, the project on Bainbridge stalled out. The person who had taken the lead has moved, I heard, to Hawai'i.

The food forest in Seattle, meanwhile, has blazed ahead with staff and financial support from the city and local volunteers. It takes a variety of factors to make a project like this work.

One, of course, is a dedicated leader, like Anita Rockefeller at the Rock Farm. Another might be proximity to a population center. In Todmorden, the town center itself was landscaped with edible plants. I saw Brian MacWhorter and his daughter putting edible plants around our commons two years ago, but the plants were not maintained by city staff, or anyone else. The food forest on Bainbridge would have been located about three miles from the town center, and right now, because of traffic patterns, it is almost impossible to walk there. I know, I tried it.

Another factor is that the Beacon Hill Food Forest is located in an area where the culturally diverse residents—including farmers relocated from Vietnam and Cambodia—have been subsistence farming for years, are used to the vagaries of urban farming, and understand that they will benefit directly from the food that grows there. Many of them have been selling their produce at farmers markets in Seattle for over twenty years. They see access to the land in terms of how much food it can produce, as opposed to how many houses will fit on it.

For now on Bainbridge, Friends of the Farms has put out a request for proposals for use of the 13.5 acres that had been slated for the food forest. One of the farmers on the island will probably add it to his or her domain of lands under more traditional cultivation. Now, food activists are concentrating their efforts on a new piece of land that is slated for development just north of downtown. It is a large, privately owned property that will be partially developed for housing, and is a natural area for a community garden of some sort. As far as I am concerned, each new housing development should have land set aside for growing food. This will afford people outdoor exercise, a practical way to socialize, and a guarantee that we won't be completely dependent on the grocery store if we needed to grow more of our own food.

As it happens, the newly renovated Town & Country has planted apple trees and rhubarb in raised beds along the west side of the building. Customers and passersby are free to collect the apples and rhubarb. I like the idea of customers picking apples for a pie, then going inside the store to buy the ingredients for crust and the rest of their dinner. This is yet another way of giving back to the community at large.

WHAT COMES IN, MUST GO OUT

Oddly, for a society that is currently predicated on scarcity, we throw away an abundance of food. Some communities have gleaning programs to collect the fruit from neglected trees and share it with the community. On Bainbridge, a program called Zero Waste, an initiative of Sustainable Bainbridge, collects the waste generated at public events, recycling paper and plastic to their proper places, and channeling the food scraps back into compost. As you can imagine, getting rid of waste on an island is an important issue. Fortunately, recycling is profitable enough (and required by state law) to keep at least one business owner going, and there are related businesses that channel their waste back into the composting cycle, including Town & Country. The island's Zero Waste program is so successful, it served as the model for the recycling program used at the Super Bowl held in Phoenix in 2015, which in turn kicked off a long-range recycling program for that city.

What else can we do together? Besides the many people working on the state-mandated comprehensive plan, there are plenty of committees that work on the day-to-day needs of Bainbridge Island. A community defined by the fact that it is surrounded by water has entirely different needs than a mainland community. We need to acknowledge, more than mainland dwellers, that we live here by choice, and must strike a balance with nature that doesn't necessarily pay us back in monetary compensation.

"Native people," says Roger Fernandes (Lower Elwha Band of the S'Klallam) in *Feeding the People,* "see that they live in a world where everything is given to them with love, generosity and abundance. They say to themselves, 'How can we live a life that is any different? We too must give with love, generosity and abundance.' So even the central cultural tenet derives itself from the generosity of the salmon."

Reexamining our housing options might be a place to start. There has been a lot of high-density development near downtown, in accordance with the state plan for growth, but it is definitely changing the quality of life in our downtown area as residents watch the green space around them disappear.

Density is good in some respects, in that it is less expensive and more energy efficient to deliver power, water, and sewage services to closely packed housing. But even since I moved here, the long walks next to green and shady patches have been reduced by about half. The community needs to remind the state that Bainbridge Island is exceptional, but also needs to demonstrate a commitment to making the island work as population and development continue to grow. Tempting as it is for city governments to allow developers to rapidly change the land, generating tax revenues in the process, overdeveloping the island might just kill the golden goose.

Every yard of concrete that is poured reduces the amount of water the land absorbs back into the aquifer. Every tree that is cut down removes habitat for birds, insects, and other animals that we might really miss one day. Farmers might be pitted against the municipal water supply if things are not carefully managed. It is a precarious balancing act that all the citizens have a role in maintaining, from the grade school student discovering the origins of potatoes in the dirt, to builders who invest millions in the future, and future livability, of the island.

Much remains to be done, but a growing awareness that the place we live in is fragile and finite is prompting some innovative thinking. Now if we can just get some of these ideas implemented. Including people with expertise as arborists and agriculturalists on the city staff might save a lot of public time and money in monitoring the use of land on our island, and maintaining the balance of trees, buildings, farms, and public land, both developed and undeveloped.

If we needed to become less reliant on outside food sources, we might have to get over a wheat-centric diet, and return to the sources of carbohydrates that naturally grow close to home, like camas root. This would involve restoring the prairies that were once cleared and maintained by Native groups. In the meantime, farmers and Extension agents continue to experiment with wheat, grape, and even tea varieties that might offer us a way to assuage our joneses for toast, wine, and caffeine.

We might consider a partnership with the Suquamish to manage an indigenous garden, offering a way for the tribe to expand its existing programs, and for other islanders to learn how to restore and manage land in ways that have survived the ages. It might be an opportunity to bring back some of the plants and trees that have been displaced, such as the native Pacific Northwest crabapple (*Malus fusca,* from which many domestic varieties of apples are descended), filberts, and even a camas prairie if the conditions are right on some part of the island. People with experience canning or preserving foods in other ways could show schoolchildren how to do it safely and efficiently.

An important idea for Bainbridge to consider is the commons. This is an innate manifestation of the gift, in that it provides a place where we publicly exchange goods and services in a way that we all acknowledge as having value. We understand that we hold access to our aquifer in common. Although there are private water systems at the south and north ends of the island, it is ridiculous to manage them as though the water is not derived from the same source. But we also hold the air, the saltwater, and the land underneath the saltwater in common.

If we set aside land on which to grow a permanent forest, we could protect air and water quality as well. In addition, many plants and animals only grow under old-growth conditions, so it is possible that we could start one with some of the trees that are left on Bainbridge. As the Suquamish understand, very large, old trees can be harvested for wood and bark, food and basketry without killing them. While Suquamish currently keeps a few gardens close to the tribal offices, they once groomed the surrounding meadows and forests for maximum yield—berry bushes were trimmed, meadows were kept open with controlled burns, and clam gardens were built and regularly harvested for the health and proliferation of the clams.

All this makes me think of Native understandings of the gift. In Coll-Peter Thrush's article "The Lushootseed Peoples of Puget Sound Country," he says that "*Sgwigwi* is a word that simply means 'inviting,' and corresponds to the more familiar term potlatch, in which wealthy people displayed their social status by sharing their wealth with others." Taking a *sgwigwi* approach might spare us a lot of heartache in an uncertain future.

OUR OWN MEDICINE

When I look at the population of the island, I see a lot of elderly people. Those who can afford it move to be near, but not too near, their children and grandchildren in Seattle. Others join their adult children for their final years, and reside in supported living. This seems to be growing as a business on the island, and a new Alzheimer's facility was recently built for specialized care.

The average age of a farmer in the United States is sixty-two. That said, at the farmers market I often see farmers in their twenties apprenticed or otherwise associated with established farmers—I hope they are prepared to step in and continue the tradition. Every single one of the farm interns with whom I have spoken has a college degree, so they take this seriously. They, and their parents who put them through school, have invested in agriculture as a viable way to make a living.

For the young farmers and interns I talked to, the goal is to intern for low or no wages until they can either raise the capital, partner with others, or otherwise gain the means to own farmland on a small scale, and continue to work the land. Bainbridge is expensive, so most leave the island after their internships. But if the city continues to acquire and protect farmland, there will be a greater chance that they can find a viable way to stay and we can keep the knowledge and experience invested in them.

Back to the elderly. One of the quirks of our current health care system is the preponderance of drugs that are prescribed to older people, often by physicians who don't check to see what other medications have already been prescribed. This can lead to bad, even fatal, drug interactions.

In my village, as my great-grandmother might have said, we used *te de canela* and *te de yerba buena*—cinnamon and mint tea—to soothe aches and pains. I am pretty sure that the indigenous women in this area have similar remedies for the small things in life. There seems to be a berry for everything, so perhaps there is a berry for the small aches or pains felt by older people.

Another problem is that the elderly, no matter how advanced in age and condition, are treated the same as younger people when it comes to emergency treatment and resuscitation. In many cases, the elderly patient being brought back from the edge has a history that, if reviewed, would show a gradual decline toward an inevitable conclusion. Many people in that situation just wants to be comfortable and near loved ones until that moment.

Others, of course, are vigorous and active until the last moment, which is what we all want, and Bainbridge offers a semi-active lifestyle for walkers, sailors, bicyclists, memoirists, and tennis players. There is an art museum and a children's museum, a small performing arts center, and numerous classes on every subject you can imagine.

Where am I going with this? I think there is a middle way. We can treat the elderly with respect as we ease them into the transition to death. We can also prolong their lives by keeping them active and engaged. We can do this without the tremendous pull on our overloaded health care system.

My father's transition was difficult. He had signed a living will, but as he entered his early nineties, suffered the sorts of things one expects: a heart attack, a fall, another fall. He received a pacemaker, a hip replacement, and another hip replacement.

My father loved life, but he wanted to remain independent. If he could walk without a walker again, he reasoned, he could continue his life without being totally dependent on others. He lived to the age of ninety-four. With the second fall, he landed back in Harborview hospital, and against his wishes, had a feeding tube inserted down his throat. He pulled it out.

I think a cup of tea would have suited him a lot better.

Now that it is the twenty-first century, I hope that the Affordable Care Act provides what my father would have wanted—a system that screens out unnecessary procedures, that listens to patients, that allows those who are comfortable with it to pursue traditional medicines. I hope it will allow traditional healers to participate in the official health care system, and maybe even influence the doctors and nurses who have dedicated themselves to helping us live better lives. We need to practice preventive medicine, and be able to let go when the time comes, with grace and dignity. Even on an island, we could implement a more sustainable version of health care, in which medical costs are kept reasonable by treating patients as individuals, rather than as statistics.

While attending the Our Food Is Our Medicine conference at Suquamish, I was able to sit down in a quiet corner with elder Ed Carriere and ask him about his relationship to the land and sea.

Ed is a member of the Suquamish tribe and lives in what is now the town of Indianola. He inherited a private land trust, separate from that of the tribe. Ed has woven baskets for over fifty years, taking it up at the age of fifteen when his great-grandmother said that her hands had grown too weak. Born and raised on the Port Madison Reservation at Indianola, he learned to make clam baskets from his great-grandmother, who raised him. She was the daughter of the last chief of the Suquamish tribe. Ed is now an expert weaver of several styles of baskets, including twined cedar bark and cattail baskets, and coiled root baskets. Weaving in this culture is very specialized, with specific materials that must be gathered for each type of use, such as clamming, clothing, and carrying.

When I met Ed, he was wearing a traditional conical hat he had made, with a fishing lure dangling off the back that danced like a whirligig. I asked him a few questions I had asked other Suquamish elders, as a way to get perspective on our relationship with food on Bainbridge today.

Did you grow up harvesting food?

"Yes. For example, horse clams. Our favorite way to eat them was roasting them over a bonfire on the end of a stick. Absolutely delicious. We cut it into strips. It is referred to as 'Indian candy.' Very nourishing. It was one of our most important foods, and people came clear from Idaho to trade for it. Once it was dried, we put it on a string or in baskets, and they were good as long as they did not get damp."

Here was the connection I had heard about, the inland people coming out to meet the coastal people for trade. When people trade food, they also trade stories, dance, find marriage partners, and exchange knowledge about the land.

"We used to fish for bottom fish: sand dabs, sole, mullheads, and chicken halibut.

"Once I caught a big skatefish. My great-grandma said to cut off the outer part. I brought it to her, and she fixed a wonderful meal, boiled in a stew. Otherwise, we ate crab, salmon, rock cod, lingcod, French sole, and striped flounder.

"I know when I eat bottom fish, crabs, and clams, a lot more energy is coming through those foods. There is nothing like the taste. It is awesome.

"Little huckleberries were our favorite berries. I've been picking berries ever since I was old enough to walk. We canned them or ate them fresh. We ate native blackberries and dried them, kept them in dried form. Salmonberry you have to eat fresh. They are red or orange, depending on the DNA of the plant. We ate black caps that tasted like raspberries. Thimbleberries. All those berries were collected, used fresh or eaten. Little wild blueberries grow close to the ground. A good patch was kept secret."

"We ate a few mushrooms. I didn't learn about mushrooms until later. I've picked chanterelles."

Could we live off food grown on Bainbridge Island? I asked.

"I think we could. I used to grow a huge garden every year, living off the beach and Puget Sound. I used to hunt ducks. I ate every kind of duck in Puget Sound. You clean it and make a big pot of duck stew with vegetables, dumplings, potatoes, and carrots. You can only get so much from a garden. We would need to hunt deer.

"We might run short in winter. I leave my potatoes in the ground in the winter. But if they are close to the surface, they will rot."

For certain foods, he told me, people from the Suquamish area traveled west. This depended on the weather and the season, of course, so they had to track the storms. Snowfall can be sudden and deep in the Olympics.

"I used to travel with my family in the summer to the Olympic Mountains for blueberries. We would camp for a few days. I was always fishing in the Olympic Mountains. I fished for trout. We would go out to the coast, Neah Bay, to gather stuff like razor clams."

I asked if he traded for the materials he uses in his weaving. "All my basket-weaving materials come from the coast: spruce root, bear grass (coastal mountains), and sweetgrass. I don't trade for anything. Once in awhile I traded cedar bark for other things when I had more than I needed."

Do you have anything else to say about food in the area? I asked.

"I think they ought to try to live on the traditional foods around here, rather than food from the store. There used to be a Canadian radio program called *The Store outside Your Door.*

"I still dig geoducks—it's a sport. I started a clam farm at my house. I planted a bunch of little ones. They all lived and got big. I'm going to do it again, because my son is working for the geoduck farm at Suquamish Seafoods. It is one of our main sources of income. Japan will buy them all. We can't satisfy the market."

Is it okay, I asked, that the markets are so far away, as far as Japan?

"It's okay, because the beds need to be harvested. So it's good. They keep the beds harvested, keep the new clams coming in. The more harvesting there is, the more clams.

"I learned to hate clamming as a teenager. I now realize it is because all the beaches had been dug over and over. It's like the timber industry. Trees grow in one third the time they used to. In the future, we will grow more than we can harvest.

"All of Indianola was trust land. I own the last waterfront, 110 feet. My trust land is in my own name. It is part of the Suquamish Reservation, but it's my land."

Ed is just one example, but I have met other Suquamish elders who actively teach their precious skills at weaving, carving, or gathering native plants for food and shelter. Along with the salmon, the cedar tree acts as a primary resource, providing materials for shelter and tools. Everything from canoes to sewing needles comes from the cedar tree. The gift is celebrated in many ways, and the seasons act as the great wheel of time upon which their lives are played out. My father would have liked Ed Carriere for his continued, bright interest in the world, and above all, for the resourcefulness with which he transforms the materials provided by the land around him into personalized, useful objects.

I would like to see people like my father transformed from the frail and burdensome (he thought) elderly, to the respected elders of their communities. This is not to say that the Suquamish and other local tribes are doing everything right. But the recent infusion of cash provided by the casino—cash that is free of federal government restrictions and paperwork—has allowed the tribal government to begin actively working to improve the lot of its residents and members in a timely and culturally appropriate manner. The Suquamish offer an example of what we can do together to preserve and improve the land while offering the people who live on it an active way to engage with it and each other. In the end, taking responsibility for the production and consumption of our food offers the best way to do this.

RENEWAL

Renewal might be the part of the puzzle that we have not paid enough attention to. All things mortal must die, but in dying, they provide a beginning for the next generation. One of my ancestors in Mexico, Manuel Acuña, wrote a famous poem in the 1800s that addresses our place in this cycle. Called "Before a Corpse," it is an elegy that reminds us that we are part of a greater cycle, and that once we are subsumed into the earth, we might yet return as flowers, wheat, or even bread for our loved ones. It is an ancient idea that we must be reminded of each generation, each cycle of the seasons. But if dead things are left to fester, they can engender rot, disease, and infection. Many of our modern-day ills are due to the fact that we have dumped waste, poisonous matter, back into our water and food streams. We are spending billions of dollars trying to right these wrongs, but we do much less to prevent them from continuing.

Suquamish has begun not only to recover its deep knowledge, but also to pass it on to its young people. At the Our Food Is Our Medicine conference, artist Kevin Paul (Swinomish) noted that if we lose part of the seafood spiral, we lose part of the knowledge that goes with it. In Puget Sound, a yearly canoe journey, revived in 1989 by master carvers and canoers, has proven to be a way to reclaim the young people of the tribe, everyone working in unison to pull off one of the biggest *sgwigwi* activities you can imagine. Young people build the boats, set the itinerary, and make plans to visit tribes up and down the coast. The paddlers are called "pullers," and upon arriving at their destination, the journeyers formally ask permission from the host to come ashore. Songs, dances, food, and gifts are then exchanged.

Much like the pilgrimage journeys of Europe, each individual on a canoe journey is there for a specific reason—it is a life-changing experience. Some participate as part of a coming-of-age spirit quest, while others are there to acknowledge an anniversary of sobriety. It is an opportunity for the elders to share songs and customs with the young, and for members of different tribes to get to know each other.

Thousands of hours and tons of food and supplies are donated by whites and Indians alike. One woman I know volunteered to help, and ended up making breakfast for three hundred people. All this is a manifestation of the gift. One of the lessons of the canoe journey is that we are all in this canoe together.

Only recently did I realize that the long-distance runs organized by members of the Opata nation are the equivalent of these canoe journeys, bringing people together for long periods of time, and bringing them back in contact with the earth.

The Powel property, located very close to Haleets, is a showcase example of a successful restoration. The property is still privately owned, but the family opted to partner in the restoration with Washington Sea Grant on the project, with Jim Brennan, a marine habitat specialist, serving as their advisor. I took a tour of the property one rainy day. The first step in the restoration had been the removal of a bulkhead constructed from ship ballast—it had probably brought with it some of the invasives found along most shorelines today, including anemones, barnacles, and arthropods. A swimming pool fed by a stream was opened back up to the tidal flow—Olympic oysters favor the brackish water that results. Saltbush, pickleweed, wild rose, and snowberries now hold their own on the upper reaches of the shoreline. In and close to the water, yellow verbena, gumweed, and of course, eelgrass provide shelter for insects, fry, and other aquatic animals.

Where does all this beauty come from? The fields, the trees, the insects making their way from plant to plant, like villagers or traders traveling between towns. At the Powel property, the eye can follow the natural progression of plants from the top of the hill, where the house is located, down to and right into the water.

Haleets

The male hovering over her, stroking her body with his fins, the female clears out a clean patch of sand and lays her eggs. This nest is called a redd. The male then sprays out his sperm across the bed of eggs, fertilizing them.

They are almost finished. The pair is exhausted. As they cover the eggs with gravel, a great weariness overcomes them. They can no longer strive, leap, and fight against current and predator. The fish fall prey to bears, to fishermen, to nets and hooks and claws and teeth. They surrender their bodies, secure in the innate knowledge that they have almost completed their part in this world.

All that is left is to impart their nutrients to the biological beings around them. In some communities, humans carry the salmon queen, the first returning salmon of the season, with great ceremony on a bed of cedar bows. They thank her for returning, for bringing with her the ingredients to sustain life for another season. As her eyes dull and the dazzle of her scales begins to fade, the queen is honored with prayers and song. As the drums increase in volume, the voices of the singers soar. In other communities, the return of the first salmon is the occasion for a blessing of the boats by the clergy. There is thanksgiving and feasting. Everywhere, even if silently over a cup of coffee by a fisherman who is not sure what he believes, there is prayer.

Haleets is one people's attempt to document the sense and beauty of the world. I see stories being passed from mouth to ear, grandmother and grandfather to daughters and sons and grandchildren. I see cedar planks carefully cut from standing, living trees for canoes, the salal and blackberries cleared with fire, the camas prairie expanding the following spring as sunlight reaches the damp earth. Fry of many fish species nestle under the roots of a fallen tree, darting out to capture small insects that land on the surface, bits of matter that fall from the plants above, worms and pupae and nymphs and eggs swirling in a glorious spiral of organic matter, settling at last to the bottom to provide a rich bed for the next season of growth and renewal.

Potlatch, *sgwigwi*, is symbolic of the gift given by nature to humans—the gift of food, salmon in particular, which goes away, then comes back again to offer itself to us. It represents an understanding that the gift manifests itself in cooperation, that if we work together, we can make many things happen.

All around, up every river, stream, creek, and trickle that has not been ruined, or has been restored, the salmon queen's subjects return to their places of birth—to wash ashore, be carried off piecemeal by crows and bears, coyotes and otters, broken down by mice and insects, soaking the earth with nutrients, until nothing is left but the good earth upon which we all live out our mortal lives.

What human can say that her life has accomplished as much as one salmon returning from such a long journey?

Brendan McGill of Hitchcock Restaurant wields a pastry cone.

−7−

Otaku

IT HAS BEEN ABOUT FOUR YEARS since I dropped nearly all meat from my diet. We eat fish and shellfish at home, and whatever we want when we eat out, but I never choose beef, and for the most part, neither does my husband. I have added some eggs and butter back into my diet, and I eat lots of kale from the garden.

I have my cholesterol level tested again. It is at 220, and my new doctor, a naturopath, says that is fine. She adds that 240 used to be considered the top of the normal range, but pressure from pharmaceutical companies caused the medical establishment to lower it to 200. The lowest I achieved while on medication was 215, and I felt terrible. I now take no prescription medications.

I've also dropped about eight pounds of weight without thinking about it too much. It was probably chicken fat! Since I cannot test my cholesterol on my own, I figured that keeping my weight down was the easiest way to control it.

I've returned to a yoga practice of two or three hours a week. "Just breathe," says my doctor, who also practices yoga.

And so, I breathe. It is calming. It teaches me to focus not only on the places in my body that hurt, but to set my intent for each day, each week, each lifetime of work. I am still thin in the arms and squishy in the middle, but there is no reason to think I will not live a long life. Long enough for me, anyway—I have no desire to live indefinitely, or to have my body outlive a useful mind.

Raising a vegetable garden keeps me outdoors during the warmer months, makes me conscious of the movement of weather and seasons, the placement of the sun in the sky, the warmth on my face. I notice the tiny bugs that feast on the same plants I hope to consume. I crumble the dirt between my fingers and marvel at the sheer rockiness of this place. I am still on the waiting list for a plot closer to my house, at Red Pine Park; I would feel better about the whole idea if I could walk to my garden, rather than drive.

Our son has grown up and lives on his own. He has learned to cook and frequents the farmers markets close to his apartment. Ben moved back to the Seattle area from the San Francisco Bay Area, after forming a company with his friends that allows him to work from anywhere in the world, at least as long as the Internet is available. Land and rent are scarce and expensive in the Bay Area, even more restricted than in our water-filled region. California has suffered drought for several years now, and we cannot count on it to fulfill the fresh food needs of most of North America.

I'm not sure Bainbridge will ever overcome the pollution problems of our waterways. The EPA has decided to inject wet cement into the ground in order to keep the creosote at the bottom of Eagle Harbor in place. This will cost between seventy-one and eighty-one million dollars and take about ten years to complete. It will be many years before we can safely eat shellfish from the harbor, more generations before people like the Rapadas, Nakatas, Loveritches, and Selfors can sustain themselves on food from it.

Rockfish are slowly making a comeback. More enlightened homeowners are restoring their shorelines and planting clams and oysters. Within months of the removal of the last dam on the Elwha River, about two hours west of here, candlefish appeared. How did they get the memo? We share the island with a variety of wildlife that have managed to adapt to our presence, as well as a few, like pheasants, that were deliberately brought along for the ride. We breathe some of the best air and drink some of the tastiest water I have experienced in the world. None of this is to be taken lightly. The food we enjoy is pretty amazing as well. Here is a hypothetical dinner that we could sit down and eat sometime, probably in the fall when all of these ingredients are available fresh, just off the vine, out of the water, out of the cellar, picked from the garden. I've used the heading *otaku*, a Japanese term for people with obsessive interests because, by now, you probably figure I am obsessed with what around me is edible. Well, sort of.

Think of this as the ultimate tasting menu, fit for our great-grandchildren on Bainbridge Island.

Menu for Otaku

Water

Wine

Shellfish

Salmon

Potatoes

Carrots

Blackberries

Apples

Honey

Coffee

MIX SOME WATER WITH THE WINE

Let's start with water and wine.

When I visited with Gerard and Joanne Bentryn of Bainbridge Vineyards, it was clear that water was a topic that had been on their minds. As Bainbridge fills up with people, and developers are allowed to build without regard to the availability of water, our water table is dropping.

Already, Whidbey Island and San Juan Island, both north of us, are converting saltwater to freshwater to fill their needs. This process generates a residue of extremely salty water that is dumped back into Puget Sound, poisoning the shallows where sensitive shellfish are trying to stay alive. Desalination roughly doubles the amount of salt in the water.

"Desalination of seawater is often touted as a solution to water shortages," says a study commissioned by the League of Women Voters on Whidbey Island. "However, present systems require large amounts of energy and produce many gallons of concentrated brine for every gallon of fresh water produced. Direct return of concentrated brine to the Sound may be toxic to sea and shore life, and on land it may need to be treated as hazardous waste. Desalination does not appear to be a viable solution to Whidbey Island's water needs until more energy efficient and safe methods of desalination are developed."

When the aquifers are allowed to refresh naturally, rainwater is captured by trees, groundcover, soil, and sand. The more immediate threat to the water quality on Bainbridge is infiltration of saltwater, which happens when the amount of freshwater in the aquifer is lowered to the point that it does not exert enough outward pressure to keep saltwater out.

The Bentryns figure that before any other resources run out on Bainbridge, the lack of water will do us in.

Gerard is not known for keeping his opinions to himself. He tells me that he was a water resource planner for the Army Corps of Engineers before he began "working on his knees" as a farmer. He was stationed overseas in the service and was intrigued by meeting German farmers who served the produce of their land and drank the fruit of their own vines. Gerard describes most of the farms on Bainbridge as hobby farms. "Making your living growing stuff is not popular," he says. "Putting on a bib overall and going to Bay Hay and Feed to talk about it is popular." The term "hobby farm" could be applied to some of the more recently established farms, in that the owners made their money in other businesses, and have now turned their attention to farming. It also embraces secondary businesses that encourage agricultural tourism, such as cooking classes, and that process some of their own food, which increases the price that farmers can demand for their products. As is always true of farming, the real test will be in times of scarcity—low yields, low prices, blight, or water shortages. "The difficulty is, we have a precious resource in this farm," he says.

When my family moved to the island, Bainbridge Vineyards was a popular tourist destination. There were always people walking up our street, which parallels the highway, looking for it. But Gerard claims the only money he ever made was in selling the land for development.

When I ask Gerard about the future of Bainbridge Island, if we could support our current population on food grown on the island, he referred me to a booklet published in 1993 by the University of British Columbia Press, *How Big Is Our Ecological Footprint?*. It breaks out how much land it takes to support each person. "On reasonably good soil," it says, one acre will support one person.

There are big differences within that estimate. If all the people are vegetarian, one acre will support five people—that is, five times as many. Raising a modest amount of meat brings the ratio to three people per acre, one third as many. This matches with what the Rapadas initially told me, that each of them grew up on a five-acre farm supplemented by hunting, fishing, and two bags of rice from Seattle's International District each year. It's remarkable to think about now.

"Thirty percent of the land on Bainbridge is roof and driveway," says Gerard. "We also have bad soil, but can get around that if we have enough water."

Gerard told me that he has looked at aerial photos of the Day Road property. The eastern half of it is on glacial till, scraped clean of most of its soil. The hardpan takes lots of water. Akio Suyematsu, said Gerard, created soil there by scraping the hardpan over and over again with the antique tractors he maintained and adding manure to the results.

The western half of the property, by the highway, is where the glaciers melted, and the ice dam dumped all of the soil. This is where Karen Selvar grows corn and pumpkins, as well as other produce. These two conditions exist within yards of each other. This explains the poor soil at my house, which is directly south of the hardpan Akio Suyematsu worked every day.

Gerard was probably the first person to use the word *terroir* when talking about Bainbridge Island. When asked to describe it, he ticks off three things on his fingers: "dirt, climate, people."

"It's the cultural history of a place. Just the choice of what to plant; the soil, does it fit the climate? And what is everyone else doing? What is the history of food in the area?"

Gerard is irked by the local restaurants. "Locovore restaurants buy a token amount of vegetables, but not local wine. Our wine goes with local food."

The definition of local wine has gotten a bit tricky on Bainbridge. In recent years, a dozen or so wineries have sprouted like blackberry vines. All buy their grapes in Eastern Washington, but process them here on the island. It's a local industry, but is it local wine? Not according to Gerard.

Gerard is warmed up now. "The other word that bothers me is *organic*. The government inspectors don't have the budget to check whether or not food is grown organically. We use copper posts with our vines, so it's not considered organic." Really, buying organic food or wine is a matter of trust between consumers and farmers, he insists.

Joanne joined us at this point, and Gerard directed my question, could we support ourselves, to her. According to the ratios given in *How Big Is Our Ecological Footprint?*, there is no way that we could support our population. "Water will limit what we can do," adds Joanne.

"I can see people doing light farming [on their own], but others demanding more," of the existing farmers, says Joanne, if we had to support our population by growing our own food.

I ask what the island will look like one hundred years from now.

In one hundred years, the Bentryns say, there will be fewer people here. Fuel for cars will all run out in forty years, eliminating the commuters who drive onto the ferries every day to work in the Seattle metro area. Fuel might not run out in forty years, I think, but there might well be other reasons we will no longer use fossil fuels.

Economic collapse will ensue, says Gerard. After the stores are cleaned out, people will look to the farmers to feed them directly. But the farms themselves will be in trouble, he says, since farmers like Brian MacWhorter are "heavily indebted to gasoline and diesel fuel. Little farms have no idea how to produce more calories than they consume." According to "Do the Math," a site run by the physics department at the University of California, San Diego, one gallon of gasoline equals thirty-one thousand calories—but I don't know where to go from there. Apparently farmers like to do these conversions, and it must make sense to do so, from their point of view. An active young man can burn up to three thousand calories a day, so it seems to me that a gallon of gasoline offers quite a bit of energy, even if converted through machines and plants. So we will definitely seek alternative sources if gasoline is not available.

In one hundred years, no one will know what to do, says Joanne, with the skyscrapers in Seattle. The Bentryns visited South Africa recently, where tall office buildings sit empty for lack of water. Johannesburg suffers water shortages, power outages, and contamination of the existing water by runoff from the mines.

But water is the main thing, says Gerard. In one hundred years we will have selective water outages first, then the wells will run dry. Or rather, they will fill with saltwater.

Given those dire predictions, the first thing on the tasting menu is a tall glass of cool water pumped from the ground and treated by the city. If this water has any discernable taste, it is slightly sweet, pleasant. It's the second-best water I ever tasted—after the water in Paonia, and that came directly from nearby snowmelt.

This precious glass of water will be followed by a Bainbridge Vineyards wine made from grapes grown on the island. Let's say Ferryboat White, the bottle they have marketed the longest, an oak-aged white wine, a dry blend of Pinot Gris, Madeleine Angevine, Siegerrebe, and Müller-Thurgau grapes. The finish is sweet.

THE TABLE IS SET

Next, geoducks we've gathered ourselves.

Neil threw himself full-length on the sand, reached into the muddy hole, and grabbed the geoduck by the neck. I was sure he would make me pull up the next one. One winter, Neil Johannsen and Hilary Hilscher, our next-door neighbors, had invited my husband and me over to celebrate the New Year. Like most events on the island, this was a potluck. They served an amazing clam chowder that Neil had made. It turned out to be geoduck chowder, with lots of pepper. The flavor was richer than regular clam chowder, meatier, a perfect antidote to our dark, damp winters. When Neil sat down, I complimented him on the soup.

"Doesn't this make you want to go out and hunt for food?" he asked.

"No . . ." I answered. Was this a trick question?

"Don't you just want to go out and hunt and fish and gather, to stalk your prey and bring it home?"

"Not really," I answered carefully. "After all, we live next door to you. Why should I hunt and gather when you do such a good job of it?" We even got the occasional chard or zucchini from their garden.

This did not satisfy Neil. He got up and went across the room, where I heard him ask my husband the same question. And my husband gave him, more or less, the same answer. I'm sure he did not hear our earlier exchange.

But many people, it seems, do feel this way. As Nabhan says in

Coming Home to Eat, "there is something primordial about the pursuit of these foods and medicines in their natural habitats. It is an
elixir for the soul, this drinking in of forest and marshland."

The geoduck (pronounced *gooeyduck*) is the hardest local clam
to dig. It has a long, thick neck and, using its foot, can dig its shell
three to five feet deep into the sand and extend its siphon up to the
surface. I had seen them dug once before, during a low tide at Golden
Gardens Park in Seattle. The digger shoveled as quickly as he could,
getting in the hole as he went, until he was completely covered in
mud, sand, and slimy seaweed. Somehow, I didn't think this was
going to happen to me. But when Neil invited me out on a geoduck
expedition, I took a towel just in case. Mostly, I just hoped that it
didn't rain.

All year, Neil had bragged about the special place where he found
geoduck, someplace no one else dug. He made a mystery of it, but
said he was willing to share it with me. Foraging and harvesting
wild foods are a big deal around here, so I decided to take him up on
the offer. When I e-mailed the day before to see what time to meet,
he seemed reluctant, although he had already instructed me to go
to Wal-Mart and get a shellfish license. Instead, I went online and
bought a license for shellfish and seaweed for twelve dollars. It was
good for ten days. There are all these rules around harvesting crabs
and shellfish in Washington State, and a lot of disputes about who
owns the rights to the tidelands and their products. The principal
players are the state and federal governments, Indian tribes, and
private landowners. In the case of geoducks, there are high stakes
commercial interests as well. I guessed that Neil's secret geoduck
stash was on public land, if I needed a license. I was right, sort of.

Neil loaded a spade and a bucket and two pairs of waterproof
gloves into his Ford Explorer. He ate a muffin and drank coffee as
he drove.

It turned out I was familiar with this park, which was a typical
Northwest shore: a long steep trail through deep woods that broke
out onto the open beach. Because you can't really see ahead, the end

of the forest trail is always a surprise. You feel as though you are in the middle of the woods, then you are standing and blinking at the open sky.

Neil grew up on a farm in Petaluma, California, the fourth generation on that land. His parents, he said as we drove, were commercial farmers, raising poultry and other livestock, as well as growing most of their vegetables. Neil also had a friend whose father owned a small plane, and used to take them thirty-fives miles out to the coast near Point Reyes, to harvest shellfish. This is where he learned to stalk and hunt the elusive clams.

We were looking for three kinds of clams that day: the geoduck, the Nuttall's cockle, and the horse clam. The forest ranger in Neil— he's a retired director of the Alaska State Parks—kicked in and he assured me that by the end of the morning, I would be able to identify all three.

We parked and got out of the car. Neil put on waterproof pants and a bright orange jacket. He and Hilary have a sailboat, and they always look to me as though they are going sailing.

"Let's see. It's around here somewhere," he said, veering left down the road.

I led Neil in the other direction, where the trailhead was clearly marked. It turned out he had not visited this spot in over a year. The chowder served at New Year's had been made from clams he had harvested and frozen earlier. A weathered sign warned against harvesting butter clams because of PSP, or paralytic shellfish poison. The beaches are almost always closed, said Neil, to the harvest of butter clams, which concentrate toxins from phytoplankton and reach toxic levels faster than other shellfish. Entire villages in Alaska had been wiped out by PSP, Neil said. Recently, toxic algae blooms severely curtailed the Dungeness crab season in California. This was due to a persistent weather condition, "the blob," that has kept the waters just off the coast unusually warm in recent years. As climate change speeds up, we will probably have more and more of these weather events.

As we made our way down the trail, brushed by person-sized ferns and sheltered by firs and hemlocks one hundred feet tall or higher, Neil told me that he and Hilary had retired to Bainbridge Island a couple of years before they bought the house next to ours. They realized that their home on the north end of the island was too large and too remote, so they sold it and moved into town. Hilary worked for the Washington State Audubon Society at the time and they travel to places like Mexico and Costa Rica on birding expeditions. In retirement, Neil has taken more responsibility for their meals, keeping a kitchen garden and collecting runoff from the carport to water it.

When a winter wren spoke up, Neil explained that its name had been changed to Pacific wren, the name *winter wren* staying with a bird in the East that had been differentiated from it by genus. He planned to continue calling the bird a winter wren. I was happy to find that the trail had been improved since I visited a couple of years earlier, when I scrambled down the rocks of a small stream to make my way to the beach. I didn't relish doing this while carrying a shovel. Only the last part of the trail was steep, stepping down about fifteen feet to beach level.

Upon climbing over a large, fallen log at the end of the trail, we could see the hand-like prints of raccoons on the sand, and a couple of places where they had dug. This far back from the tide line, it was probably worms or insects they had been looking for. We walked toward the receding tide, facing a Marine facility across the water at Keyport that tests missiles, Neil said. North a little and much closer, breaking up the dense green trees, was the Indian casino at Suquamish, across the bridge that ties us to the rest of the Kitsap Peninsula.

Washington State has few smooth, sand beaches. This is one of them, with a gradual slope going west, and a substantial tide flat that invites marine life to dig in. As we walked out of the woods and closer to the water, the sand took on a rippled surface that held small pockets of brackish water. When seaweed appeared, we began to search for clams.

It was still an hour before low tide. I had remembered to check the newspaper for the timing of low tide. Life in the Northwest is so dependent on the tides that checkout stands at grocery stores have booklets with the tide charts for sale, along with gum and other "point of purchase" items. The optimum level for digging geoducks is at least a minus-1.5 tide; today was a minus-1.1, which meant the clams would be close to the water's edge even at the lowest point.

Neil paused at what appeared to be a small pile of gravel on the surface of the sand. Bending over, he pinched it, and a small stream of water shot upward before the protuberance slowly withdrew. This was the siphon of a geoduck, and Neil was pleased to find it. He wanted to wait until low tide before making any serious investment in digging. We picked up a couple of the Nuttall's cockles, which are prized for their ease in harvesting, since they hardly bury their shells, but provide plenty of meat. He also picked up a couple of long, dark-red oval shells that resembled mussel shells, but that he said came from some other type of clam.

We wandered north along the shore, crossing the outlets of small streams that drain the cliffs above, into an area that fronts on large, expensive houses. Two men in their sixties or seventies emerged onto one of the docks and one called "Good morning!" Neil answered him, but I don't think he heard. I wondered if they considered this their property. A long history of litigation simmers in this state over the ownership of these lands. It has been settled that private land ends at the midpoint between high tide and low tide, and that Native Americans have the right to harvest shellfish on all the tideland properties. The latter right was spelled out in treaties, but never enforced. It took a landmark federal court decision in 1974, *United States v. Washington*, and years of litigation to reestablish it. Still, on Bainbridge, private owners of adjacent lands go out of their way to hide public beach accesses designated by the city, even gating and padlocking them and posting "No Trespassing" signs.

The end of the dock was well above and away from the low tide, so the two men had to drag their small, inflatable dinghy to the water. Again, the first man called "Good morning!" a little more belligerently, and I answered him. He was making sure we knew he had seen us. I realized why Neil made sure we had licenses, in case we were confronted by people like this. In Oregon and California, no one owns the beaches, although I'm sure people use similar tactics. The two paddled out to a small sailboat anchored offshore and sailed away.

Finally Neil found a geoduck he liked. I'm not sure what he was gauging, probably size, depth, and distance from the tide line, but how he could tell the first two from the surface, I didn't know. Starting a couple of feet from the spout, he began to dig rapidly, circling the clam as he threw sand behind himself. The clam spouted water and withdrew its siphon farther into the sand as more and more of the neck was exposed. The first time I had watched this, I thought the clam was digging itself farther into the sand, and would get away.

Not true, Neil said later. The clam is not going anywhere. The need for haste is because the hole immediately begins to fill with water, and then collapses. When the hole was over three feet deep, he set his shovel aside and threw himself full-length upon the sand, reached down into the excavation, and grabbed the geoduck by the neck. The trick is to extract both the neck and the shell. If you sever the neck, you cannot legally keep it. Otherwise, it would be too easy to cut off the necks and leave the maimed geoducks to die deep in the sand. Pulling mightily, Neil was able to bring up the shell. The neck was about a foot long, and the shell, brown and roughly oval, about six inches.

Commercially farmed in parts of Puget Sound, the geoduck is a valuable animal. Highly prized for its tasty meat, it can sell for over one hundred dollars a pound in the Tokyo fish market. Seattle's own sushi houses serve the pale, slightly yellow flesh sliced in overlapping ovals that can be picked up with chopsticks, dipped in sauce, and nibbled. The geoduck is richer than most clams, and shellfish lovers are quickly won over by the taste. Rather than digging each clam up, commercial growers use giant vacuums to suck up the clams. I'm sure this is tough on the habitat.

Geoducks are also a favorite seafood display at the Pike Place Market in Seattle, a major tourist destination. The young, almost always male fishmongers throw fish at each other and sometimes pull an especially vicious-looking fish, like a monkfish, across the display table by a string to scare children. The geoducks are often surrounded by tittering teenage girls, or their mothers, because of their resemblance to a human penis. In the bucket, they just looked like really sad clams.

Neil was visibly tired from the effort. I filled in the hole, mostly for aesthetic reasons. Later I learned that doing so is required, although the tide would soon even out the beach. Other clams live alongside the geoducks, and leaving the holes unfilled damages them.

Neil remarked that the Native Americans say that the clams offer themselves to us, that they give of themselves for us to eat—yet they are so hard to dig. Well, I said, they are available to us, even if they don't like it. There is a saying around here, "When the tide is out, the table is set."

When we found the next geoduck, I dug part of the hole, but it was too close to the water, and the sand began to collapse as we dug. Each geoduck seemed to be surrounded by lots of big, tough butter clam shells, mostly empty, that made it difficult to dig. The combination of silt, sand, and water created a slurry as heavy as wet cement. I could barely lift each small shovelful. I realized why Neil had tired after digging the first hole so quickly. A third dig also resulted in failure, so we began to wander back the way we had come.

Neil showed me a different kind of siphon, delicate and lip-like compared to that of the geoduck. It belonged to a horse clam. Although horse clams are large, they do not bury themselves as deeply, and this one was easier to retrieve than the geoduck. Horse clams also make good eating, but are not as prized as geoducks. They are tougher, less delicate in flavor than geoducks, and some diggers keep them solely as bait for crab traps.

By the time we were back near the park, Neil was talking to the clams as we examined each siphon. Another of my rules about food is that people talking to their food, or naming it, leads to trouble. Nancy and Bob Fortner bought a turkey chick to raise for Thanksgiving several years ago, and named her Turkey Girl. She roosted with the laying hens and was the first to call out to them each morning. When the day came to slaughter her, they couldn't do it, and had to give her away to grace someone else's table. By then, said Nancy, the turkey hen was eating too much anyway.

Neil noted the neat holes drilled in many of the white butter clam shells littering the beach. These were made by radula, the small, circular saws that the giant moon snails and razor clams, both predators, use to gain entry into other shellfish. They then suck the other shellfish out of their shells. I looked back and saw that a seagull was feasting at one of the holes we had dug, eating the damaged butter clams left behind.

Finally, Neil noticed a geoduck that had several inches of neck sticking out. On the chance that it was not buried as deeply as the others, he began to dig. Sure enough, the clam, a young geoduck, came up easily. I walked out into the shallows and rinsed it, as Neil had done with the others. The long neck was rough like a callused hand. It was rigid when I picked it up, but seemed to relax as I carried it. Otherwise, there was no movement. I could not tell if it was dead or alive.

By now, Neil was dripping sweat. He walked up and down the beach trying to catch his breath. I could see why he had been reluctant at the last minute to go clamming: it's a lot of work. Neil had been too polite to make me lie down on the wet sand and pull out a clam. It was a perfect morning for being on a Northwest beach—overcast, but no wind or rain. For once, I felt just right outdoors.

We examined a few more spouts, but most of the remaining clams were located in heavy, wet sand that would have been difficult to dig. Neil was considering names for each clam we looked at, and it was time to leave. We had about six large shellfish, and I was perfectly happy. I hoped to create something like Neil's chowder from earlier that year. His mother, he said, used to grind the clams, mix the meat with sweet onions, and fry them as patties.

Once the clams are rinsed, he said, you remove most of the shell and plunge them in boiling water for a few minutes. Then you trim off the end of the siphon and strip back the rough skin.

At home, we showed off the shellfish assortment on the lawn to my husband and another neighbor. We hosed them off along with Neil's jacket and my boots. Then Neil said he would take the clams home and clean them. A couple of hours later, he returned, showered and in clean clothes, with four pounds of ground clam meat in a bowl. He had decided that the mussel-like shellfish probably were a type of mussel, maybe an invasive species, and left them out of the mix until he could identify them. They turned out to be the northern horse mussel, *Modiolus modiolus*—edible, but mostly used as bait.

The ground geoduck meat was white and almost fluffy. I gave him back at least a pound to use before he and Hilary left for an extended sailing trip up the east side of Vancouver Island. The rest became chowder in my kitchen. Some of it went into my freezer, awaiting the New Year.

SALMON AT HOME

At this point, I would love to add salmon to the menu. But the only salmon that comes from the island today is Atlantic salmon raised in a fish farm, and shipped to the East Coast for consumption.

So while salmon should be our main source of food, it will have to come from somewhere else until we can restore our streams and shorelines to the point that a viable population of fish are returning to the island.

As for preparing it, although I have a recipe in one of the local cookbooks for tortilla soup, I don't think of myself as a chef or even a good cook. But a happy combination of fish and a neighbor's visit to Morocco brought together the go-to recipe for salmon at our house.

If you do come by some fresh salmon, probably Chinook or Copper River from Alaska, here is the way I have been fixing it:

- ½ to ¾-pound salmon fillet, skin on
- 10 drops sesame oil
- 1 teaspoon olive oil
- 1 teaspoon harissa (Middle Eastern spice paste)
- kosher salt
- 1 teaspoon anise seeds

Heat medium skillet. Add olive oil and 5 drops sesame oil, and heat through. Place salmon skin-side down in the oil. Sprinkle top with ¼ teaspoon harissa, a little salt, and remaining 5 drops of sesame oil. Cook on medium heat for three or four minutes. Turn salmon over, and peel away the skin with a fork. Sprinkle salmon with remaining harissa, salt, and anise seeds. Once the salmon is seared on both sides, turn down the heat and cover until just cooked through, maybe ten more minutes. The spices and oil will give the salmon a lovely crust. Do not overcook.

Drizzle with a sauce made from fresh or frozen raspberries.

Serve with Ozette potatoes, carrots, and fresh greens. Serves two. To serve more, get more fish.

Another fish alternative would be the sustainably caught tuna that Paul Svornitch supplies, but it comes from waters off the coast of Oregon. He has the knowledge to catch ground fish in our inland waters, and some that were fished out have recently bounced back. But they are probably too fragile a population at this point to think that we would not do the same thing to them—harvest so many that they become scarce again.

THE OZETTE POTATO

How about potatoes? Brought from Peru to the coastal villages of the Makah out on the coast at Neah Bay, the little blue potato has "naturalized" and adapted to the Northwest's cold, wet climate. Intensely blue, almost purple, Ozette potatoes don't look as though they would necessarily be edible—at least not to someone who grew up eating russets or other white potatoes. However, they are nutritious and easy to grow. And they taste good.

Not long ago, the Washington State tribal librarians held their annual meeting. One of the topics was Native foods. Tracy Hosselkuss of the Lower Elwha tribe talked about the Ozette potato. She said that lots of folks in her area were growing these fingerling potatoes with their distinctive nutty taste. Hosselkuss said they are wonderful roasted in a fire pit, the traditional way of preparing them, along with shellfish gathered on the beach.

The Makahs have preserved and have been enjoying the potato for two hundred years. It turns out that Spanish Jesuit missionaries came up to the Olympic peninsula from Peru in the late 1700s, bringing potatoes with them. The Jesuits spent one winter in the rain forest and left when their ship returned in the spring: it was too wet for them! The potatoes, which did not mind the climate, remained and the Makahs kept planting and eating them. Genetic tests by Washington State University verified this oral history, confirming that the potato came directly from Peru.

The popularity of the Ozette potato probably coincided with reduced availability of the camas lily (*Camassia quamash*) and its edible root. Camas root was once the most common form of starch in the Northwest, and was unknown outside of the region until Lewis and Clark described it. To cultivate camas, meadows need to be burned off and maintained, and this practice has not been allowed on public land for many years. There was once a camas prairie, according to Dennis Lewarch of the Suquamish Museum, on Restoration Point on Bainbridge. Some research shows that large camas meadows were maintained in southwest Washington and used for trade along with dried salmon. It is important to cook the camas root, and it is even more important to eat only those plants with blue flowers—those with white flowers are poisonous. At present there is a preserve in the Wenatchee Mountains where a camas meadow can be viewed, but it is considered too fragile to walk on. I have yet to taste this root vegetable, but I hope to soon.

I recently grew organic blue potatoes, a variety called Purple Majesty, the only blue potatoes available when I stopped by our local farm store, Bay Hay and Feed. I could not tell if they were related to Ozette potatoes, but they do not look the same online. At Bay Hay and Feed, I purchased starts, a little bag of potato pieces, presumably each holding the "eyes" from which potatoes sprout. I planted them. We had a hot spring and summer, and the potatoes grew quickly, with a little water and a lot of sun. Each time I checked, fist-sized, intensely blue potatoes were nesting just below the surface of the soil. The plants continued to produce smaller tubers all summer and well into the fall.

Typically, I slice potatoes into rounds, fry them a little in oil, then layer other vegetables and beaten eggs on top to make a frittata. This is like a quiche, but without the crust, and the potatoes on the bottom hold the whole thing together. Ozettes are small potatoes, and can easily be steamed as well. Traditional cooking in the Northwest did not involve much frying—people mostly cooked their food in stews, or hard-smoked meat for preservation.

THE PERFECT CARROT

Carrots are not indigenous to the Northwest, but I like them, and they do well in this climate. My carrot story started the summer of 2009 in San Miguel de Allende, in Guanajuato, Mexico. While visiting there, I rented a small condominium with a kitchen. The furnishings were basic, and I ate simply when at home, mostly breakfasts and salads.

In San Miguel, the stores are clustered by type along the narrow, cobblestone streets—pharmacies on Insurgentes, clothing stores on Relox, and produce stores on Mesones. One day, I bought some carrots. I didn't eat them for a couple of days. Then I washed and peeled them, although at home I probably would have left the peels on. Hungry, I cut one into rough chunks and took a bite.

This was my Proustian moment, the madeleine of my vegetable experience. I didn't think of myself as a carrot fan in particular. I do like most vegetables, raw or slightly cooked. If anything, I favor dark greens—broccoli, kale, spinach, even Brussels sprouts. But the flavor of this carrot was overwhelmingly good. There wasn't a hint of bitterness. It was rich and clean tasting. The texture was crisp and tender at the same time. I sliced it up and ate it with sliced tomatoes and lime juice. That carrot tasted of the essence of the color orange.

I bragged to my Facebook friends, some of whom are foodies, and most of whom just like good food. Who doesn't? I made some of them so hungry they had to leave their computers and go have snacks, called *antojitos* in Spanish. Then I forgot about it.

A couple of months later, back at home, I remembered those carrots. I buy both regular and organic foods at our grocery store, depending on the price, the appearance of freshness, and my level of virtuous feeling that day. I looked for a fresh-looking bunch of organic carrots and took them home.

Later, I washed and sliced a carrot. I took a bite and waited for that special flavor to revive my memories of sunny San Miguel. Instead, my mouth was flooded with bitterness. This can't be right, I thought. I took more bites. Still bitter, as well as tough. I finished the carrot because I don't waste food, and eventually the bunch, although I probably cooked most of them. I was hugely disappointed, especially when subsequent carrots yielded similar results. What was wrong with them? What was wrong with me? And who really cares about carrots, anyway?

An additional wrinkle to this story is that, about two years prior, I had lost most of my sense of taste. At first, I assumed the loss was temporary, and waited for it to return. When it did not, I mentioned it to my doctor, who insisted on taking a magnetic resonance image of my head. She wanted to make sure I didn't have a brain tumor, or a lingering sinus infection, or some other malady. The twenty minutes of metal-pounding-metal of the MRI yielded nothing but a headache. My brain was fine, only my taste buds had taken a hike.

I could taste in a very general way, as though my sensory nerves were remotely describing things to me through a headset. All subtleties were lost. This extended to my sense of smell as well. This absence persists to this day.

So you can see why I got so excited about this carrot. After two years of weak signals, the channels were open and clear. The message was "delicious."

What did I know about carrots? Not too much. They are orange, although I have seen them in different colors. It is possible to grow them in North America. We call redheads "carrot tops." Oh yes—they are supposed to be good for your eyesight.

According to the website of the Carrot Museum (of course there is a carrot museum, in Belgium), "carrots originated in present-day Afghanistan about five thousand years ago, probably originally as a purple or yellow root. . . . Nature then took a hand and produced mutants and natural hybrids, crossing both with cultivated and wild varieties. . . . Purple carrots were then taken westwards, where it is thought yellow mutants and wild forms crossed to produce orange. Finally some motivated Dutch growers took these mutant orange carrots under their horticultural wings and developed them to be sweeter and more practical."

The wild carrot and the domestic carrot are not the same species, but the wild carrot has been used for approximately ten thousand years for medicinal purposes. Naturally, because of their shape, carrots have often been prescribed as an aphrodisiac. Carrots were cultivated in Europe by the thirteenth century, when doctors prescribed them for ailments as varied as syphilis and animal bites.

This brings us back to eyesight, and an interesting story. Few vegetables have much Vitamin A. You can get Vitamin A from some animal products (such as fish and liver), but not from most veggies—except for yellow vegetables, like butternut squash—and fruits such as dried apricots and papaya. All these are yellow because they contain the pigment carotene, as do the feathers of canaries and the reddish shells of lobsters. When you eat yellow vegetables, your liver converts the carotene to Vitamin A. Vitamin A promotes healthy skin, a healthy immune system—and good vision. This last item was the basis of a rumor started by the Royal Air Force during World War II.

In 1940, during the Battle of Britain, the British fighter pilot John Cunningham became the first person to shoot down an enemy plane with the help of radar. His nickname was "Cat's Eyes." The Royal Air Force put out the story in the British newspapers that Cunningham and his fellow night pilots owed their exceptional night vision to carrots. People believed this to the extent that during WWII they started growing and eating more carrots, so they could get around more easily at night during blackouts.

This story was a complete invention by the RAF to hide their use of radar, which was what really located the Luftwaffe bombers at night—not carrot-assisted super-vision. The German Air Force, in spite of the obvious radar towers on the English coast, fell for this story because the myth that carrots improve eyesight already existed in German folklore. With more recent stories, I am starting to think the RAF successes were more likely due to people like Alan Turing and Hedy LaMarr.

I described my carrot moment in Mexico to a couple of local farmers. Why were the carrots in Mexico so sweet—sweet and tender enough to cut up and eat raw with tomatoes and lime juice? Cliff Wind and Marilyn Holt of Holt Ranch explained that vegetables bought in grocery stores in the United States must withstand shipping, whereas the carrots I ate in Mexico were probably grown for local consumption. In order to end up with a carrot that will survive shipping, growers choose varieties in which the sugars are pulled from the inside to create cellulose in the outer wall.

Barbara Kingsolver, in her book *Animal, Vegetable, Miracle,* says something similar: "Most standard vegetable varieties sold in stores have been bred for uniform appearance, mechanized harvest, convenience of packing ... and a tolerance for hard travel. None of these can be mistaken, in practice, for actual flavor."

This is also one of the problems with patented seeds, Cliff and Marilyn said. Organic produce certifiers give farmers a hard time unless they use seeds from certain companies, which do not always produce the tastiest produce. Earth Company and Seed Foods are two of the companies preferred by certifiers, and if you trace their ownership, said Marilyn, they go back to the same companies, like Monsanto, that have put a big emphasis on patenting and monopolizing seed sources.

I told this story to farmer Brian MacWhorter. He does not always use organic seed, he said. If he finds a conventional seed of better quality, he can petition his inspector for an exception. As for my search, "cold can affect the taste," he said. He suggested the Napoli as a carrot variety I might like that is suitable for this climate.

Online, I found an article by Kristen Corselius of the Rodale Institute. Corselius says that, bred to be mechanically harvested and to store for long periods, the average carrot travels 1,774 miles to our dinner plates. "It's no wonder that 'flavorful' is a word rarely associated with this woody root crop," she says. "'Average' is more like it." According to the USDA, carrots are the fifth most-consumed vegetable in the country; the average American consumed 9.5 pounds of carrots in 2003. Chances are, at least 7.2 pounds of those carrots came from California.

In her research into more flavorful carrots, Corselius discovered farmer Gary Guthrie, who has made carrots his specialty. According to Guthrie, variety selection, more than anything else, is the key to tasty carrots. Among his favorites are Bolero, Napoli, and Nelson, depending on the season. The soil matters, too. "It starts with nice loose organic soils," says Guthrie. Fortunate to farm on Iowa's famously fertile, black prairie soils, Guthrie makes every effort to conserve and enhance his soils with green manures, cover crops, and long rotations. His farm is close to a college town, which makes it ideally situated for direct local marketing.

So there were two votes for the Napoli carrot.

The next summer in San Miguel, I bought two more carrots. I got lost on my way to somewhere else and ended up at the poorest market in town, down by the railroad, which also featured used clothing and cheap, plastic children's toys. Like a summer romance, these carrots were unable to live up to my glowing memories of the year before. Only a peso each, these carrots were grown for cash, not for love. My first San Miguel carrots must have been loved.

Still, even these lowly carrots were better than the California-grown carrots I had eaten on Bainbridge Island. The one-peso carrots were not bursting with flavor, like that first bunch, but they were not bitter. A little smaller, a little more crooked—I could taste the rocky soil they came from, turned by hand or by a horse-drawn plow. I had arrived with the first of the summer rains that year, and every bit of soil that could be cultivated was under the plow.

Suddenly, everywhere I went, I heard conversations about carrots. Was I obsessed? Or were carrots suddenly a hot topic? At Vía Orgánica, a fancy grocery store at the north end of San Miguel, an American woman in a headscarf left in a huff because the carrots for sale had been washed.

Behind me in the café at the library, two women discussed a third who had cut carrots from her diet when she discovered that she was borderline diabetic. Apparently, carrots have naturally occurring sugar in them. A quick search of websites recommended carrots for diabetics because of their high fiber content. However, one website advised caution at drinking too much carrot juice, because the high glucose content can cause levels in the patient to rise too quickly.

Back home for the second time, I continued my search for the golden carrot. When I interviewed the Nakata cousins about T&C, I told them my carrot story.

They agreed that the taste and quality of produce can vary quite a bit, and is affected by how fresh it is. "Vegetables are alive after they are harvested, but refrigeration stops that. That is when they begin to lose flavor," Rick said.

As we walked out of the conference room, I heard Vern say, "People are looking for that taste, that special something. That is why they overeat. If we could just provide that taste . . ."

MORA

Just north of our neighborhood is a deep, wooded ravine that runs under the nearby highway to join a salmon stream. Just south are five acres of open land, privately owned. When I say open, I don't mean empty. The land is dense with salal, invasive blackberries, and scrub trees. Our neighborhood, on a dead-end street, serves as a wildlife corridor between the two areas, one of the reasons we love it. On a regular basis, the neighbors sign petitions, write letters, and attend city council meetings to protect the Cave Avenue neighborhood from the encroachment of developers.

One summer, when the blackberries were particularly dense, our cat disappeared. This is not uncommon, but Pearl had lived with us for over fourteen years. She was a rescue cat from the county, and we figured her combination of caution and her ability to climb trees quickly had kept her safe.

When the blackberries are ripe, the bushes are especially prickly, as though to give up the purple-black fruit to only the most worthy seekers. Right now deer, songbirds, crows, blue jays, raccoons, and yes, rats are feasting on the fruit. There is so much that many berries will simply fall, staining the road with their bloody juice. One summer evening I passed two Russian Orthodox priests in full regalia reaching to snatch berries from the closest vines, putting them directly into their mouths over their long white beards and pale albs, heedless of stains.

I waited a couple of days for the cat to turn up. After all, I thought, she is an indoor-outdoor cat, and although she tends to stick close to home, she is entitled to a little adventure. Only on the third day did I reluctantly put up "Have You Seen Pearl?" posters around the neighborhood, feeling both worried and foolish. Maybe she was in somebody's garage.

The rugged nature of the vines meant that, unless I came into possession of a moonsuit, it was impossible to enter either the ravine or the five acres to look for Pearl. Four days after her disappearance, several of us admitted that we could smell a rank odor by the side of the road. Narrowing it to a particular patch of berries, we returned with garden hoes. Gingerly, we pulled back the spiky vines, expecting to find the remains of our cat. Even wearing long sleeves and gloves we suffered bloody scratches and pricks. The vines are armed with a chemical irritant that keeps the scratches from healing quickly. The blackberries that cover Bainbridge are *Rubus armeniacus,* Himalayan blackberries, and along with invasive Scotch broom and English ivy, they have crowded out the native blackberry, *Rubus ursinus.* Work parties are held on a regular basis on other spots on the island to fight back the encroaching plants, especially where they climb trees or overrun the natural undergrowth around streams. No such work is ever done on these five acres.

Instead, every summer, we neighbors take our colanders and gather berries. Entire families come from tamer neighborhoods, and the more industrious use footstools or stepladders to reach the fruit that hangs at a tantalizing distance, always just beyond arm's length. The blackberry canes can reach out and grab you, soon entangling a foot or an arm in vicious thorns. Vine cutters or garden clippers are good tools to bring along. The plants I see don't usually reach more than six feet in height, but they can, supposedly, grow up to fifteen feet tall, with canes up to forty feet long. Abandoned buildings in our region are soon engulfed by blackberry vines—they are to the Northwest as kudzu is to the South.

The more ambitious harvesters pick buckets of berries to freeze and use over the winter months. They will bake cobblers, cookies, breads, and preserves. The grasshoppers among us buy ice cream to accompany the fresh berries, living just for today. Or maybe we sprinkle them on our cereal in the mornings.

The five acres are currently owned by descendants of early white settlers on the island. Before that, the property was part of the Hall Brothers Shipyard, along with our neighborhood. We sometimes find old bottles gone blue with age among the roots of the second-growth fir trees.

After the first-growth forests were logged, salal, then invasive blackberries and ivy took over the spaces opened up to sunlight. With these new meadows, and most of the predators killed or banished, deer have proliferated. A doe and her two fawns move regularly through our yard, biting off rosebuds and nibbling the tender leaves of the hosta until my husband, infuriated, goes outside and throws rocks at them. They move on, hardly perturbed, to return the next night.

At dusk, the raccoons emerge, drink from our birdbath, and continue on to the five acres to gorge. These raccoons are huge, easily twice the size of Pearl, who weighs only seven pounds. Still, they are not known to be aggressive unless cornered. Many times I have watched the cat and the raccoons look straight through each other. At first light, they will return to their nests in the ravine.

A few years ago, a Chilean family on the island opened an ice cream parlor named Mora, offering fresh fruit flavors and interesting flavor combinations. Their website says, "We churn Old World flavors—Gianduja, Marron Glacé, and Dulce de Leche—that are traditional in our hometown, as well as new-school favorites—Goat Cheese with Fig, Banana Split, and Lemon Bar." This is a perfect business for Bainbridge, since we have many day visitors from Seattle, here mostly to ride the ferry round trip. You can't go wrong selling sweets to tourists. Since the family was from Chile, I figured that Mora was a family name. Recently, my son told me that *mora* means blackberry. I had to stop and think, because I associated that word with a big tree from my childhood. We looked it up. *Mora* means blackberry, but it can also mean mulberry.

I knew only one grandparent, my father's mother, Refugio Ramirez Alcalá Gutiérrez. A refugee from the Mexican Revolution, she owned a stone house in East Highlands, California, a short drive from our house in San Bernardino. She had transformed the property, nearly an acre, into a lush garden over the years, presided over by a spreading mulberry tree with big, dark green leaves. When I was in second grade, my class at school raised silkworms, and I supplied the voracious eaters with mulberry leaves, bringing useless bags of leaves even after they had spun their brown cocoons and transformed into frail moths.

I spent many hours in that yard, nibbling berries and pomegranates and other fruits that seem impossibly exotic to me now. I would invent kingdoms among the flower stalks and medicinal plants, build bug houses on a scale that made the adults look huge when I returned to them. It was a garden of earthly delights for a solitary child, while the joys and sorrows of an only son and his twice-widowed mother raged inside. Their conflicts were mostly about money. Late in the afternoon, I would sit in the kitchen with my grandmother and drink tea with milk in it and eat graham crackers. That is what *mora* meant to me.

The rancid smell in the blackberries turned out to emanate from a rotting log that had probably attracted too much dog pee. We found no sign of Pearl. Later that day, unable to resist the abundance, we went farther down the road, away from the log, to gather berries for ourselves. Two days later, we consumed grilled salmon followed by blackberry pie at our neighbor's house. When Hilary lifted one of their indoor-only cats to her lap later that evening, I had to look away. A feeling of physical craving had come over me, the same I sometimes feel when I see mothers with their young sons, still small enough to pick up. I missed my cat.

After two weeks, I stopped checking each door on a regular basis to see if the cat was waiting to be let in. I no longer called "Here kitty kitty, here Pearl," as I walked down the street. All but one poster of her, a compact gray tabby with a white bib and boots, has been taken down. No one called our number, or tried to collect the reward.

What I have avoided saying is this: Pearl was probably eaten by a coyote. She was snatched away in the dark sometime between 10:30 P.M., when I fell asleep, and 6:30 A.M., when she would normally enter the bedroom to see if anyone was willing to come downstairs and feed her.

People stopped telling us heroic cat stories of returns after a month, six months, a year. We washed Pearl's blankets and brushed our chairs and couches. Her dishes were put away, dismantling the miniature ecosystem in which a spider waited for tiny insects to visit her water dish. This might have been a form of magical thinking, as Joan Didion would call it—that if we put her things away, Pearl would surprise us and return. But mostly, it just made me sad to see them.

The blackberries I eat with ice cream harbor a complicated flavor—not only sugars but also something darker, peaty, organic. It is a tangle of story lines, thousands of summers of growth and decay, the soaring song and the abrupt squeak. Somewhere in those brambles may lie Pearl's remains, already nurturing the growth of next season—sweet, and bitter.

ROXBURY RUSSET

One October I stopped by the Secret Spring farmstand at the farmers market. They had some interesting-looking apples for sale, and I asked about them. "These are the oldest American apples," said Felix Williams, one of the farm owners. "Roxbury Russet."

I knew they were not the oldest apples, since there are crabapples indigenous to the Northwest, but I didn't want to start an argument. I tasted a slice. The apple tasted green and earthy, a little mineral. "Nice," I said. "I'll take a couple of pounds." That worked out to four apples of varying sizes. Most of the commercially grown apples in North America come from Eastern Washington, and the ones we see in supermarkets are intensely uniform in size, color, and shape. I have purchased Red Delicious from Washington while in Mexico. These Roxbury Russets were bumpy and greenish-brown, varied from very small to very large, and were eccentric in shape.

The Roxbury Russet was probably brought to the Secret Spring Farm by Felix and Eric's great-grandfather, Frank Williams, who homesteaded the place near Rolling Bay, and planted the trees in 1920. Felix and Eric are cousins, and they are married to sisters Sola and Maia. And now there is baby Aime. They all look very young.

At home, I sliced up the apples, peels and all, and cooked them with a little cinnamon, sugar, and water. I rolled out dough and cut rounds to fill with apple before baking them until brown. We ate a couple of these empanadas immediately, and I mailed the rest to my son for his birthday.

I'm glad that Frank Williams's great-grandsons, who grew up in California, decided to come to Bainbridge and revive his farm. There are neglected trees in every neighborhood on the island, planted by people who understood the value and necessity of local fruit. Now, on almost every street, the apples fall and rot on the ground while we buy apples in the store. This is food that could be gathered and shared. Maybe we will figure out a way to do that in the near future.

I am going to add honey in here, too. Chuck Schafer already told me about cultivating bees and honey on the island. I want to add that for Rosh Hashanah, Jews offer each other apples and honey, to ensure a sweet new year.

SISTER ISLAND

And finally, a little nonnative coffee to balance out our wonderful meal. The story of Ometepe is also that of a resilient community, one from which we can learn a lot.

Kim Esterberg first visited Ometepe, an island in Nicaragua, during the Contra/Sandinista era. In 1986, many people opposed the U.S. involvement in Nicaragua. "People had different attitudes" about going there, Kim said. He and his wife, Ela, were part of a peace movement that included opposition to nuclear armaments in Kitsap County. "I thought we could do something more positive," Kim said. "We were listening to people who really lived there."

Kim, Ela, and I sat outside their home on the northeast side of Bainbridge, listening to birds and watching three deer pick their way past the property. I wanted to know what we could learn from Ometepe in terms of self-sufficiency. But I also wanted to talk about Ometepe because the coffee that grows there has become such a strong part of our food identity here on Bainbridge. Our island has purchased coffee directly from the Ometepe farmers for twenty-five years. In fact, our program served as the model for Seattle's Best Coffee when its owner decided to skip the coffee brokers and deal directly with farmers.

When Kim joined a trip to Nicaragua organized by a fact-finding group from the Managua-Seattle sister city program, he had no idea if he would be able to visit an island as a potential sister community. "It was Ela's idea to ask for ten dollars from each friend to send me," Kim said.

"That way, they would be invested in it," Ela added.

Kim and Ela already had a history of helping others. Ela, who grew up in Kenya, met Kim when they were both students at Washington State University. A friend of theirs from that time was one of thirteen college graduates in the entire country of the Congo, and wanted to start a school in his home village. Kim and Ela helped him start a nonprofit organization for this purpose, setting a pattern for the rest of their life's work in grassroots organizing. Later, both were active in the antiwar and antinuclear movements in the Northwest and Kitsap County, where they have lived since 1985, raising a son and daughter here.

When Kim got to Managua with the Seattle delegation, he was directed to Ometepe. He met with the mayors of the island, and took a lot of pictures. "At the time," Ela said, "Ometepe had two telephones and three trucks, and phone calls were very expensive." Because of its left-leaning government at the time, "Nicaragua was under a U.S. embargo, so we worked with a Canadian group to send them tools. It was very difficult to communicate."

Upon their return, the delegation "met with a lukewarm reaction on Bainbridge Island. But a few people were quite excited" that Kim had been able to make contact with an island, and that its people were eager to form a cultural and practical exchange program.

In 1988, Kim, Kim and Ela's teenage daughter, Asha, and another volunteer, David Mitchell, traveled to Ometepe and stayed at the coffee co-op. At the time, the Nicaraguan government was helping the farmers, who had been abandoned by the landowners who had fled during the revolution. The government bought the coffee beans and helped the workers to organize a co-op. In turn, the co-op gained title to the land. But because of the U.S. embargo, they had no market other than the Nicaraguan government.

"It was David who made the coffee connection," Kim said, "because we have a roaster, Pegasus Coffee, on Bainbridge." The reaction on Ometepe to David and Kim's efforts to bring Ometepe coffee beans to Bainbridge was always very positive. "They made a big distinction between the people of the United States and our government," Kim said. "I don't know why. They had no access to radio or television, and did not have a broad sense of the world."

Before leaving Ometepe, Kim and David emptied out their suitcases of clothing and bug spray and filled them with pounds of raw coffee for the very first import to Bainbridge. It was two years later, in 1990, after the Sandinistas lost a highly monitored election, that the embargo was dropped and shipping containers, rather than suitcases full of coffee, were imported.

Now, the Ometepe coffee is purchased and brought by ship to Bainbridge in one full shipping container each year. Some of it goes on to two companies in Canada that buy and roast the coffee as well. Once a week, a rotating group of about fifty volunteers on Bainbridge gather to roast, package, and label it as Café Oro, golden coffee, to be sold in Town & Country stores. All Café Oro proceeds are returned to the Bainbridge Ometepe Sister Island Association (BOSIA), who make it available for development projects on Ometepe.

Groups or organizations on Ometepe propose projects, and a committee consisting of people from both islands approves them. The first project funded was the installation of a water system on the island. BOSIA hired an engineer from Managua who lived on-site during the course of the construction project. "They know how to fix it themselves," says Kim, "since they built it." The people of Ometepe provided the labor to bring water from the two mountains to the villages, where the system serves about ten thousand people. "This was all coffee money, by the way."

When the BOSIA association was formed, the Esterbergs envisioned it as fostering a long-term relationship of equals, and all aspects of the program emphasize this approach. High school students from Bainbridge visit Ometepe each year, where they stay with host families and see how resources are cultivated and used. They see that everything is recycled and repurposed, as needed—there are no transfer stations on Ometepe, no off-island disposal.

BOSIA has now sent over twenty delegations from Bainbridge to Ometepe, consisting of about thirty-five students each time. They have stayed in all of the communities on Ometepe, which now has a few paved roads. "People there know each other better as a result," Kim said. Because the American students live with families on Ometepe, "the student becomes a part of the host family, and so ties are very strong." I know of one marriage between a Bainbridge Island resident and an Ometepe native. The couple resides in the United States.

Some years ago, a third grade teacher on Bainbridge, Alicia Mendoza, started a calendar project. Her students illustrated and produced a calendar about Ometepe, sold copies for ten dollars apiece, and voted on how to spend the money. One year, the students raised over ten thousand dollars, which they donated to various BOSIA proposals, including cutting windows into a concrete block school on the island to improve light and air circulation, and seeding a sister-school relationship between the elementary school and a school on Ometepe. To make comparisons is difficult, but it costs about one thousand dollars to build a house—a basic concrete cube—on Ometepe, compared to perhaps two hundred thousand or three hundred thousand on Bainbridge—and that's on top of the cost of land here.

BOSIA pays one staff person on Ometepe to coordinate activities there and to act as a central contact point. In the past, that coordinator has been an American from Bainbridge, but now is a local. Until the advent of cell phones, communication between the two islands was difficult, and mail is still slow. From Bainbridge to Ometepe, mail is sent to the coordinator, who can send it on or wait for people to pick it up from her office.

While farmers on Ometepe grow coffee for export to the United States, the main export from the island is plantains, which are sold to other Latin American countries. Families also raise rice and beans for their own consumption and for sale. Bags of these commodities furnish the living rooms of their modest homes, like beanbag chairs. "Those are their bank accounts," says Kim. Each family tries to own land on each of the two nearby volcanic mountains, since one, a caldera, has a moist climate suitable for rice, and the other, a cone, has a dry forest climate suitable for beans.

Islanders also fish in the surrounding Lake Nicaragua, which they call Cocibolca. It is one of the largest freshwater lakes in the world, and separates Nicaragua and Costa Rica, much as Puget Sound divides Seattle from the Olympic Peninsula. Ometepe has three times the land mass of Bainbridge, and supports forty thousand people, compared to our twenty-three thousand. Like Bainbridge, Ometepe struggles with pollution and water conservation, but is more progressive than Bainbridge in that removal of any tree within a town must be approved ahead of time. There has been no bee die-off, but its bees are Africanized, which means they are more aggressive. The biggest environmental threat to these communities, currently, is a proposed canal that would bisect Lake Nicaragua as an alternative to the Panama Canal.

BOSIA "has changed lives there," Ela said, "but the world has changed, too." There are now cell phones all over Ometepe, but islanders on both sides still send mail with delegates. Revenue from BOSIA coffee sales have sent about one hundred Ometepe students to college in Nicaragua. One is now the first psychologist on the island, working with women and children, including street children from Managua who live at a shelter on Ometepe.

I wondered, if we needed to survive on our own resources on Bainbridge Island, what we could learn from the people of Ometepe.

"Community," said Ela. The most valuable resource on Ometepe is the ability of people to cooperate and work together. "There are no street children," Ela said, "because other families take them in."

An important change brought about by the Sandinistas was literacy. Teachers were sent out to every community in Nicaragua to teach people how to read and write—much like the barefoot doctors trained in Cuba—and now the people of Ometepe see education as a right, not a privilege. Organizing as a collective in order to purchase land after the revolution taught people how to accomplish large tasks collectively; they were ready to work with *los Americanos* when they came to the island offering friendship, island sisterhood, and cash in exchange for coffee.

People on Ometepe have led a subsistence lifestyle since time immemorial, and could easily adapt to the sort of scenario about which I have asked people on Bainbridge to speculate.

"As for coffee," said Kim, if left to our own devices, "we would have to substitute something else."

I noticed a camellia bush at Bay Hay and Feed advertised as having leaves suitable for tea. Sakuma Brothers have been growing and selling *Camellia sinensis* tea in the Skagit Valley for over ten years, so maybe we can have our caffeine fix after all. But we all know it would not be quite the same. Throughout my research, I waited for someone to tell me what Native Americans in the Pacific Northwest used instead of coffee or tea to wake up in the morning. There are species of holly that can be prepared as stimulants, the most widely known today being yerba mate from South America, and chocolate was prepared in what is now Mexico. Maybe that is why long-distance trade with the Southwest was invented, to bring chocolate and yerba mate north. Coffee was not introduced to the Americas until the 1600s.

Haleets

Deep in the gravel, safe from foraging raccoons, rats, and other animals, the salmon eggs rest in their redds. There are from five hundred to twelve hundred eggs in a single nest. The winter is dark and long. In some streams, the water freezes. Not until the temperature rises, bringing more streams and rivulets together, do the eggs begin to hatch. The hatchlings, called alevins, don't need to eat at first. Each carries a little potbelly of yolk to sustain it for a few weeks. Then it must find food or starve.

I am getting closer to figuring out the meaning of Haleets, those carved figures rocking hats and labrettes, staring at Suquamish from across the pass. It didn't take staying up to observe its function under the light of the summer solstice or the winter moon. I didn't interview even more elders, or even more farmers, or even more fishermen.

Haleets was never meant to be a secret, since its location could not be more public. And so its meaning cannot be a secret either. It has to be evident to someone coming across it from land or sea. It faces the passage, but also faces the land just across it, the heart of Suquamish.

I used my head. I also used my heart.

After all these years of trying to figure out what Haleets has seen, and will see in the future, I realized that it allows us to project both backward and forward in time—to what is possible on this piece of rock.

If we conserve the land and the people linked to it, we will be able to see Haleets in the future. Shoreline erosion will slow down if we manage the forests and houses and farms on the island. Perhaps one dark night or bright morning, someone at Suquamish will find a basket or a robe or a pair of boards, once part of a spiritual practice, that remind that person what a grandmother or grandfather once said about Haleets, maybe who was supposed to take care of it, or a song that goes with it.

Years ago, I was part of a chat group among some Native American academics. I had to get off the list because they chatted so much, but before I did, I heard one story that I remember every spring.

We were talking about our gardens, about honoring the earth by cultivating and taking care of it, and thanking the Creator for giving it to our people. How, I asked, can I honor the earth my ancestors sprang from if I am fifteen hundred miles away?

One woman answered that her sister sends a little dirt each year from their original home, and she mixes it into the soil of her present garden. She nourishes that little bit of dirt as part of the larger garden she maintains in the place she now lives. And she consumes the essence of that soil with her food.

It made me realize that we need to nourish the dirt we live on as though it were our ancestral garden. We have taken, and taken over, the land we live on now, so it is our responsibility to not let it die. We cannot load it up with chemicals and overtill it. We cannot ignore it or use it as a waste dump. We can nurture it and care for it, and enter into a partnership with the land that will benefit it and ourselves.

An important aspect of the gift is that we must accept it from a willing environment, or from willing hands. Using resources or labor extracted by force sets up a system that is not sustainable. Sooner or later, people will revolt, and take back their freedom. The same is true with nature—if we take more than we give, the system breaks down—the soil, air, and water become unhealthy and can no longer sustain us. The environment will "free" itself of us by refusing to support us.

Years ago, the nature writer Aldo Leopold started an experiment. He purchased a played-out farm in Wisconsin, and slowly brought back the natural systems that had probably attracted the original farmer to settle there in the first place. Leopold and his family replanted woods, undammed streams, cleared out fallen fencing and barbed wire. Wild groundcover grew back, streams and seeps ran again, and fish and wildlife returned to what had been tapped-out acreage. That farm is now a preserve and a living testimony to his work.

What is not much known is that in the thirties, Leopold also visited the Southwestern borderlands, home of my ancestors, and wrote about that, too. He loved the wild woods, the abundance of birds and animals, the shocking sunrises and gentle nights of the place. He regarded the stars that, to this day, shine more brightly there than almost anywhere else. He had a really good time, riding horseback and camping out. Leopold realized even then that he would be among the last to see this abundance, before wider trails were carved in, followed by roads and government officials who would trap and kill the last big black bear, and finally give all the water away upstream.

More recently, Gary Paul Nabhan, together with indigenous people, environmentalists, and a few hardy reporters, walked across this space to draw attention to the link between human health, culture, and the environment. We can do this. I don't know if any Opata were along for the walk, but I hope so. I'm sure Gustavo Gutiérrez, in the spirit of our ancestral captains of peace, was with them in some form. Even now, a Buddhist priest walks the length and breadth of Bainbridge Island, beating a hand drum and praying for peace.

Recently, the Opata people held a reunion. Many of us have only met online, and we understand the gap that can be filled only in person, on our land. We are modern people. We work as tribal police, artists, and academics. We live all over the United States and in northern Mexico. Another woman and I flew from Seattle to Tucson, and rented a house for the meeting when we could not get any organization to loan us a room for this historic event. It turned out to be just right, offering a living room just big enough for all of us, a kitchen for snacks, and a yard shaded by pepper and jacaranda trees.

Our experiences and politics are not identical, but we were open and respectful. A pressing need, we agreed, is for a practical dictionary of the Opata language, as the last fluent speakers are beginning to pass on. Some members want to push for recognition and land right away. We would need to apply on both sides of the border, and the process is completely different in Mexico. Sitting in that little house with the big yard, I thought, this would be enough for me—a reservation the size of this property where people could take classes, find refuge, or tell stories.

Each of us can only hope that someone will treat our ancestral homes with love. More people are moving today—as immigrants, as refugees, as adventurers into the realms of physical space opened up by their relationship to cyberspace—than at any other time in history. Those who stay behind, or move in behind them, are charged with saving the earth—their earth, our Earth.

A rubbing of Haleets (x̌alilc), a glacial erratic at
the north end of Bainbridge Island associated with
the Suquamish (su?qwabs) people.

Postscript

Last Song

SAY YOU LIVE ON AN ISLAND in a temperate, maritime climate. One day, out of the blue, the ferry sinks to the bottom of Puget Sound, and the bridge across Agate Passage falls down. You are now on an island with twenty-three thousand other people, assuming they all made it back from their jobs in Seattle. If it was during the day, they did not. Power is down, of course. Eventually, the cars will run out of fuel, the generators at T&C will give up, and you will need to affirm yourself as a member of the community worthy of having something to eat.

Say that a few months earlier, several hundred people joined you from another country, refugees from their own disaster, and were settled at Battle Point Park, where tents and portable toilets were set up. When it became clear that we would need to share our limited resources with them for the long term, there was some resentment on the part of the residents. But the new people, or the old people, I forget which, divided the park into rice paddies, restored the nearby creeks so the salmon would run again, and planted mulberry trees from tiny starts, the only food for silkworms, which they brought over as cocoons in padded boxes.

Eventually, we will tear up and plant the two golf courses with crops. You will dig up the lawn. You will plant pieces of a potato you found at the bottom of the refrigerator when you cleaned it out, looking for anything at all to eat. You will try to figure out what part of the salal plant is edible, and how to fix it. One day, you will follow a deer for hours through the ravine, taking note of what plants it pauses to eat, and which ones it passes by. You will scour the beaches for clams, and start eyeing that squirrel in the yard in a new light. The neighbor's dogs will cease to be a problem, because the neighbors will have eaten them.

You will try to defend your hundred-foot Douglas firs, but eventually the neighbors will prevail, and the trees will be cut down for heating and cooking. It will open up your lot to more sunlight. The road, once slated for drastic improvements, will be left alone.

Most likely, you and your neighbors will form a co-op, the kind that meets and takes hours to decide anything, in order to distribute food and other necessities. You will realize that those in the workforce who were stranded in Seattle might have included some of the most capable of farming. Fortunately, the neighborhood still includes two doctors and a forest ranger. Once we realize how much time and labor it takes to grow food, we will become quiet and work on our calluses.

Across the island, we will form specialty co-ops, or guilds. Canning, cheese-making, winemaking, herbs and tinctures, and beekeeping will be developed as specialties, to be traded between groups. The latter guild will be more an act of faith than a practicing group, since the bees disappeared with the initial incident.

Members of the bee guild will stand every day, deploying binoculars east and west, in hopes of spotting returning bees on the horizon. The Watchers, as they will come to be called, will dress all in white, and people will bring them food offerings as they work. In our hothouses, tomatoes and other vegetables will be pollinated by hand. Olaf Ribeiro will develop a tool that resembles a very long duster for pollinating fruit trees.

People who understand how to work the land will be greatly revered. Those who have inherited Akio Suyematsu's legacy, and preserved or inherited knowledge of the old ways, will be sought out for their expertise in repairing and using ancient mechanical equipment. All of them will have cadres of apprentices who watch their every move with fascination and urgency.

Your husband will rig an electrical generator to his bicycle and recharge small batteries in exchange for food. Although you won't see them much, since they live on another part of the island, you will hear that Linda and Stephen have become fabulously rich by selling meat and eggs. In exchange for what, you are not sure. The earth continues to tremble, and there are flashes visible across the water at night.

If you are a middle-aged writer with a bad back, you will begin to tell stories. Nothing too extravagant, nothing that will alarm people or give them false hope, but stories about the land. This land, this *terroir*, and maybe stories about the land your people came from. It had a different air, different soil, and different tastes. You will describe oranges, lemons, and limes. You will describe freshwater fish, *chilaquiles*, wild greens that grow on the edges of cultivated fields in Sonora. They have quail and rabbits, much like ours. You learned most of this out of books, just like the farmers on the island. Your library of printed books, almost lost in the transition to digital media, will be good as gold, and their stored knowledge will earn you a few meals. Tilting the pages toward the last light to read at dusk, you will remember your father's complaint about studying by kerosene lamp, and his insistence that it had ruined his eyes.

You will read the old stories, and then you will tell stories of *gaman*—of people who succeeded through patience, perseverance, and cooperation—as we must do now.

If you are lucky, someone will bring you a little wine or a tincture for your bad back. They will trade you a clam for ten potatoes, and offer to split some of the wood left when your neighbors cut down all the trees. A clam, a potato, dandelion greens, and blackberry wine will be considered an excellent meal. It will rain, and you will get very cold. The doctors will tell you to wash everything carefully before eating it, but which is cleaner, the water from the ground, or the water from the sky? You will probably not die of high cholesterol.

You will stand in a cornfield holding the hand of a little girl—maybe a granddaughter, or the daughter of a friend. Across from you will be a pheasant—as foreign to the island as you—eating the corn. You hope that there will be enough corn for all three of you.

One day, two or three people will show up in a boat. I can't see this part too clearly. If they have food with them, you will welcome them, especially if it is honey to sweeten your black lichen loaves. If not, you will probably push them back into the water. But first, you might let them tell you a story or two about the rest of the wide world in the shimmering distance—what they grow, what they eat, and the tastes they miss the most.

The language about how we consider our landscape and our relationship to it is changing. Words like sustainable and renewable are being displaced by restoration and rewilding. I would like to add adaptation, compatibility, and emulation. Scientists realize that nature still does a better job of managing the earth than we do. All the processes and chemicals in China or the United States do not clean the water as well as a few plants in a bog. If anything, the chemicals make it worse. Scientists have made an honest effort to "capture" the value of nature in ways more specific than the gift metaphor I have used here. Economists need this tool in order to convince developers and third world countries that the mangrove swamp is as valuable as the shrimp farm, the forest as necessary as the thirty-seven houses, even though it does not generate revenue in the short term.

The more I learn about this, the less I think that placing monetary value on undeveloped land and water will necessarily protect it. It might offer a way to plug certain transactions or descriptions into an Excel spreadsheet, but I think the "gap" offered by the gift notion is probably more accurate. The idea of the gap allows for the immeasurables of beauty, a relationship with the natural world, and all the things that we do not yet know—dark matter, dark energy, where the salmon go and what they do when they are not close to us—and so cannot measure. In the not-so-long term, if we manage to suffocate ourselves for lack of air and water, the monetary value of the land will not be of benefit to us.

There is a call for a renewal of reverence for the natural world—from indigenous cultures to modern green religious practices—now that we have all but destroyed it and ourselves.

Haleets

Let me try to sing this song one last time: the tide rushing in and out of Agate Passage, a boat rising and falling over the wake of another boat, the clanking of hardware against a mast, the chop-chopping of a chef's knife preparing vegetables for yet another meal.

The world is made of stories, and stories are made of the sea. She is tainted, scarred, sticky, and stinky with the effluence of humans. The dry land has been tapped of its nutrients, while we flush our own biowaste out into the bay.

This won't always be the case. More people will move here, and demand power, water, food, and shelter. We will plug directly into the sun's rays, and recycle our water and waste. We will walk the shoreline looking for evidence of life renewing itself.

All will not be well. More of us will develop cancers, and only the very wealthy will be able to afford the treatments for it. No matter what we start doing now, the air, the sea, food, and water around us are irrevocably tainted.

If Haleets is anything, it is a warning about the underside of things. "Beware the Undertoad," said John Irving in *The World According to Garp*. When I finally got out to see Haleets in person one foggy day, the surface was so worn that only parts of the faces were visible under the tenacious barnacles. Current thinking over at Suquamish is that Haleets is a directional marker for canoes, so its place on the beach is important. My family and I took photos of each other standing next to Haleets, this glacial erratic sent down through the ages to confound us.

I was a little disappointed as I picked my way among the fist-sized rocks that dot the beach where Haleets rests. There is so little left. There is so little time. But as I neared the path up to the road, I began to hear voices, the way they can carry in fog. I heard laughing, then drumming. A party, I thought, over at Suquamish Village. It was a Sunday afternoon. There was the high sound of a horn. A *zuzuvela*? Or a conch? Then I remembered it was Rosh Hashanah, and the sound transformed itself to the call of a ram's horn. Every day is a struggle between light and the dark, the world we live in and the world to come. Some days, the membrane between them is thinner than others.

I've decided, finally, with no authority other than that which I grant myself, that Haleets is a time machine. The petroglyphs face the direction of the future. By portraying the dangers and powers of the unseen world, the ancestors have posted both warnings from the past and predictions for the world to come. Each of these faces portrays the personal experience of a single person. While each is the result of a private encounter with the divine, it was posted in the most public place available at the time. We were meant to see these.

If Haleets goes under, is no longer visible above the waterline, we are in serious trouble. If we can create a world in which Haleets remains visible, even restored, we will have saved our favorite species, ourselves. I think this is what the ancestors had in mind all along.

And Haleets says, *"Haboo!"*

Notes

Sources are listed in the order in which their related material appears in the text.

INTRODUCTION

James Lovelock, from *The Vanishing Face of Gaia: A Final Warning* (New York: Basic Books, 2009), quoted in Ray Ring, "Doomster Chorus," *High Country News* Communities, Sept. 27, 2010, www.hcn.org/issues/42.15/ doomster-chorus.

CHAPTER 1

For more on Suquamish history, see "History and Culture," on the Suquamish Tribe website, www.suquamish.nsn.us/historyculture, accessed April 2016.

For more on Göbekli Tepe, see Elif Batuman, "The Sanctuary," *New Yorker,* Dec. 19 and 26, 2011, www.newyorker.com/magazine/2011/12/19/the -sanctuary.

Doreen and Daniel Rapada, interview with author at the author's home, July 20, 2010.

For more on Filipino American history, see H. Brett Melendy, "Filipino Americans," *World Culture Encyclopedia*, www.everyculture.com/multi/

Du-Ha/Filipino-Americans.html#ixzz3HYovAmhf, accessed December 2015; and Brian Roberts, *They Cast a Long Shadow: A History of the Nonwhite Races on Bainbridge Island* (Bainbridge Island, WA: Bainbridge Island School District, 1975).

Dennis Lewarch, Suquamish tribal historic preservation officer, lecture and interview with the author during circumnavigation of Bainbridge Island, July 15, 2012.

Gary Paul Nabhan, "Collaborative Conservation to Restore America's Wild Food Diversity," lecture at the University of Washington, Nov. 16, 2010.

Gary Paul Nabhan, *Renewing Salmon Nation's Food Traditions* (Corvallis: Oregon State University Press, 2006).

For more on Croatian immigrants, see Gary Loverich and Barbara Winther, *Let It Go, Louie: Croatian Immigrants on Puget Sound* (Bainbridge Island, WA: Bainbridge Island Historical Society, 2009).

Paul and Lorraine Svornich, interview with author at their home, Bainbridge Island, Nov. 19, 2012.

For more on the Japanese American history on Bainbridge Island, see Bainbridge Island Japanese American Community, www.bijac.org, accessed December 2015; and David A. Takami, "Japanese Immigration to the Puget Sound Region," *HistoryLink*, Oct. 26, 1998, at www.historylink .org/index.cfm?DisplayPage=output.cfm&file_id=300.

Lilly Kodama and Kay Nakao, interview with author at Bainbridge Bakers, Bainbridge Island, April 30, 2014.

Arthur Kleinkopf, "Relocation Center Diary," 1943, War Relocation Center, Hunt, Idaho. Transcribed from the Twin Falls, Idaho, library copy and made available by the National Park Service through the Bainbridge Island Historical Museum.

For more on food storage policies of the Church of Jesus Christ of Latter Day Saints, see "Food Storage," www.lds.org/topics/food-storage, accessed November 2015.

Mark Glickman, interview with author at Kol Shalom, Bainbridge Island, Jan. 20, 2010.

Jeffrey K. Salkin, *Being God's Partner: How to Find the Hidden Link Between Spirituality and Your Work* (New York: Jewish Lights Publishing, 1997).

Michael Pollan, *The Omnivore's Dilemma* (New York: Penguin Press, 2006).

Spencer Wells, *Pandora's Seed: The Unforeseen Cost of Civilization* (New York: Random House, 2010).

David Kraemer, *Jewish Eating and Identity through the Ages* (New York: Routledge, 2002).

"First TV Interview with German Cannibal: 'Human Flesh Tastes Like Pork,'" *Der Spiegel Online International,* Oct. 16, 2007, www.spiegel.de/international/zeitgeist/0,1518,511775,00.html.

For more on Haleets and other petroglyphs in the Northwest, see Dan Leen, "A Gallery of Northwest Petroglyphs: Shamanic Art of the Pacific Northwest," www.danielleen.org/petroglyphs.html, accessed December 2015.

CHAPTER 2

Joan Didion, "Dreamers of the Golden Dream," in *Slouching towards Bethlehem* (1968; reprint, New York: FSG Classics, 2008).

Robert Kenner, *Food, Inc.,* Robert Kenner Films, 2008.

Nancy and Robert Fortner, interview with author at Sweetlife Farm, Bainbridge Island, March 4, 2010.

For more on Helen and Scott Nearing, see their *Living the Good Life* (1954; reprint, New York: Schocken Books, 1990); and Helen Nearing, *Simple Food for the Good Life* (1980; reprint, New York: Chelsea Green Publishing, 1990).

Marilyn Holt and Cliff Wind, interview with author at Holt Ranch, Kitsap County, March 11, 2010.

For more on Barbara Damrosch and Elliott Coleman, see www.fourseasonfarm.com.

Betsey Wittick and Sallie Maron, interview with author at Laughing Crow Farm, Bainbridge Island, Oct. 1, 2010.

Fred Kirschenmann, *Cultivating an Ecological Conscience: Essays from a Farmer Philosopher* (Lexington: University Press of Kentucky, 2010).

For more on Judy Wicks, see http://judywicks.com.

For more on David Suzuki and his foundation, see www.davidsuzuki.org.

For more on Sound Food, see www.soundfood.org.

For more on FoodHub, see www.ecotrust.org/project/foodhub.

For more on the history of the Washington State Grange, see John Caldbick, "Washington State Grange," HistoryLink.org essay 10717, March 3, 2014, www.historylink.org/index.cfm?displaypage=output.cfm&file_id=10717, accessed December 2015.

Brian MacWhorter, interview with author at Day Road Farms, Bainbridge Island, June 17, 2010. For more about Brian MacWhorter's work, see "Our History from the Roots," Organically Grown Company, www .organicgrown.com/about/organically-grown-history; and Jon Garfunkel, "An Interview with Farmer/Partner Brian MacWhorter," *Educulture*, Oct. 21, 2014, http://educultureproject.org/interview-farmer -partner-brian-macwhorter.

Akio Suyematsu, interview with Debra Grindeman, Dec. 3, 2006, on Densho Digital Archive, archive.densho.org, segment 17, accessed December 2015.

Akio Suyematsu, interview with author at Day Road Farms, Bainbridge Island, June 17, 2010.

Wayne and Patty Nakata, interview with author at their home, Bainbridge Island, July 24, 2014.

Kay Nakao and Lilly Kodama, interview with author at Bainbridge Bakers, Bainbridge Island, April 30, 2014.

Rick Pederson, interview with author at Town & Country Market, Bainbridge Island, May 27, 2010.

Gene, Rick, and Vern Nakata, interview with author at Town & Country Market, Bainbridge Island, June 9, 2010.

For more about Town & Country Markets, see Russ Banham, *Town & Country Markets: Nourishing the Quality of Life* (Bainbridge Island, WA: Fenwick Publishing, 2007).

Annie Leonard, *The Story of Stuff*, 2007 official version, www.youtube.com/ watch?v=9GorqroigqM, accessed December 2015.

Brendan McGill, interview with author at Hitchcock, Bainbridge Island, Sept. 21, 2010.

Ed Carriere, interview with author at Our Food Is Our Medicine conference, Kiana Lodge, Suquamish, Washington, Sept. 24, 2014.

For more on the General Allotment Act (Dawes Act) of 1887 that granted
Carriere his land, see Krohn and Segrest, *Feeding the People, Feeding the
Spirit*, 22.

CHAPTER 3

Aida Laughlin, interview with author by telephone and email, March 2011,
and in person, March 2015.

For more on the Green Revolution, see Daniel Pepper, "The Toxic Consequences
of the Green Revolution," *U.S. News and World Report*, July 7, 2008, www
.usnews.com/news/world/articles/2008/07/07/the-toxic-consequences
-of-the-green-revolution.

For more on the World Trade Organization, see www.wto.org.

For more on Farm Aid, see www.farmaid.org.

For more on NAFTA, see "North American Free Trade Agreement," U.S.
Customs and Border Protection, www.cbp.gov/trade/nafta, accessed
December 2015.

Jonathan Garfunkel, interview with author at Day Road Farm, Bainbridge
Island, Sept. 13, 2011.

Jim White, interview with author at IslandWood, Bainbridge Island, Sept. 27,
2011.

Jen Prodzinski, interview with author at IslandWood, Bainbridge Island, Sept.
27, 2011.

Linda Versage, interview with author by telephone, Sept. 28, 2011.

For more on Mochi-tzuki, see Luciano Marano, "Mochi Tzuki Returns to
IslandWood," *Bainbridge Review*, Dec. 24, 2015, www.bainbridgereview
.com/entertainment/363482831.html.

Kleinkopf, "Relocation Center Diary," 1943.

Chuck Schafer, interview with author at Bainbridge Island Farmers Market
and his home, Bainbridge Island, July 23, 2011.

For more on the Bloedel Reserve, see www.bloedelreserve.org.

For more on the Hartman Group, see www.hartman-group.com.

For more on lobbying, see Open Secrets, Center for Responsive Politics, www
.opensecrets.org.

Michelle Obama, *American Grown: The Story of the White House Kitchen Garden and Gardens across America* (New York: Crown Publishers, 2012).

Marco Hatch (Samish), keynote speech at Our Food Is Our Medicine conference, Kiana Lodge, Suquamish, Washington, Sept. 24, 2014.

For more on traditional Hawaiian fish ponds, see Luka Mossman, "Restoring Hawaiian Fishponds Important Step toward Seafood Security," *HumanNature*, Aug. 24, 2016, http://blog.conservation.org/2014/08/restoring-hawaiian-fishponds-important-step-toward-seafood-security/.

Carol Smith, "Unsafe to Consume: Despite Warnings, People Fish the Duwamish," *Investigate West,* March 20, 2011, www.invw.org/content/unsafe-to-consume-despite-warnings-people-fish-the-duwamish.

Luz Calvo and Catriona Rueda Esquibel, *Decolonize Your Diet* (Vancouver: Arsenal Pulp Press, 2015).

Coll-Peter Thrush, "The Lushootseed Peoples of Puget Sound Country," American Indians of the Pacific Northwest Collection, http://content.lib.washington.edu/aipnw/thrush.html.

CHAPTER 4

Betsey Wittick, interview with author at Laughing Crow Farm, Bainbridge Island, Oct. 20, 2010.

Gerard and Joanne Bentryn, interview with author at Bainbridge Vineyards, Bainbridge Island, Sept. 13, 2011.

Linda Meier, interview with author at Chateau Poulet, Bainbridge Island, Sept. 1, 2010.

Minnie Rose Lovgreen, as told to Nancy Rekow, in *Minnie Rose Lovgreen's Recipe for Raising Chickens,* 3rd ed. (Bainbridge Island, WA: NW Trillium Press, 2009).

Stephen Hubbard, interview with author at Chateau Poulet, Bainbridge Island, Oct. 29, 2010.

Rebecca Slattery, interview with author at Persephone Farm, Indianola, Oct. 3, 2011. For more on Rebecca's work, see Kipp Robertson, "Persephone Farm Offers Organic Alternatives," *North Kitsap Herald*, Aug. 16, 2013, www.northkitsapherald.com/business/219978371.html#.

Betsey Wittick, "Samantha's Passing," *Laughing Crow Farm* (blog), Sept. 28, 2010, https://laughingcrowfarm.wordpress.com/2010/09/28/samanthas -passing/.

Joel Salatin, public address, Day Road Farms, Bainbridge Island, June 2, 2012.

Aida Laughlin, interview with author by telephone and email, March 2011.

For more on the contested "French GMO study," here is one of many articles: "Study on Genetically Modified Corn, Herbicide, and Tumors Reignites Controversy," *CBS News*, June 25, 2014, www.cbsnews.com/news/ study-on-genetically-modified-corn-herbicide-and-tumors-reignites -controversy.

For more on Norman Borlaug and the Green Revolution, see *Freedom from Famine: The Norman Borlaug Story,* Courter Films and Associates, 2009, www.courterfilms.com, accessed January 2016.

Lewis Hyde, *The Gift: Creativity and the Artist in the Modern World* (1979; repr. New York: Vintage, 2007).

CHAPTER 5

Jamaica Kincaid quoted in Leigh Habor, "Ten Questions for Author Jamaica Kincaid," *O: The Oprah Magazine*, March 2013, www.oprah.com/ entertainment/Jamaica-Kincaid-Interview-See-Now-Then.

For the high occurrence of diabetes among Tohono O'odam, see Dorothy Gohdes, "Diabetes in North American Indians and Alaska Natives," in National Diabetes Data Group, *Diabetes in America,* 2nd ed. (Bethesda, MD: National Institute of Diabetes and Digestive and Kidney Diseases, National Institutes of Health, 1995), 683–701, www.niddk.nih.gov/ about-niddk/strategic-plans-reports/Documents/Diabetes%20in%20 America%202nd%20Edition/chapter34.pdf.

For more on hypertriglyceridemia, see Lars Berglund, John D. Brunzell, Anne C. Goldberg, Ira J. Goldberg, Frank Sacks, Mohammad Hassan Murad, and Anton F. H. Stalenhoef, "Evaluation and Treatment of Hypertriglyceridemia: An Endocrine Society Clinical Practice Guideline," *Journal of Clinical Endocrinology and Metabolism* 97, no. 9 (2012): 2969–89, www.ncbi.nlm.nih .gov/pmc/articles/PMC3431581, accessed December 2015.

Brian Kelly, "Neighbors Oppose Cave Avenue Subdivision Proposal," *Bainbridge Island Review*, Oct. 8, 2010, www.bainbridgereview.com/news/104579234.html.

Olaf Ribeiro, interview with author at Bainbridge Island Historical Museum, Oct. 7, 2011.

Susan Warren, "God Can Make a Tree, but Olaf Ribeiro Can Save Its Life," *Wall Street Journal*, Oct. 13, 2006, www.wsj.com/articles/SB116067823679190943.

Jay Zischke, lecture at Bainbridge Island Museum of Art, June 4, 2012.

For more on how the allowable salmon catch is determined, see Washington Department of Fish and Wildlife, Puget Sound Treaty Indian Tribes, *Puget Sound Chinook Comprehensive Harvest Management Plan: Annual Report Covering the 2012–13 Fishing Season,* Aug. 13, 2013, http://wdfw.wa.gov/publications/01539/wdfw01539.pdf.

For more on farmed fish on Bainbridge, see Associated Press, "Fish Farm Kills Stock after Virus Found," *Seattle Times*, www.seattletimes.com/seattle-news/wash-fish-farm-kills-stock-after-virus-found, May 26, 2012.

Martha Bellisle, "Conservation Group Sues to Stop Commercial Salmon Farms," *Kitsap Sun,* Nov. 4, 2015, www.kitsapsun.com/news/conservation-group-sues-to-stop-commercial-salmon-farms-ep-1352799211-353910911.html.

For more on standards for farmed fish, see Mary Clare Jalonick, "USDA to propose standards for organic seafood raised in U.S.," *The Rundown* (blog), April 16, 2015, www.pbs.org/newshour/rundown/usda-propose-standards-organic-seafood-raised-u-s.

Phil Rockefeller, email communication with author, December 2015 and January 2016.

For more on the restricted fishing season, see Pacific Fishery Management Council, "Council Announces 2016 Salmon Seasons," April 14, 2016, www.pcouncil.org/2016/04/41860/council-announces-2016-salmon-seasons.

Frank and Mary Stowell, group walk that included the author, Old Town Woods, Bainbridge Island, Oct. 11, 2015.

For more on the Bainbridge Island Land Trust, as well as Frank and Mary Stowell, see www.bi-landtrust.org/default.asp?ID=20, accessed April 2016.

For more on the Puget Sound Partnership, see www.psp.wa.gov, accessed January 2016.

For more on Squamish adaptation to the new economy, see Andrew Parnaby, "Indigenous Labor in Mid-Nineteenth-Century British North America: The Mi'kmaq of Cape Breton and Squamish of British Columbia in Comparative Perspective," in *Workers across the Americas: The Transnational Turn in Labor History*, edited by Leon Fink (New York: Oxford University Press, 2011), 119.

Tom Reiss, *The Black Count: Revolution, Betrayal, and the Real Count of Monte Cristo* (New York: Crown Books, 2012).

For more on Sakuma Brothers, see http://sakumabros.com.

Rosalinda Guillen, presentation at Our Food Is Our Medicine conference, Kiana Lodge, Suquamish, Washington, Sept. 24, 2015.

For more on the Rural Development Center, see "Timeline" in *Cultivating a Movement: An Oral History Series on Organic Farming and Sustainable Agriculture on California's Central Coast*, oral history database, http://library.ucsc.edu/reg-hist/cultiv/timeline.

Nancy Turner and Alison Davis, "When Everything Was Scarce: The Role of Plants as Famine Foods in Northwestern North America," *Journal of Ethnobiology* 13, no. 2 (Winter 1993): 171–201.

Gary Paul Nabhan, *Why Some Like It Hot: Food, Genes, and Cultural Diversity* (Washington, D.C.: Island Press, 2006).

Dan McShane, "Indian Population, Camas, and Prairie," *Reading the Washington Landscape* (blog), Feb. 10, 2012, http://washingtonlandscape.blogspot.com/2012/02/indian-population-camas-and-prairie.html, accessed Dec. 2015.

Justin Gillis, "Climate Change Seen Posing Risk to Food Supplies," *New York Times*, Nov. 1, 2013, www.nytimes.com/2013/11/02/science/earth/science-panel-warns-of-risks-to-food-supply-from-climate-change.html?_r=0.

For more on social justice activist Gustavo Gutiérrez, see "Gustavo Gutiérrez, Opata Nation," *Indigenous Peoples Forum on the Impact of the Doctrine of Discovery* (blog), Sept. 5, 2012, http://doctrineofdiscoveryforum.blogspot.com/2012/09/gustavo-Gutiérrez-opata-nation.html, accessed April 2016.

Lillian Pitt, "She Who Watches," *Lillian Pitt: Pacific Northwest Native American Artist* (blog), www.lillianpitt.com/culture/native_legends.html, accessed December 2015.

R. S. Ludwin, C. P. Thrush, K. James, D. Buerge, C. Jonientz-Trisler, J. Rasmussen, K. Troost, and A. de los Angeles, "Serpent Spirit-Power Stories along the Seattle Fault," *Seismological Research Letters* 76, no. 4 (July/August 2005): 426–31.

For some colorful maps of the Seattle fault, see Robert S. Yates, "Earthquakes in the Crust: Closer to Home," in *Living with Earthquakes in the Pacific Northwest: A Survivor's Guide*, 2nd ed. (Corvallis: Oregon State University Press, 2004), interactive version at http://oregonstate.edu/instruct/oer/earthquake/07%20chapter%206_color.html. Yates also notes that tribes in the Northwest may have recorded the 800 CE earthquake, pointing out that Ruth Ludwin of the University of Washington has collected "oral traditions including a story about the horned serpent, Psai-Yah-hus, a spirit that lived underground and caused landslides and earthquakes. The locations of some of these tales line up along the Seattle Fault. In addition, the origin of Agate Pass at Bainbridge Island has been attributed to a climactic battle between the Giant Serpent and the spirit power of Chief Kitsap, the Double Headed Eagle."

Dennis Lewarch, *Haleets*, DVD, October 2012, Bainbridge Island Historical Museum.

CHAPTER 6

For more on the City of Bainbridge Island Comprehensive Plan, see City of Bainbridge Island, "Navigate Bainbridge: Comprehensive Plan Update," www.ci.bainbridge-isl.wa.us/615/Navigate-Bainbridge-Comprehensive -Plan-U.

Anita and Phil Rockefeller, interview with author at the Rock Farm, Bainbridge Island, July 7, 2013.

Marco Hatch (Samish), keynote speech at Our Food Is Our Medicine conference, Kiana Lodge, Suquamish, Washington, Sept. 24, 2014.

Rudolph Ryser, quoted in Elise Krohn and Valerie Segrest, *Feeding the People,*

Feeding the Spirit: Revitalizing Northwest Coastal Indian Food Culture (Bellingham, WA: Northwest Indian College, 2010), 22, 23.

Elise Krohn and Valerie Segrest, *Feeding the People, Feeding the Spirit: Revitalizing Northwest Coastal Indian Food Culture* (Bellingham, WA: Northwest Indian College, 2010).

For more on food for elders at Suquamish, see "Elders Honoring at Kiana Lodge Houses a Wealth of Knowledge," *Suquamish News,* October 2012, https://issuu.com/suquamish/docs/suquamish_news_10-2012_web.

For more on Red Pine Park, see Cecilia Garza, "Park, Community Garden Donated to Parks District," *Bainbridge Island Review*, Nov. 1, 2014, www.bainbridgereview.com/news/281184101.html.

For more on Todmorden, see Vincent Graff, "Carrots in the Car Park, Radishes on the Roundabout: The Deliciously Eccentric Story of the Town Growing All Its Own Veg," *Daily Mail*, Dec. 10, 2011, www.dailymail.co.uk/femail/article-2072383/Eccentric-town-Todmorden-growing-ALL-veg.html#ixzz1h6LneMBz.

Chuck Estin and Debbie Rasmussen, class at Bay Hay and Feed, Bainbridge Island, Nov. 2, 2012.

For more on the food forest in Seattle, see Indian Country Today Media Network, "Seattle to Offer Food Forest for Foraging," *Indian Country Today*, March 12, 2012, http://indiancountrytodaymedianetwork.com/2012/03/12/seattle-offer-food-forest-foraging-102623.

For more on recycling at the Super Bowl, see Seraine Page, "Bainbridge Island Company Looks to Clean Up at Super Bowl XLIX," *Bainbridge Island Review,* Jan. 31, 2015, www.bainbridgereview.com/news/290426361.html.

Roger Fernandes quoted in Krohn and Segrest, *Feeding the People, Feeding the Spirit*, 93.

For more on native Northwest apples, see Elizabeth Dickson, "Native American Apples," *World and I School*, article 11299, Sept. 1993, www.worldandischool.com/public/1993/september/school-resource11299.asp.

For more on *sgwigwi*, see Coll-Peter Thrush, "Weaving a Life Together: Body, House, Community, Cosmos," in "The Lushootseed Peoples of Puget Sound Country," American Indians of the Pacific Northwest Collection, http://content.lib.washington.edu/aipnw/thrush.html.

Ed Carriere, interview with author at the Our Food Is Our Medicine conference, Kiana Lodge, Suquamish, Washington, Sept. 24, 2014. For more on Ed Carriere, see "Southern Northwest Coast Weavers," www.burkemuseum.org/static/baskets/artists/snwc1.html.

Manuel Acuña, "Ante un cadáver," *Poemas del alma* (blog), www.poemas-del-alma.com/manuel-acuna-ante-un-cadaver.htm, accessed April 2016.

For more on the seafood spiral, see Jamie Donatuto, "Rounding the Home Stretch: Learning Experiences from the Bioaccumulative Toxics in Native American Shellfish Project," *Proceedings of the 2005 Puget Sound Georgia Basin Research Conference*, August 2005, 3, www.swinomish.org/media/5301/d1_donat.pdf.

For more on the canoe journey see, Brittany Patterson, "Suquamish Once Again Host Pacific Northwest Tribes," *Kitsap Sun*, July 19, 2013, www.kitsapsun.com/news/local/tradition-comes-ashore-during-tribal-canoe-journeys-ep-416143158-356018781.html.

CHAPTER 7

For more on the Superfund site, see Tristan Baurick, "Wyckoff Superfund Site's 'Final' Plan Proposed," *Kitsap Sun*, May 5, 2016, www.kitsapsun.com/news/local/wyckoff-superfund-sites-final-plan-proposed-321faa5f-0034-37a2-e053-0100007f1954-378354121.html.

Gerard and Joanne Bentryn, interview with author, Bainbridge Island Winery, Bainbridge Island, Sept. 13, 2011.

League of Women Voters, *Water Resources on Whidbey Island, 2003*, April 2003, www.lwvwa.org/whidbey/pdfs/water_resources41503.pdf.

Wackernagel, Mathis, J. McIntosh, William E. Rees, Robert Woollard, *How Big Is Our Ecological Footprint? A Handbook for Estimating a Community's Appropriated Carrying Capacity,* discussion draft of the Task Force on Planning Healthy and Sustainable Communities, University of British Columbia, Vancouver, 1993.

For more on converting gallons of gasoline into calories, see "MPG of a Human," *Do the Math* (blog), Nov. 29, 2011, http://physics.ucsd.edu/do-the-math/2011/11/mpg-of-a-human.

Neil Johannsen, interview with author at Fairy Dell Trail, Bainbridge Island, Sept. 6, 2010.

Gary Paul Nabhan, *Coming Home to Eat: The Pleasures and Politics of Local Foods* (New York: W. W. Norton, 2002), 243.

Carolyn Peterson, "The Long Journey of Ozette Potatoes," *Between the Lines: Washington State Library Blog*, Nov. 16, 2012, http://blogs.sos.wa.gov/library/index.php/2012/11/the-long-journey-of-ozette-potatoes, accessed January 2016.

For more on camas prairies, see Washington Trail Association, "Camas Meadow Preserve," www.wta.org/go-hiking/hikes/camas-meadows, accessed January 2016.

For more on the World Carrot Museum and the RAF, see www.carrotmuseum.co.uk.

Barbara Kingsolver, with Steven L. Hopp and Camille Kingsolver, *Animal, Vegetable, Miracle: A Year of Food Life* (New York: HarperCollins, 2007), 48.

Kristen Corselius, "Carrots to the Core," *Dig Deeper* (blog), April 19, 2004, http://rodaleinstitute.org/carrots-to-the-core/.

Ela and Kim Esterberg, interview with author at their home, Bainbridge Island, May 4, 2011.

For more on Ometepe and BOSIA, see http://bainbridgeometepe.org.

For more on the salmon cycle, see "The Salmon Life Cycle," *Puget Sound Shorelines* (blog), www.ecy.wa.gov/programs/sea/pugetsound/species/salmon_cyc.html.

Aldo Leopold, "Chihuahua and Sonora," *A Sand County Almanac* (1949; repr. New York: Ballantine Books, 1996).

For more on the desert walk, see Anne Raver, "Human Nature: Finding Desert Blooms that Heal," *New York Times*, March 20, 2000, www.nytimes.com/2000/03/30/garden/human-nature-finding-desert-blooms-that-heal.html.

Acknowledgments

Portions of this book were first published in different form in the *Jack Straw Writers Anthology*, vol. 16 (Seattle: Jack Straw Productions, 2012), 8–12; in the anthology, *What to Read in the Rain,* vol. 3 (Seattle: 826 Seattle, 2010); and *Soundings Review*, Fall/Winter 2013 (Whidbey Island: Northwest Institute of Literary Arts, 2013).

Additional information and assistance came from Barbara Winther, Deborah Rudnick, Wayne Daley, Gerald Elfendahl, Tim Bird, and the Bainbridge Island Historical Museum. Thanks also to Maradel Gale, Jon Quitslund, and Jennifer Sutton for information, and for their dedication to the health of the island.

Special thanks to first readers Elizabeth Wales, Ana Maria Spagna, Kristen Iversen, and Gary Paul Nabhan for giving me the nerve to complete this book. And to Joel Sackett, photographer extraordinaire.

Thanks to the Island Treasures program of the Bainbridge Island Arts and Humanities Program, especially Cynthia Sears and Frank Buxton; the Hedgebrook residencies on Whidbey Island, Washington, and Nancy Skinner Nordhoff; the Storyknife Writers Retreat in Homer, Alaska, and Dana Stabenow; the residencies at Centrum in Port Townsend, Washington; and the Jack Straw Foundation.

Thanks also to the staff at the University of Washington Press, including Regan Huff, Nancy W. Cortelyou, Casey LaVela, Rachael

Levay, Kathleen Pike Jones, the art department, and copy editor Caroline Knapp.

And of course, thanks for the support of my family.